Why **Empathy Matters**
More Than Ever

SELL
SMARTER

Harnessing the Power of AI
and Emotional Intelligence
to Drive Sales Success

JAMES L. MURRAY

SELL SMARTER

HARNESSING THE POWER OF AI AND EMOTIONAL INTELLIGENCE TO DRIVE SALES SUCCESS

WHY EMPATHY MATTERS MORE THAN EVER

JAMES L. MURRAY

SELL SMARTER

Harnessing the Power of AI and Emotional Intelligence to Drive Sales Success

ISBN. 979-8-9893065-5-8 (Ebook)

ISBN. 979-8-9893065-6-5 (Paperback)

ISBN. 979-8-9893065-7-2 (Hardcover)

First Edition

SELL SMARTER

PRAISE FOR

INTERSECTION OF AI & EQ - THE PATH TO ELITE SELLING

Murray has always had a fantastic approach to technology selling. He possesses high emotional intelligence and offers valuable insights regarding the upcoming intersection with AI.

Dr. Pram Vindal, Architect, AMD Labs

Having worked with James during the COVID-19 pandemic, I learned the importance of active listening, empathy, and persistence. His style is exemplified through leadership by example.

David Pearson, Vice President, Technicolour

I hired James during the B2B sales craze and needed someone who could be a differentiator, a collaborator, and work effectively in a highly dynamic, rapidly growing environment. He was an instrumental part of our leadership team…

Karen Sheehan, CMO, Leadership Consultants, Inc.

I am always amazed when I meet someone like James Murray with a very high EQ. He managed strategic selling across multicultural audiences and consistently delivered successful outcomes for both parties. As we traveled together across Asia and the US, I witnessed his charisma as he communicated sophisticated technical material with ease and composure.

Alex Wei, CTO, Advanced Semiconductors

Complex technical selling can be an art with sophisticated audiences who have no time to waste on slide decks. I worked on several government-funded programs with James, and he managed the delicate balance between technology, value, and timing. He is the ideal author to provide insights into the relationship between artificial and emotional intelligence.

Thomas B. McKee, CMO, Honeywell Technologies

As a student, educator, coach, and leader, Murray brings competitive grit to selling and a path to win. Sell Smarter is an eye-opener and brings a fresh perspective on the new influences of AI on professional selling.

Cheryl Anderson, President, Palmarium Partners

I had the pleasure of working with James on several team-building projects, including consultative selling, account-based marketing, and a mix of competitive gaming. He is brilliant at sales psychology and reveals the unique aspects of AI and EQ for elite salespeople.

Richard Giles, VP Marketing, Focus Point

James has a unique way to bring numbers to life. His passion for sales leadership is woven throughout this book and is a testimony to understanding how our intelligences influence our everyday life.

V.V.K. Data Scientist, Stanford Medical Associates

Artificial Intelligence is revolutionizing our future and redefining the landscape of robotics and humanoids by integrating emotional intelligence, which enables machines to perceive, interpret, and respond to human emotions. Murray brings a fresh perspective on the emergence of intelligent selling as collaborative robots look to outperform average humans.

Peter Wells, VP Engineering, Automated Robotics Corporation

Murray is one of the first authors to expand the horizons of emotional and artificial intelligence through relatable topics, including ADHD, alcohol, diabetes, divorce, and sleep, across the spectrum of emotional general intelligence. He even included the sales-drive influencers Batman and Robin, and the Tortoise and the Hare.

Paula Van Horn, EVP Marketing, Stone Consulting Group

This book is dedicated to those who have been supportive and influential in my life—many thanks for all your energy and praise. You've always been my g.e.m.

I've always been a fan of creative juices that help build character and are instrumental in a variety of intelligences that make up our persona.

Sell Smarter is for those who are experiencing the excitement and challenges of artificial intelligence and wondering how it may impact their sales career. Leveraging your inner emotional intelligence can significantly improve your success with a path to elite selling.

Relax, your heightened emotions will become your superintelligence.

Twins are twice the fun.

CONTENTS

AUTHORS NOTE

Imagine reaching the final pages of this book energized by the powerful influences of artificial and emotional intelligence—two forces that are radically shaping the future of sales and human connection. Today's buyers and sellers stand at the threshold of transformation, equipped to harness data, empathy, and technology to elevate every interaction. In this new era, decisions unfold with confidence and speed, driven by sharper insights and a richer understanding of what truly matters.

Past distinctions between the characteristics of hunters and farmers are giving way to a dynamic fusion: the best sales professionals blend relentless drive with genuine care, adaptability, and self-awareness—qualities strengthened by both AI and emotional intelligence (EQ). Outdated professional selling labels don't define tomorrow's leaders; they champion progress, remain humble, and stay alert to innovations that not only enhance performance but also build lasting trust.

Embrace this journey not as a shift in tactics, but as an awakening—one where every seller and buyer unlocks new levels of possibility. The future will reward those who combine insight with heart, technology with empathy, and strategy with authentic connection.

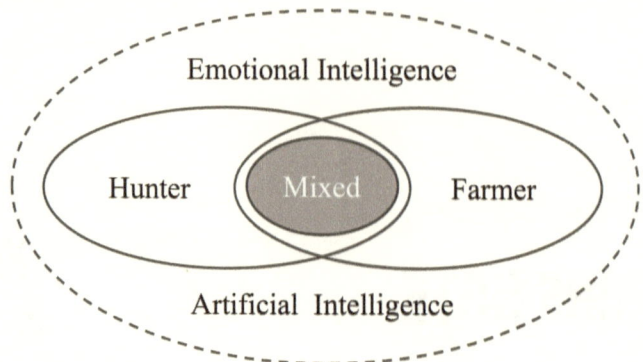

A transformative storm is sweeping through the sales world, fueled by AI woven into every aspect of our work—from CRM systems and precision forecasting to intelligent content, and from buyers empowered by instant access to supply chains, tariff intelligence, and competitive analytics. The landscape is shifting fast, demanding new levels of adaptability and insight.

Growing up with a nurse and a physicist as parents, I navigated a crossroads of technology and empathy. Early exposure to both intelligence and compassion shaped my journey; I pursued art, athletics, engineering, and medicine, searching for where I could truly excel. Whether winning an art competition without formal training, breaking the three-hour marathon barrier, or leading teams that thrived through leadership by example, each experience brought me closer to a career that blends strategic rigor with a creative heart— the hybrid sales leadership.

Today's top sales professionals master a hybrid form of selling called emotional general intelligence, where artificial and emotional strengths combine to empower decision-making and build authentic relationships. Sales leaders must cultivate multi-dimensional teams, training people to listen actively, adapt with empathy, and manage their own emotions under pressure. Modern deals demand deeper collaboration and communication, forging trust as never before. In this AI-powered age, those who lead with emotional intelligence will consistently deliver exceptional outcomes and drive superior revenue performance.

PART I

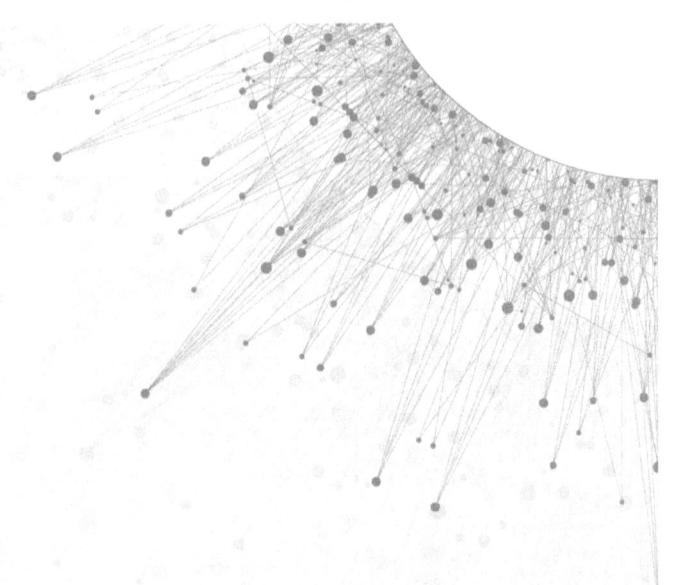

CHAPTER 1
EMOTIONAL GENERAL INTELLIGENCE

"Manage your thinking and manage your world."

THE TWO MOST powerful influences in a salesperson's life are about to collide. These two forces will shape everything we do in ways that are unstoppable — like a hot knife through butter — and will "carve us" into individuals who must effortlessly manage an unpredictable future filled with daily challenges in how we operate as sales leaders. If you thought you were ready for a little challenge, a new boss, or a software update, think again.

What if I told you that technology will replace you? As a cafe barista, a tire installation mechanic, a postal worker, a dog walker, a trash man, and almost any profession that is threatened by automation of repetitive tasks, you've already heeded the warning signs, and your boss has told you that the technology is too expensive or not ready to replace humans. Wrong.

However, if you're reading this book, it is because you're aware of how technology has advanced into the fabric of sales, so you can no longer participate. Instead, you must be aware, understand, retool, and rethink your approach to selling.

This book is not a "how-to" or "follow these seven successful habits."

Being prepared for what is to come cannot be explained in a simple, step-by-step methodology. What makes you successful today changes by tomorrow, and again the next day. Numerous sales books are offering new approaches, frameworks, methods, negotiation strategies, management tools, and business strategies. You may already have a portfolio of books and sales training manuals, making you well-versed in the art and, hopefully, a top performer. You are well-equipped for everything leading up to today, but you may wonder about how to manage your future.

If the title resonates with you, then you may have already explored the individual paths of emotional and technical selling and wondered about how much of your activities overlap and how you can combine your skills for better results. Your individual Venn diagram has overlapping circles that influence you every day. The challenge of the future is to replace overlapping ellipses with a single ellipse that allows two liquids, such as oil and vinegar, to coexist in the same space. In "The Art of Selling to Humans & Humanoids," it is noted that each day the dish of oil and vinegar changes, and you, as the bread, are immersed in the balsamic mix.

The collision of artificial and emotional intelligences is akin to nuclear fusion, where atoms combine to form a larger molecule. In this case, the intelligences are stronger together and will be considered emotional general intelligence (EGI) in the future. Not to be confused with AGI (Artificial General Intelligence), EGI is neither a subset of AI nor a new psychological aspect of emotions; rather, it is a true blend of the creative and logical parts of your brain that work stronger together.

1.1 OIL & VINEGAR

Balsamic vinegar is a dark, intensely flavored vinegar made from grapes, known for its sweet, tangy flavor. As a potent ingredient, it can be combined with flavors such as mustard, honey, lemon, salt, and pepper to enhance the overall taste. Devouring artichoke leaves with a blob of mayonnaise can be immensely improved with a dash of balsamic.

There are three main categories of balsamic vinegar: traditional, balsamic vinegar of Modena, and condiments. These three make up most of the common variants, which include white balsamic or other flavored versions, such as berries, ginger, or other fruits. Similarly, olive oil is available in three main types: virgin, extra-virgin, and refined. Extra-virgin oil is considered the highest quality, produced by cold-pressing olives without heat or chemicals, and has a low acidity level. Just as the lovely hobby of wine tasting made its way from the vineyard to the tasting rooms and to specialized retail stores, there are now olive oil tasting bars around the world. Some of the oil stores are dedicated to their oils, while others add cheese, nuts, crackers, grapes, or a full charcuterie board. Interestingly, when you enter an olive bar, the extra-virgin oil is just a teaser to pair with one of hundreds of specialty vinegar flavors. Grab your cup of sourdough breadcrumbs and start dipping.

Mixing balsamic vinegar and olive oil is a treat when you are seated at a restaurant, and the waiter pours the oil on a flat plate, creating a small dabble. There is no wrong amount; just a simple hand-pour to get the excitement started. Your mouth waters at the sight of the sourdough in the basket as you wait for the following motion. The waiter pours the dramatic balsamic, and the dark liquid separates the oil in its path. Independent small and medium circles of dark vinegar form on the dish, just waiting to be stirred. A nod from the waiter gives you the green light to dig in with an absorbing sponge of sourdough.

This culinary metaphor offers meaningful insight for sales leaders today. Artificial intelligence is the balsamic: sharp, quick, analytical—cutting a clear path through complexity, revealing patterns, and making precise decisions. Emotional intelligence is the oil: smooth, intuitive, human-centered—infusing warmth, empathy, and understanding into every connection.

When combined, AI and EQ don't just yield more innovative strategies but also deepen engagement and trust within organizations. AI informs the choices to consider, while emotional intelligence guides how those choices are executed, especially in nuanced areas such as customer relationships and team leadership.

We can view olive oil as our emotions, and balsamic vinegar as artificial intelligence. It immediately makes itself at home on our plate, and the two bodies remain separated by a thin layer of liquid friction. The sourdough is like a chatbot prompt, immersing itself in the liquids and, like an LLM response, providing a mixture of balsamic and oil. For now, we can appreciate the delicate nature of vinegar and oil, as well as the pouring rituals, as a way to enjoy each flavor as if they are stronger together.

1.2 STRONGER TOGETHER

Peanut butter is just butter until we add jelly. There is no Bonnie without Clyde, Batman without Robin, Tom without Jerry, and fire without water. These are simple pairings we have fond memories of. The invention of processed peanut butter predates jelly by nearly 25 years; yet they were paired in a cooking magazine long before they became a staple as "PB&J" for soldiers during World War II. The original recipe included: flour, sugar, mustard, pepper, egg, vinegar, water, and peanuts.

Heating this mixture created a "peanut butter" consistency, and it tasted like a vinegar-based peanut butter sandwich. Today's peanut butter ingredients include: roasted peanuts, sugar, hydrogenated vegetable oil, and salt. In 1997, a paper was published in the Journal of the Academy of Nutrition and Dietetics that showed vinegar and peanut products could lower postprandial glycemia without altering mealtime glycemic load. Chronic postprandial glycemia is a sign of insulin resistance or diabetes and typically increases after eating a meal.

When you operate from a mindful state—grounded in emotional intelligence—you begin to experience life's challenges not as overwhelming obstacles, but as part of a natural rhythm. Rather than reacting impulsively, you respond with intention and clarity. The highs and lows of the sales cycle—the pressure of monthly quotas, the scrutiny of quarterly reports—become more manageable when you're anchored in empathy, self-awareness, and self-regulation. Emotional intelligence enables you to read the room, adjust your tone, and lead conversations authentically, all while staying aligned with your purpose and drive. This rhythm isn't about coasting—it's about moving with presence and precision, even under pressure.

As a top performer, you've already learned to manage sales-specific emotions, such as resilience after rejection, energy during the pitch, and confidence in the close. You've tuned your mindset for success in the world as it was—a human-centered, relationship-driven arena. However, with AI rapidly changing how we prospect, analyze, and engage, a new layer of complexity has emerged. Emotional intelligence remains your differentiator, but it must evolve. It's no longer just about reading people; it's also about interpreting data without losing humanity, blending technology with intuition, and adapting to new workflows while maintaining a personal edge. The fundamentals stay the same, but the tools are shifting—and your ability to integrate both will define what top performance looks like from here forward.

As salespeople, retooling is what we do. Often, it is driven by a management, job, or career change, where new circumstances require you to update your approach, such as implementing a new CRM or another reporting system to track your sales pipeline. You bring your rich network of contacts and relationships to the latest set of company rules. Even if you have "no changes" at work, you will still see changes in your audience's behavior, including buyers and key decision-makers. They are equipping themselves with new tools and information, making them even more challenging to work with, and the obstacles to obtaining new business have increased. Only a fool will think things are getting easier.

The careful blend of artificial and emotional intelligence will make you a better salesperson, and, like oil and vinegar, the mixing phase is crucial. Initially, you should appreciate the "liquid friction" as elements of AI start to integrate into your workplace, such as standalone tools like chatbots or improved spell-checking. Buttons will guide you in improving your spelling, wording, voice, tone, and even your intelligence. You might decide to write your emails with a more assertive tone or ask the prompt to: "Please rewrite with the message as if sent from a CFO." Your alter ego awaits as you become stronger together.

1.3 A DOZEN INTELLIGENCES

You probably didn't realize that you are filled with many sorts of intelligence. Psychologist Howard Gardner's Theory of Multiple Intelligences proposes that there are nine distinct types of intelligence, including: linguistic, logical-mathematical, spatial, musical, bodily-kinesthetic, interpersonal, intrapersonal, naturalist, and existential.

In "Successful Aging[1]," a book by Daniel Levitin, he simplifies intelligence by first referring to the test used by early cognitive psychologists, the intellectual quotient, IQ. However, evidence suggested that this test may be flawed and was only assessing a particular aspect of intelligence. Levitin suggests that we need to separate the learning experiences a person has had, or knowledge acquisition, from their innate ability to utilize the information they have. Scientists call the things you've already learned crystallized intelligence, and they call your potential to learn fluid intelligence. A third is called acquisitional intelligence, which refers to the speed and ease with which you can acquire new information.

Cyrstallized intelligence is the knowledge you have already acquired, regardless of how easy or difficult it was for you to obtain it. It includes aspects such as your vocabulary, general knowledge, skills, and any mathematical rules or formulas you may be familiar with. Crystallized intelligence also depends on educational experience and opportunity. Crossword puzzles and Sudoku are examples of this sort of intelligence.

Fluid intelligence is your ability to apply any information you have to new contexts. It is your innate ability to reason and think, to identify patterns, and to solve problems. It is the intelligence that enables you to think quickly on your feet.

Broadly speaking, a focused specialty that is driven by the brain can be considered an intelligence. Gardner defines intelligence as "the ability to solve problems, or to create products, that are valued within one or more cultural settings. And when you think you've got a handle on the intelligences, we add a few more, including creative, digital, emotional, existential, moral, musical, practical, and visual. The intelligence becomes context-specific, implying the capacity to excel in a particular domain in life. If you spend the majority of your time developing software code, you certainly have some form of coding intelligence.

Artificial Intelligence

Body-Kinesthetic	Existential	Moral
Coding	Fluid	Musical
Creative	Interpersonal	Naturalist
Crystalized	Intraprersonal	Practical
Digital	Linguistic	Spatial
Emotional	Logical-Math	Visual

Figure 1.1 Dozens of Intelligences

A decoder ring is required to map these specific intelligence types in the practices of artificial, customer, emotional, and social intelligence. Artificial intelligence has many layers, including AGI (artificial general intelligence), narrow AI, and artificial superintelligence (ASI). Lisa Earle McLeod describes customer intelligence in her book, "Selling with Noble Purpose[2]," as understanding your customer in terms of their environment, goals, challenges, and the meaning of success or lack thereof. Emotional intelligence encompasses a range of attributes, including self-awareness, self-regulation, motivation, empathy, and social skills. And this is an ideal segway to social intelligence and Daniel Goleman's book "Social Intelligence[3]," where he describes the science behind social interactions, stress, sexual attraction, narcissism, and psychopathy.

1.4 SELF-INVESTMENT

In life, we should be prepared for whatever comes next, just as we should be prepared for significant life events such as marriage, a job change, or retirement. But if you're like most people, you have concerns about the future, as there seem to be more or fewer paths to follow, and future planning, while a steady and reliable habit in the past, no longer provides the confidence it once did. The dramatic alternative is to live your life as a reaction to whatever comes along, a bit like a piece of drift-wood on the beach.

The most influential resource and best investment in the future is you. No matter your perspective, career timing, or the positive or nega-tive situations in your life, the opportunity to become a better person, a better decision-maker, and to have a connected, healthy, and prosperous life is available now. This book takes a closer look at emotional intelli-gence as a foundation for building your "house," including how you respond to the immense pressures and technical advancements of artifi-cial intelligence. We examine resourceful tools and attributes that enable us to be high performers, as well as strategies for managing life's distrac-tions, including self-diagnosis, prescription medication, alcohol use, divorce, sleep, time management, active listening, and human-to-human contact.

We explore some key elements of artificial intelligence, including automation, robotics, deep learning, prompts, devices, and lawsuits that encompass and extend well beyond privacy protection. This is about effective leadership and how we respond to significant changes, such as the influence of intelligence. AI will impact every market and every person involved in business. It will be part of society, starting with add-ons and plug-ins, and eventually with entire applications that have an agent that does your thinking for you. The science experiment is over. We have self-driving cars, spell-checking on steroids, auto-generated everything, and an ever-increasing number of computer-generated responses that look more human every day. One day, that robot will be so nearly human that we can't decipher it otherwise.

We must rely on our strengths of human emotions. The art of selling to humans and humanoids is not a cliche. Suppose you have relied on your high emotional intelligence to manage selling in human-to-human transactions. In that case, you will need to expand your capabilities to manage the influences of artificial intelligence, which introduces human-to-robot, robot-to-human, and perhaps robot-to-robot communications. Today, we often put up with long hold times when calling customer service to fix our home appliances or report that we have lost a credit card. In the future, we will tell our "agent" to solve it. They/them will have perfect memory, and a simple prompt will set them on a path to fixing the problem.

Top salespeople make *self-investment* a habit by constantly seeking new knowledge and skills and by adapting to changing markets. They treat learning as an ongoing process, not a one-time event. Remember, self-investment includes self-assessment, and truly high performers routinely reflect on their strengths and weaknesses, seek feedback, and analyze their own performance. Self-awareness helps identify areas of improvement and ensures that growth is intentional and measurable.

Self-investment as a salesperson is much like crafting an investment portfolio—your time, energy, and mindset are the capital. In one mode, it mimics the behavior of selecting high-growth stocks, reflecting the spirit of a sales hunter. This path involves taking calculated risks, betting on bold opportunities, and pursuing quick wins with aggressive strategies. It's fast-paced, volatile, and demands a high level of agility, adaptability, and emotional resilience. Hunters are constantly seeking the next break-through, investing in cutting-edge tools, rapid learning, and high-impact relationships that may pay off big—or not at all. Success in this mode requires comfort with uncertainty, strong instincts, and a sharp focus on emerging opportunities.

On the other end of the spectrum, self-investment can take the form of mutual fund investing, aligning more closely with the sales-farmer mindset. Here, the focus is on slow, consistent, and sustainable growth. Salespeople who operate this way invest in long-term relationships, skill mastery, process refinement, and personal development with a steady hand. Like a diversified fund, their approach is disciplined and resilient, focusing less on explosive gains and more on compounded results over time. This path rewards patience, routine, and emotional intelligence—qualities that nurture client trust, deepen account value, and cultivate repeat business. Whether you lean toward the risk-taking hunter or the steady-growth farmer, both forms of self-investment are vital—what matters most is knowing your style and being intentional about where and how you grow.

1.5 CHALLENGER SALE

One of my colleagues recently compared the key messaging in this book (the combined effects of AI+EQ) to "The Challenger Sale[4]," by Matthew Dixon and Brent Adamson. In their book, they define five profiles: the hard worker, the challenger, the relationship builder, the lone wolf, and the reactive problem solver. After extensive research involving over 6,000 individuals, it was determined that the most valuable traits of a salesperson were not necessarily those related to relationship building. This was partly due to the decoupling of the relationship from the purchasing decision, as more customers were demanding greater depth and expertise. It was the challenger profile that attracted top performers, who learned to provide additional value and often teach customers things they didn't know.

The challenger trait represents a powerful fusion of artificial intelligence (AI) and emotional intelligence (EQ), combining the precision of data with the nuance of human connection. These sales professionals are strategic learners—they gather detailed, high-value information about their prospects through advanced AI tools, thoughtful prompts, and predictive analytics. With a few well-placed queries, they can quickly synthesize a customer's needs, industry shifts, behavioral patterns, and pain points. This enables them to walk into every interaction with a strong command of context, positioning them not just as common salespeople but as informed advisors.

Leveraging EQ

What sets challengers apart is what they do with that information. Leveraging EQ, they engage customers in dynamic, two-way conversations—offering fresh perspectives and insights that challenge conventional thinking. Their approach isn't pushy; it's provocative in the best sense. They earn trust by demonstrating an understanding of the customer's world and then offering bold, differentiated ideas that deliver real value. This combination of data-driven insight and emotionally attuned delivery allows challengers to take control of the sales conversation—not by dominating it, but by guiding it with confidence and credibility. In a market increasingly shaped by AI, it's the human ability to deliver relevance with empathy that gives the challenger its edge.

The challenger also uses emotional intelligence, but with a slight twist. Where the relationship builder often looks to resolve customer issues and reduce any tensions, the challenger is okay with constructive tension and uses customer situations to teach, draw out customer issues, and build a framework to win over the customer. Challengers are assertive, but not aggressive, and employ coaching and teaching methods rather than just participating. They use constructive tension with empathy by challenging the customer's assumptions and encouraging them to view their problems from a different perspective. However, this is done with "control, diplomacy, and empathy," ensuring that the customer feels understood rather than attacked or dismissed. The goal is to guide, not bulldoze, the customer toward a better solution.

1.6 BUYERS & SELLERS

The relationship between buyers and sellers is about to undergo a dramatic change. The history of buyers and sellers dates back to medieval European transactions, primarily centered around land ownership and reciprocal obligations, such as labor and security. Early commerce originated with skilled artisans and tradespeople who entered into contracts for specific tasks, essentially selling their skills or labor for compensation. They acted as service providers, while employers served as buyers. Then came the shift from artisan to factory worker, supporting the Industrial Revolution, in which mass production in factories led to a rise in unskilled labor and a natural decline in the number of artisans. This fundamentally changed the nature of work, with workers becoming more like parts of a machine. Labor unions soon followed, engaging in negotiations and collective bargaining, which gave workers more power in "selling" their labor. Employer-employee relationships became more balanced, leading to the development of labor laws and regulations that favored workers.

Over the past 25 years, automation has advanced significantly and is gradually replacing workers, creating a skills gap. Mechanical automation, from parts placement and sub-assembly to light-out factories with vision systems for inspection, and complete start-to-finish assembly without human intervention. Robots are performing tasks such as assembly, welding, painting, material handling, and packaging. Industries including aerospace, agriculture, automotive, electronics, Healthcare, logistics, military, and mining leverage robots in their workforce. An operator may need to be retrained to assist the robot in fine-tuning the operation until the robot eventually replaces them.

As long as humans exist, there will be distinct differences in the psychology of buyers and sellers. The core concepts for buyers include motivation and internal needs, perception with emphasis on brand, learning from experience, beliefs and personal feelings, and emotional triggers such as joy, fear, and pride. Buyers may also exhibit cognitive biases related to pricing, social pressures, the fear of missing out or losing a deal, and varying perspectives on value. Most salespeople engage with buyers who exhibit routine buying behaviors, as well as those who engage in habitual or impulse buying, particularly when influenced by factors such as urgency, limited-time offers, risk assessments, and personalized elements related to their purchasing experience. Their decision-making process typically follows a flow of problem recognition, information search, evaluation of alternatives, purchase decision, and post-purchase rationalization.

The seller's mindset can be easily summarized as understanding the buyer's psychology and anticipating their needs, motivation, and objections. They must communicate value and benefits and appeal to the buyer's emotions through storytelling and empathy. Skilled sellers anticipate and address buyer concerns, often reframing objections as opportunities to reinforce value. They should navigate the value proposition carefully to avoid overestimating their product's appeal or buyers' expectations. Buyer feedback can be instrumental to the seller's ability to adapt and improve—see the Challenger Sale. Sellers who understand these psychological drivers can better tailor their messaging and build trust, and increase sales effectiveness.

When we understand emotional intelligence (EQ) as it applies to both buying and selling behaviors, we begin to see sales as a profoundly human exchange—not just a transactional one. For sellers, EQ empowers them to build authentic relationships, tune in to customer needs, and adapt their communication style to the emotional tone of each interaction. It's not just about knowing what the customer wants, but understanding why they want it—what pressures they face, what they're afraid of, and what success looks like from their perspective. Salespeople with strong EQ skills can read subtle cues, manage tension, and shift gears between consultant, problem-solver, and challenger. This emotional agility creates trust and connection, which are often the deciding factors in a crowded marketplace.

Buyers EQ

On the other hand, emotional intelligence also plays a significant role in purchasing behavior. Buyers with high EQ are better equipped to recognize and regulate their own emotional triggers—whether it's the fear of making a bad decision, the excitement of a new solution, or the skepticism that comes from previous negative experiences. They're less likely to be swayed by hype and more capable of evaluating offers through a balanced lens. At the same time, emotionally intelligent buyers are more attuned to the seller's motivations—they can sense authenticity, detect pressure tactics, and appreciate consultative approaches. This creates a more transparent and productive exchange where both parties are aligned not just on price and product, but also on mutual understanding and shared outcomes. In this way, emotional intelligence becomes a bridge between value creation and value perception on both sides of the table.

Now we introduce AI to the mix, and it will undoubtedly affect both sides of the negotiation. Salespeople, or sellers, will use every tool in their toolbox to sell, and if there are advantages to adding artificial intelligence to the arsenal, then load up the truck. And if your standard tools were shovels and pitchforks, you don't have an "Elon Musk chainsaw" to shred with. Enough of that graphic, let's see how effective AI can be in setting up and closing deals.

Most experienced salespeople have perfected their craft, knowing how to prospect, navigate obstacles, and have several pitches at their disposal. They've closed enough deals to say experience and wisdom are on their side. Whether they are selling widgets or multi-dimensional, complex machinery, the art of selling is complete. In the age of AI, never has a statement been so wrong. It's like showing up for a tennis match with a wooden racquet, or to a horse race with a donkey. The real question is, do I need an oil change, a tune-up, or a whole new motor to drive my sales car? The best answer, assuming your "check engine" light is not on, is to take inventory on your approach, use a critical eye on your methods, and continue to ask yourself whether you are truly engaging with buyers and deal flow. A vast, but dormant pipeline is just filler in the CRM. However, if there is significant activity among your key targets, you may need some adjustments or genuine enhancements to achieve some wins.

After reviewing your previous quarterly results, is there anything you could have done differently to improve the outcome? You can measure this quantitatively or subjectively, but the important part is to make some measurements. Perhaps you had a deal that stalled, and you are wondering how to approach the buyer to determine the cause of the delay or if there is anything wrong with your proposal. Make this exercise a priority and gather as much feedback as possible. Understand that this is more than just a data collection task; it involves outward-facing communication and maintains active customer touchpoints. If you prefer to communicate via email or text, consider using an AI agent to assist you with your approach and take advantage of your new computer friend. Try asking nontraditional questions in your prompts, such as: "Please help me draft a program status update from the buyers at 'Company' who are responsible for purchasing commodity electronics." Remember, the average query is under nine words, and you should strive to add more context before hitting the send button. Many AI models will not have up-to-date information on your specific issue, but they may have some additional information that you may have never thought to ask. A starter prompt would be: Is there a problem with selling manufacturing services to "Company?" And a much better prompt is filled with as much detail as you can, including: "I am selling manufacturing services for Company X and want to present our offering to Company Y. My recent activity with the procurement team has slowed, and there may be some reason for the delay. Before I approach them again, would you help me draft a status email to the buyers, keeping an open mind, soft tone, and understanding voice?" Soon, you will start dictating to your AI agent, and you will see that the more detailed your queries, the more informative the responses will be, allowing you to further a stalled engagement. Now you're in the AI game.

As a buyer, you've likely been using AI to gather information before sending out any RFPs. Using an agent to collect supplier information has never been easier or more comprehensive. You may ask a simple prompt to be: Please provide me with the top 10 electronics manufacturers who have experience with my widget." AI will provide you with the 10 suppliers by name or present them in a table with any other pertinent information, such as recent revenues, manufacturing locations, competitors, and more. Unfortunately for the sales team, buyers may have gained a leg up on their knowledge of who and what is selling and have become a much more innovative and efficient buying community. Remember, it's what they are not saying that is important. If you're noticing any trends where your buyers are leaving you behind, it may mean they have moved on, and you need to catch up. Add this type of messaging to your communication. If you need help, have your agent work on a more effective script for you.

1.7 ENGINEERED MARKETING

Whether you want to avoid, rely on, or endure technology, almost everyone is subject to technical selling through "engineered marketing." This is not a commonly used term, but it refers to a systematic, data-driven approach to marketing that leverages technology and models to inform decision-making and implement strategies effectively. Sounds a lot like artificial intelligence.

Let's break it down into the primary elements of data-driven, technology-enabled, systematic, model-supported, and long-term growth. This involves leveraging engineering skills — such as organization, content, and thought leadership — to fuel marketing. The background includes rich case studies, articles, podcasts, and other technical reporting. Front and center are tools such as search engine optimization (SEO), keywords, social media, and the development of a sales platform with strategic direction.

Imagine a marketing team composed predominantly of engineers, math whizzes, and a select few computer scientists. They are tasked with launching a new product: cotton-candy-flavored Pop-Tarts. A second marketing team is comprised of individuals from business school with compelling writing and communication skills, and the challenge of marketing a new electric vehicle (EV). The Las Vegas odds would likely favor the business team, with communication as the lead skill, offering strategies for differentiation, brand, and excellent persona development. Meanwhile, the engineering-based team would rely on the story origin (1963 Kellogg chairman William LaMothe and the "Fruit Scone"), metrics (such as calories and competition), and positioning (between the top-selling sugar cookie and the strawberry milkshake). Pop-Tarts meet engineered marketing.

In 1984, a Super Bowl commercial directed by Ridley Scott, conceived by the marketing agency Chiat/Day to promote the new Macintosh, was one of the most successful product launches ever. A year prior, Ridley had directed the dystopian sci-fi film Blade Runner. The ad was a reference to George Orwell's novel 1984 and the controlling influence of "Big Brother," a reference to IBM's dominance in the computer industry. Counter to Apple board members, Jobs and Sculley decided to purchase 60-second ad time. The ad cost $600,000 to produce and air. Today, an equivalent 60-second Super Bowl ad costs over $16 million for airtime alone. The Apple ad remains one of the top-rated ads, followed by Coca-Cola, Budweiser, McDonald's, and Pepsi. Amazon Alexa has one of the highest ad spends at $26 million. A notable study for the engineering marketing team is the 2021 GM ad featuring Will Ferrell and Aquafina, which promotes an EV with an estimated production cost of $22 million. Their plot had America beating Norway in per capita EV sales—leveraged humor over battery technologies.

Disciplined Marketing

Interestingly, engineered marketing—a discipline that combines data science, behavioral insights, and structured content delivery—is poised not only to survive the AI revolution but also to thrive because of it. Its foundation in data-driven methodology aligns perfectly with how AI operates: by processing vast amounts of information, identifying patterns, and optimizing strategies in real time. As artificial intelligence continues to evolve, so will the sophistication of engineered marketing tactics. What once took days or weeks to analyze and refine can now be accomplished in minutes through AI-assisted tools, allowing marketers to test, learn, and iterate faster than ever before. Campaigns will become hyper-targeted, deeply personalized, and driven by predictive algorithms that anticipate consumer behavior with startling accuracy.

Yet even as automation reshapes the mechanics of marketing, a more profound shift is underway—one that redefines the human side of the equation. Traditional SEO is being rapidly overtaken by GEO (Generative Engine Optimization), where marketers optimize for generative AI tools rather than static search engines. This shift demands more than just technical precision; it requires a rethinking of emotional intelligence in brand communication. Consumers now expect content that feels authentic, relational, and trustworthy—not just relevant. In this environment, the brands that win won't just master algorithms—they'll master empathy. AI may generate the message, but the voice, tone, and emotional resonance must still come from a place of human understanding. In this new era, engineered marketing serves as the bridge between machine intelligence and human connection, enabling the scaling of reach without sacrificing authenticity—an AI query for Pop-Tarts.

Prompt: *Provide key marketing points for new cotton candy Pop-Tarts*

Response: *Distinctive flavor profile, limited edition appeal (novelty, nostalgia), visual and sensory experience (bright pink and blue), flavor engineering (sweet, airy, carnival-inspired).*

1.8 THINK GLOBALLY, ACT LOCALLY

The worldwide gross domestic product (GDP) is over $115 trillion (est 2025). Not surprisingly, the top 10 countries contributing to this in descending order are the US, China, Germany, India, Japan, the UK, France, Italy, Canada, and Brazil, with the US topping the charts at over $30 trillion and India with the highest growth rate of 6.7% per year. The world average is 2.9%. If you are selling high-dollar products or services, you likely have overlap in some of these 10 countries and realize that customers have a wide variety of choices. Another key element is that most organizations now have global teams that include team members from multiple countries, who will bring their biases to the process. You don't have to rush out and learn Hindu, but you must recognize who you are selling to —your company, your team, and your competition.

A salesperson may be an expert in one or two markets, knowledgeable in a half-dozen markets, and somewhat knowledgeable about many more. However, realistically, the most critical knowledge is understanding the key markets in priority order to be successful in their job.

This can be a single market, such as Healthcare, if you are selling into the medical device market, or a tangential market, such as Government Healthcare. But if you are selling rocket fuel, you may have a more selective audience, limited to liquid hydrogen.

Across the globe, there are dozens of market verticals. Depending on granularity, some of these include the following;

Agtech	Education	Manufacturing
AI	Energy	Oil & Gas
Automotive	Fintech	Pharmaceuticals
Chemicals	Food & Beverage	Real Estate
Computers	Government	Robotics
Construction	Healthcare	Software
Crypto	Industrials	Telecom
Defense	Insurance	Travel

Figure 1.2 Worldwide Market Verticals

In business school, we used the Harvard case methodology for our training, and our professor would always start the lecture by asking the crowd, "What's new in the world?" Most would answer their Yahoo home page or something tactical from a news report. However, one of the students, whose first name I remember — Bill — would always have a significant update from around the world. He would respond with an elegant update on a crisis in Asia or Europe that far outweighed the local weather report. After a quick back-and-forth with the professor, he would be asked about his sources, which would include various world newspapers and news outlets (e.g., the BBC) that took a "world view" of news. I was always baffled by Bill's intimate knowledge of topics that I felt were far beyond the scope of daily life. I later learned that he grew up in Australia and needed to stay current on activities in other countries, as his homeland was only a minor contributor. My "US" bias was not helping.

I once interviewed for a new sales position, taking a big leap from over nine years of experience as an engineer in the aerospace and satellite industry. I was a systems engineer, which meant I had to be familiar with all the various subsystems within a system. For example, in the Global Positioning System (GPS) satellite, these included: avionics, electrical, landing, mechanical, propulsion, RF, solar panel, and thermal subsystems. In the subsystem, I had experts, and I was the "glue" that coordinated and communicated between groups, leveraging my EQ to help solve cross-functional issues. It was an excellent springboard into sales.

Before the interview process, I was warned that it would be a gauntlet of people to meet and be grilled on my technical knowledge of modems and semiconductors, as well as my sales skills. My potential new boss said that at any moment during the day, if one of the managers disagreed with your skills, the secretary would fetch you and escort you to the front door, where you would take a cab to the airport. The eight or so interviews were progressively harder, and meetings included technical, sales, and marketing experts, each knowing full well that you were either going to proceed or be stopped. Fortunately, I made it to the final interview with the company's President. I had studied him and knew he was well-educated (Caltech), incredibly driven, and likely a tough interviewer. Sitting across from him as he read over my resume was intimidating as I watched him slowly read each section. He was in charge of the world's number one modem division, and I was getting my ducks in line to answer questions about modulation, forward error correction, and the inner workings of communications silicon. Instead, he said, I see you've spent a lot of time in geosynchronous satellites. How did you like that? I wondered if he was throwing me a softball. My responses were high-level and light on specifics. He then started peeling the onion and asked about launch trajectories, orbits, Earth-to-space communications, and topics specific to the satellite industry. He knew as much about space as my previous employer, and the interview focused more on my past travels than on what he might expect from me in a modern sales role. When the interview ended, he shook my hand and said he looked forward to working with me. I then took a favorable walk to the lobby for my taxi ride. In my 30 years of working in tech, this leader was one of the few mentors who recognized the value of engaging in deep knowledge and made me feel very comfortable. In the end, I secured the job and discovered that the work culture was similar to that of the division's president—a lead-by-example moment.

Thinking globally is imperative for salespeople. Taking stock of activities that influence others around the world can help you with communications, compassion, relevance, and trust. Let's discuss the job requirements of a precision vacuum ball bearing supply chain manager. Their ultimate goal is to procure ball bearings that meet their specifications for a consumer vacuum, encompassing material, size, weight, surface finish, mounting, packaging, and any supply constraints. They have a few vacuum SKUs and may require different part numbers, but their primary goal is to avoid issues with their ball bearing supplier.

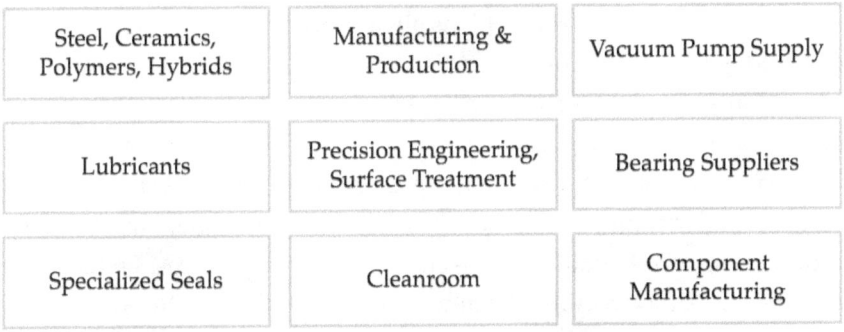

Figure 1.3 Precision Vacuum Bearing Ecosystem

As a ball bearing salesperson, "JP" sells high-tech solutions to individuals in various industries, including aerospace, automotive, agriculture, semiconductor manufacturing, scientific research, and consumer goods. You have prepared yourself with in-depth information on your precision engineering, manufacturing, and market success. Unfortunately, there is a supply constraint on specialized lubricants containing precious metals, such as tungsten, sourced from China, and you are currently qualifying new vendors in Vietnam. As you run through your pitch, you mention this constraint: the buyer is setting up key manufacturing in Vietnam while working through tariff and customs issues in real time. The constraint quickly becomes an asset, and your message back to the factory is filled with excitement and even the notion of moving full production to Vietnam. Before the day started, you were anxious about whether the customer would prefer 316-grade stainless steel bearings. Still, they were more concerned about whether your tungsten lubricant factory was located in Hanoi or Ho Chi Minh City.

Thinking globally is not getting ready for a geography quiz. It is about recognizing that nearly every product or supply chain has a presence in every region of the world. As a salesperson, your ultimate goal is to help resolve any buyer's issues so they can purchase from you. If you are selling into a high-volume situation, the buyer will want to leverage low-cost region (LCR) suppliers with lower labor rates than in the US or Europe. Many OEMs establish buying teams that specialize in the LCR supply chain by staffing them with team members fluent in Chinese, Taiwanese, or Spanish. Negotiations always occur in the native tongue. If you find yourself lacking a specific language, culture, or appropriate ways to interact, fix it. Out of politeness, you can learn a few Chinese or Taiwanese words, but 4 or 7 tone languages and their various dialects will leave you wanting. Use your words wisely to let the customer know that you understand the situation. This is why sales leaders hire country managers to handle both the spoken and nuanced gestures. Perhaps the better statement is to think globally, act locally, and avoid improvising in complex situations. You may inadvertently say the wrong thing and tell your customer to drink from the toilet, instead of asking where the bathroom is.

1.9 POSITIVE INTERSECTIONS

This book represents several intersections, including those between sales and psychology, certainty and uncertainty, innovation and problem-solving, and emotional and artificial intelligence. In these cases, the pathways intersect for good reasons, and the value is in what happens after the crossings. Most visuals of an intersection depict cars entering it with cross traffic, or two lines on a graph that intersect at the point where they cross. The following intersections are more complex than the crossing of two elements and require explanation, as they anticipate an upcoming convergence of fundamental ideas, markets, and associated behaviors that will directly impact how salespeople operate in the future.

Sales Psychology

Let's explore the most straightforward intersection of sales and psychology, revealing it as the starting point for humans selling to humans. In this case, the intersecting terms include reciprocity, commitment, social proof, liking, and authority. Note that when a salesperson offers something of value to a potential customer (such as information or a sample), the customer often feels compelled to reciprocate, thereby increasing the likelihood of making a purchase.

The psychological impact of commitment may be more significant to both parties. It is very common for people (especially buyers) to be motivated to act in ways that align with their previous commitments or stated beliefs. Persuading someone to take small actions increases the likelihood that they will follow through on a larger commitment, such as making a purchase.

Leveraging social proof can be very useful when the seller has evidence of momentum. We know that buyers are influenced by what others are doing, and although it is not explicit, they are following the trends of other decision-makers under social pressure. Testimonials, reviews, and case studies provide evidence that others are satisfied customers, reducing perceived risk and encouraging new prospects to make a purchase. We've all seen the proverbial "logo slide," which identifies other customers in the portfolio who have selected this vendor. Demonstrating expertise, credentials, or third-party endorsements makes a salesperson or company more credible, which increases buyer confidence in their recommendations.

And lastly, people do business with people, and the majority prefer working with those folks they like. Buyers are more easily persuaded by those they want or feel connected to, and have built some form of rapport that fosters a genuine relationship, which helps salespeople earn trust and close deals.

Certainty & Uncertainty

The intersection of certainty and uncertainty spans from a simple, transactional purchase decision to the depths of a long, drawn-out sales cycle. Post-mortem analysis of both cases is worthwhile for salespeople to better understand how to plan for the next intersection. Suppose you are working with a sales situation where the certainty factor is high, perhaps due to existing relationships or positive guidance from your customer. In that case, the outcome is also likely specific, and the purchase details are transactional. However, during a longer-term sales process with many hurdles to overcome, multiple audiences to convince, and high uncertainty, a history of intersecting decisions or deal flow may be instrumental. There are no shortcuts to the long cycle; a blend of endurance, patience, and commitment is required. Collect as much information as possible from the purchasing side, including inputs from buyers, engineers, operations, and finance teams. It is a take-no-prisoners approach to navigating through uncertainty until the decision moves closer to your favor. Effective salespeople will leverage multiple communication channels to win their buying audience and run what feels like a campaign when the stakes are high.

Innovation & Problem Solving

The intersection of innovation and problem-solving is defined by several core elements that enable organizations and individuals to develop more effective, creative, and valuable solutions. Generating original ideas and thinking outside the traditional framework is fundamental at this intersection. It empowers the creation of novel solutions to problems that may be ill-defined or complex. Drawing on insights from diverse disciplines, fields, and cultures allows for cross-pollination of ideas. This blending often sparks transformative solutions that wouldn't emerge in a siloed approach. Truly innovative problem-solving begins with a deep understanding of the underlying issue, usually requiring empathetic approaches to view the problem from the stakeholder's perspective. A creative salesperson may embrace experimentation and iteration by testing ideas, learning from failures, and refining approaches. This enables progress beyond conventional problem-solving limits, leading to robust innovation. And remember, innovative problem solving is not just about ideas, but about executing solutions and creating tangible value. Bridging the gap between ideation and action is a distinguishing factor at this intersection.

This brings us to the quintessential valuable intersection between emotional and artificial intelligence, and hence the topic of this book. As we increasingly see the impact of human-to-machine interfaces in the workplace, we need to recognize the potential changes to overall human values. Artificial intelligence systems use technologies such as facial expression analysis, sentiment analysis, tone-of-voice interpretation, and physiological signal monitoring to detect and interpret human emotions. These methods enable machines to recognize emotions such as happiness, frustration, and stress in real time.

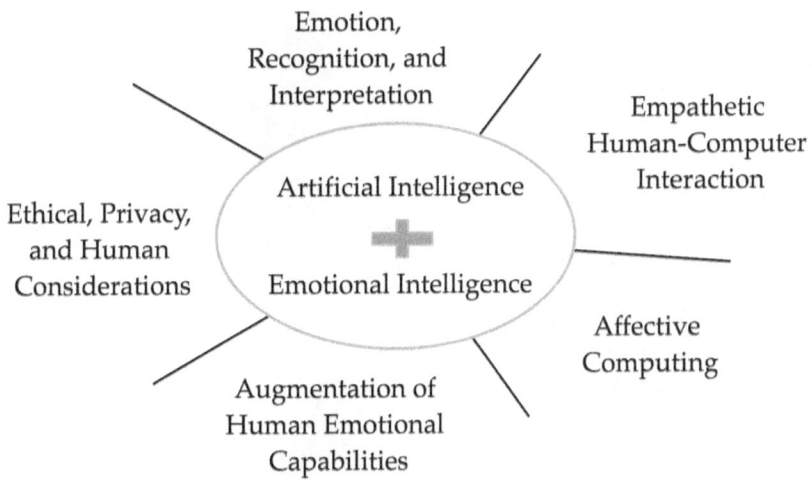

Figure 1.4 Intersection of Artificial and Emotional Intelligences

By integrating emotional intelligence, AI can engage in more natural, intuitive, and human-like interactions. This enables technology to respond more sensitively and appropriately to users' emotional states, thereby improving the user experience and fostering trust.

The field of affective computing blends AI and emotional intelligence by designing algorithms and interfaces that can both recognize and simulate emotional responses. Affective computing enables machines to adjust their behavior based on a user's emotions, making them more adaptive in tasks such as customer service, Healthcare, and education. AI tools can help people understand and manage their feelings—examples include sentiment-tracking apps and AI-driven empathy-training simulations. These applications are used in leadership development, conflict resolution, and improving workplace well-being.

The fusion of AI and EI poses potential risks, including privacy concerns, ethical use of emotional data, and the potential for dependency on machines for emotional regulation. Ensuring transparency, avoiding bias, and striking a balance between automation and genuine human connection remain essential challenges as these technologies continue to advance.

CHAPTER 2
SALES CHI

AS WE DIG DEEPER into how artificial and emotional intelligence will shape our future, it is essential to review a few key baselines from our current set of attributes, styles, and tools. We know that AI will make its way into our everyday sales lives, and how we embrace this change will determine our effectiveness in the profession. In the coming years, your teammates will be bragging about how they finished their weekly report in half the usual time, wrote a new proposal with a better pitch and graphics, and have their chatbot revise their A-B email campaigns with both nurturing and blast styles. They turn to you and ask whether your CRM is up to date, whether you've adjusted your workflows based on recent customer behavior, and whether you have a complete forecast for the quarter. It was probably good timing that you didn't mention being on top of your SEO analytics or having manual sequences queued up on HubSpot.

As you read earlier, we possess many intelligences at our disposal. Note: I have always thought that disposal is a terrible analogy, as it reminds me of food going down the drain. However, in this case, disposal means do with it as you please according to your needs. You have the power to decide how and when to use your intelligent resources.

2.1 SALES ATTRIBUTES

We all possess some percentage of sales attributes, even if you are an engineer, a soccer coach, a teacher, or a retail salesperson. On our everyday journey to the grocery store, we find ourselves on one side of the sales table. Likely, the skills are presented unconsciously as we go about our business with discipline, confidence, determination, persuasion, and negotiation. If you're buying or selling, you're in the game. Buying is a bit more like targeting, shooting, and, as you look through the crosshairs, perhaps making some adjustments to enhance your aim. You may recall that the most common transaction where you exercise both buying and selling is the sale and purchase of your home. On one side, you want the highest value—dollars per square foot —and, on the purchasing side, you want to consider the neighborhood, asking, 'Can I afford this neighborhood?' Fortunately, you have an agent to assist with the details.

The question is, how do our attributes compare to those of high performers in sales, negotiations, and business deals? Let's examine some of the most common characteristics of top salespeople and review research conducted by Matthew Dixon and "The Challenger Sale." In his best-selling book, he describes five types of salespeople. For each group, there are associated attributes that further describe each person and their direct approach to selling. For example, the challenger possesses qualities such as always having a different perspective on the world, understanding the customer's business, enjoying debate, and pushing the customer to think differently. After reading this, you might assume the challenger is one of the least successful, and you'd be dead wrong. The challenger outperformed the other four sales types in both low- and high-complexity selling. Dixon goes on to add that a combination of skills matters, and that top performers must learn to teach, tailor, and take control of the sale.

2-Way Communications

One of the challenger's key attributes is the two-way communication skills. This skill is not about getting along with everyone or hugging your customers, like a relationship builder. Instead, this is the art of active listening and assertiveness. Challenger reps excel at balancing strong listening skills with assertive, confident engagement, using probing questions and customer verifiers to control the conversation and under-value drivers.

Communication is not a one-sided activity. Challengers introduce new business insights (teaching) and then adapt (tailor) their approach based on the prospect's reactions and needs, making every exchange tailored to the prospect's needs. By challenging customers' assumptions in a respectful yet direct manner, Challenger salespeople create productive tension that motivates change, reframes problems, and fosters a deeper understanding on both sides of the communication table. Elite salespeople are often skilled at 2-way, 3-way, and "many-way" communications as they manage the delicate balance between what the customer wants and what the company can deliver.

In Daniel Goleman's Emotional Intelligence, he draws on groundbreaking brain and behavioral research to illustrate the factors at work when people of high IQ struggle, while those of modest IQ excel surprisingly well. These factors, which include self-awareness, self-discipline, and empathy, contribute to a distinct way of being smart—and they aren't fixed at birth. He states that "although childhood experiences shape us, emotional intelligence can be nurtured and strengthened throughout our adulthood - with immediate benefits to our health, our relationships, and our work."

Sales Limits

Should top salespeople have any limits? Is there a quota limit or a commission payout ceiling? How many phone calls or emails are enough? Are there ways, especially with AI, to replicate some of the work required for obvious repetitive tasks? So many unanswered questions surround a daunting yet straightforward question.

Here are some answers. There are no limits for top salespeople. They are the outliers who smash quotas, force commission plans to put payout caps, and challenge management and operations to deliver on customer demands. These individuals drive new business beyond capacity and test the customer support functions. With commissions tied directly to deliveries, they constantly push the factory. Management teams love to leverage customer demand to drive operations and utilize salespeople to their advantage, achieving results.

Just the notion of a "limit" is likely out of bounds for the elite seller. These individuals operate on the assumption that everything is a means to an end, and whether they are sending 10, 100, or 1,000 emails, it is just another step toward achieving greatness. They may make one phone call or ten (in an hour), then, after a coffee break, rinse and repeat, sending more emails, making extra calls, setting up appointments, and filling their pipeline.

During a recent interview for a WW VP Sales role, a candidate was handed a bottle of Costco Kirkland-branded drinking water and asked by the CEO to sell him on the water. It was an impromptu approach to see if they could act quickly on their feet on a subject very far from exotic semiconductors. After acknowledging the candidate's responses to chilled or sparkling bottled water, he went down the proverbial rabbit hole, asking how many calls and emails I typically make in a day and any other metrics that drive me to be a top sales leader. Unfortunately, the CEO was under pressure from his board to restructure his current sales team and bring in a new team member who could deliver high-quality sales performance metrics. He was treating sales candidates like used-car salesmen, asking questions about activities such as how many calls, contacts, emails, or other tactical items to fill up the bucket - never once asking the candidates if they had any clear path to decision makers. The role was to sell advanced semiconductor manufacturing and required a strategic approach to new customers; however, top management had run out of patience and decided to adopt a "fill the leak" approach. It was an easy "pass" for me, and the company struggled in sales for another year before hiring a skilled salesperson whom I later met at a trade show. He was a showman and a storyteller and convinced the CEO that he would be successful. I looked up the VP on LinkedIn, and he had come from a company that was going bankrupt and had a small universe of capabilities, none of which applied to the problem at hand. Remember, hiring at the executive level is often a crap shoot. In the sales department, finding the perfect solution is often even more challenging because the company may think they have a sales issue when they are actually hiding behind an operational execution or a technological roadblock.

In some situations, sales metrics can be critical to running the business, and the sheer volume of activity can make the difference in meeting revenue goals. In that case, there are no limits to how many calls, emails, or other KPI's can be achieved every day. However, be mindful of what the job requires and know the difference between strategic selling, which may have specific limits, and tactical selling, where more is better. If someone asks you to sell a bottle of water on the spot, ask them how it will be important to the sale of your product. Remember, they are trying to put you back on your heels —and better yet, ask them what work problems keep them up at night, or whiz them with a few pipeline conversion metrics that showcase your transformational leadership skills.

2.2 HUNTERS, FARMERS, HYBRIDS, AND UNICORNS

Young or old, tall or short, fast or slow, kind or selfish, your sales abilities will always be measured as if you lived in the jungle or on the prairie. It doesn't matter if you are running sales solo or in a team environment, selling complex or simple widgets, having the world's finest education and training, or simply the unique ability to win; there is still a bullseye on your back with someone above you anxious for better results. We can all aspire to be unicorns, but remember: this is not an elected role; rather, it is an appointed position.

Hopefully, you've spent some time in some competition in academics, sports, art, music, and of course at work. Perhaps you were a position player, like a pitcher or a quarterback, or you were a swimmer on the Junior Olympic team, a finalist in a mock trial state championship, or asked by your boss to present the quarterly sales update to the board; you have likely played the hunter, farmer, hybrid, or unicorn role as a matter of course. As an elite salesperson, you will need to fit into any and all of these roles, and your successes and limitations will influence your ultimate leadership.

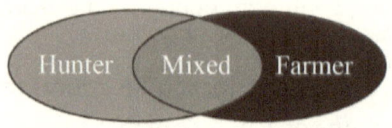

Figure 2.1 Hunters and Farmers

Sales Hunters

Early in my career, I was taught that the two most essential elements in a sales character were competence and closure. During the early days of dial-up internet, we were selling complex modem silicon, and understanding the technical features required studying the data sheet and application notes. As a sales engineer, it was straightforward, but also tedious whenever new products were introduced with exotic features that could only be dreamed up by telecommunications-savvy engineers. Who knew that facsimiles had a different, one-way dial tone than a point-to-point modem handshake and connection? And, within our best-in-region sales team, each person was expected to learn the product and update their presentations accordingly.

Being competent meant learning the product features, communicating the details effectively, and addressing competitive comparisons. To be a top salesperson, you stay on top of all details and ensure your customers have the latest information, including application notes and data sheets. Some of these documents were over 100 pages long with diagrams, tables, and formulas to remind you of textbooks past. I recall coming into work on Saturday mornings to review the material and practice my stand-up in the conference room so that I would be sharp the following week.

Closure meant having the skills to close a deal. At every turn, a salesperson may have the opportunity to close a deal, and knowing when and how to do so was an art. Leaning in too much leads to feelings of desperation, but passively waiting for results is also a path to failure. An excellent closer, he knew the right timing for closure and, indeed, how to work a deal.

This early training was the foundation for becoming a skilled sales hunter. The set of hunter characteristics included focus, competitiveness, innovation, passion, strategy, and an obsessive nature to find opportunities.

Sales Hunter: *A Person who focuses on generating new business by actively prospecting and closing deals with new clients.*

Rifleman

A rifleman is an expert hunter, known for shooting targets with bullseye accuracy. They chose their weapon with intimate knowledge of the barrel, the scope, the type of bullets, and the rifle's precision settings. They manage their shot by adjusting for wind and distance, and practice their skills, refining their technique over and over. A rifleman doesn't just shoot; they make necessary adjustments (wind, distance) and practice. A sales rifleman is a sharpshooter who maintains a steady aim on their target and closes the sale with pinpoint accuracy. No distractions, no bullshit. Just 100% focus on the goal and results. Stalking their prey is a compliment. They use their skills, such as the optics on their rifle's scope, and carefully bring their target into their crosshairs. These types of salespeople are ideal in complex, high-differentiated, and often technical selling.

There is a Civil War anecdote based on Union General John Sedgwick's last words, "They couldn't hit an elephant at this distance," uttered just before he was fatally shot with a Whitworth rifle, a weapon renowned for its exceptional accuracy and long effective range. Then there was the opposite phrase, "You couldn't hit the broad side of a barn," referring to the shotgun approach.

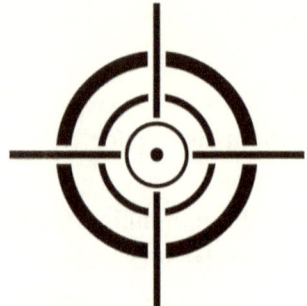

ShotGun

A shotgun salesperson has a "barn door" approach to selling. They may be selling commodities, low-tech products, or services, and regardless of the amount of selling or marketing presented, there is very little differentiation. The buyers may need to be reminded to make a sale. The shotgun approach also has a high probability of hitting many targets to make a sale. Like an email blast, you might send 20,000 emails to a large audience about a new product or service, hoping to obtain marketing-qualified leads (MQLs) to hand over to the sales team. But just like a shotgun has a big kick to your shoulder, over-messaging your customer with constant contact may put you into their spam folder or even block you. Beware of shrapnel fragments and wood chips going everywhere. Choose wisely when you aim the barn!

Crossbow

Some hunters prefer the quiet, calculated, and patient style. These people can be sneaky-aggressive and outperform other hunters who cause all the commotion. A well-crafted compound bow can manage a 25-meter kill without making a sound—stealthy wins. Don't confuse the crossbow style of shooting with the bow and arrow. A high-performance crossbow can shoot an arrow at 500 feet per second (fps) with a flat trajectory and deadly aim. Bow hunters are efficient, focused, and appreciate tools such as account-based marketing (ABM) for hunting high-value targets. If you are a planner and like to add the element of managing the hunt, the crossbow may be for you. Today's record for the longest accurate shot with a crossbow is 680 yards, and the furthest distance is 2047 yards - that's over 20 football fields.

For the most athletic, we have the Winter Olympic Biathlon, which combines cross-country skiing and target shooting with a small-bore, bolt-action rifle and .22-caliber round.

Sales Farmer

A farmer nurtures his fields with love for the soil. They plant many seeds and trust that the new seedlings will become full-size crops. These farmers are incredibly patient and kind. Their attributes include adaptability, dedication, organization, patience, process orientation, nurturing, and practicality. A good farmer is also transformational. They turn acres of dirt into fields of lush crops. On the Central Coast, our local news station is KSBW, which stands for "The Salad Bowl of the World[1]," where thousands of tons of lettuce, artichokes, broccoli, and strawberries are farmed. The growth in farming is unpredictable due to climate change, worker stability, and other factors beyond human control. However, the assertive sales farmer is shifting their portfolio into more cash crops, including cannabis and grapes.

Sales Farmer: *A salesperson who focuses on nurturing and expanding existing customer relationships, aiming to increase customer life-time value and revenue.*

Sales Hybrid

The first hybrid car was invented in 1901 by Ferdinand Porsche[2]. He combined a gasoline engine to power the rear wheels and an electric motor to drive the front wheels. It was called the Lohner-Porsche Mixte and sold over 300 vehicles. A far cry from Toyota, which, as of mid-2025, has produced over 15 million hybrids, with the Prius as its most notable model. So popular as a gas saver that it created the phenomenon known as the "Prius Effect," referring to drivers' obsession with monitoring their energy consumption on the dashboard, which led them to change their behavior and consume less gas.

So what is a salesperson hybrid? Is it simply someone who performs both roles —hunting and farming? Or someone who works both remotely and in the office. No, and no. Hunters and farmers are two distinct ways of life that are effective in their own ways; however, combining them into a hybrid sounds messy. Let's use the track analogy and assume there is a relay race that includes both sprint and distance runners. A coach would have elite runners for each distance and assemble the team accordingly.

As a salesperson, you will have specific inherent skills and naturally fall into one of two camps: Hunter or Farmer. And to avoid being a "tweener," you must be successful in managing both of these skills as you work. There are complex sales cycles that leverage both skills during the long process to close a deal, and enterprises that use different team approaches, including dedicated hunters, farmers, and a blend of both. Finally, there are the trappers. These are behind-the-scenes professionals who utilize strategy and marketing to attract customers using inbound techniques. This is the sales operations team that feeds both the hunters and the farmers.

Sales Unicorn

As a top salesperson, I was once referred to as a "unicorn" by my boss, the CEO. At first, I thought it was a jab, but later I learned it was the ultimate compliment to my performance. I had recently brought in more new business than any of my peers and was being singled out as an example of extraordinary achievement. Before I entered sales, I was a startup entrepreneur and had the DNA to achieve very high goals. It was just something you did when you were in the role.

Figure 2.2 The Unicorn Salesperson

It would be ideal if unicorn selling could be taught. Elite salespeople overachieve as a matter of course. They deliver on their own self-driven goals, often exceeding management's expectations.

In my twenties, I visited my college roommate "Happy,' at the US Olympic training site in Colorado. They were studying lactic acid production in elite distance runners from around the US. After three consecutive sub-5-minute miles and three blood draws, the elite runners were just warming up, running lap after lap, and produced no lactic acid. This high-performance group of *unicorns* ran faster than gazelles at altitudes above 6,000 ft, like a "walk in the park." More details are provided in Chapter 9, "Elite Selling."

Except for children's books, there are not many books on how to become a sales unicorn. There are sales "How To" books on prospecting (Jeb Blount), effectiveness (Stephen Covey), and influence (Dale Carnegie). They are bestsellers for a reason. They cover the most essential traits of top salespeople. Each has chapters that lean into unicorn-type behavior. However, writing an entire book on how to be an extreme overachiever would likely not appeal to many readers, and, aside from a book of examples of these amazing unicorns, it would read like a Wikipedia page.

"That's as extreme as the odds of becoming a polymath, a master sommelier, an actuary, or a (sales) unicorn."

The unicorn salesperson is someone extremely unique. You may be lucky enough to have one on your team or in your network. Unfortunately, they likely operate in their own universe with different rules and objectives. They don't look up to anyone as they set the bar very high. If the definition of dominant market share is 40-45%, they will operate in the 75-90% share. This also leaves a tiny room for improvement.

A leader in sports is nominated for the "MVP" award for their outstanding performance in a game or series. Achieving consistent high grades in school allows you to embroider "Suma Cum Laude" on your sash. And, the fastest runner in the Olympics receives a gold medal. But an exceptional salesperson is called a "Unicorn." Hmmm.

Sales Unicorn: *An exceptionally high-performing sales professional who consistently exceeds expectations, utilizing unique skills, innovative strategies, and delivering outstanding sales results.*

And a word to the fishermen in the crowd who want to be included in the hunter-farmer games. You may fish with a hook, set a crab trap, or lay a long net from a trolling fishing boat. As you consider which method to select, the sales analogies are common. Use a hook for the strategic, high-value accounts, set a trap for those looking for a deal or discount, and launch your net far and wide to pull in as many shrimp as Forest Gump. Rifle-Hook, Crossbow-Trap, Shotgun-Net.

2.3 COMMUNICATIONS AND WRITING

Name the top skills required to be an expert salesperson, and communication should be at or near the top. Every sale begins with some form of introduction and progresses to either a door opener or its alternative: silence or a response indicating disinterest. This introduction may take the form of an email, a phone call, or a face-to-face meeting, including those held in retail, at a tradeshow, or at the customer's location. First meetings include a host of "firsts": first impressions, first demonstrations, first conversations, and the chance to listen and understand your customers' needs.

For better or worse, email correspondence has become the mainstream method for communication between buyers and sellers. Assuming you are involved in a somewhat complex sales cycle that requires multiple steps to secure a purchase order, the initial stages rely heavily on your ability to be charming, engaging, and direct. If you send a certain number of outbound emails — perhaps 20 per day — your messaging needs constant revisions to stay fresh. If you are sending to a recipient multiple times in a cycle (also known as the "drip method"), you need to vary the intent to increase the odds of a positive response. Although your goal is to get started on the path to revenue, there are reasons to "plant seeds" with your buying audience who may not be as ready for engagement as you are. If you push too hard and insist on a direct message to engage, it may come across like a one-sided conversation. Conversely, a broader approach that includes status updates or check-ins may be well-received and allow for feedback on their situation.

Crickets

How do great salespeople handle unresponsive customers who ghost them or go radio silent like the dreadful crickets? There are many possible reasons for their silence, but the most common sales concern is that something is wrong. They may be busy, dealing with a work situation that keeps them away from email, taking PTO, or any number of reasons for not getting back to your inquiry. This could be the ideal time to make some adjustments to your approach and re-establish a connection via a call or text. Mixing up communication paths can easily go unnoticed and lead you to send awkward emails that elicit unnecessary responses.

A coach would say, "Be a good listener and understand your customer's needs." Ok, great, but what if they aren't saying anything — or at least not responding to your emails? More than ever, now is the time to exercise a calm demeanor, empathy, and truly active listening. Ask yourself, when was the time you landed a big deal by pushing too hard with a customer? The greater the decision, the more patience is required, and one should resist the urge to rush out another creative email. Remember, in some countries, they salt, roast, and eat crickets for a snack!

· · ·

e-Blasting

Automated messaging through email "blasts" or a CMS/CRM allows you to scale across a larger audience. A fully loaded CRM with marketing automation will allow for sequences and campaigns to surround the buyer community with rich details about your products or services. More on leveraging tools is addressed in the upcoming section, but for now, we will assume these methods are amongst your arsenal and can be both helpful and harmful, depending on your sale.

One of my favorite examples is car salespeople sending outbound emails asking if you'd like to look at a new car, complete with juicy details on the technology, inventory, or a great lease deal. These email marketing techniques are commonly sent to a massive audience to beat the odds of low conversion and support a particular brand campaign, which is amplified while watching your favorite football game. Note: Over 44% of TV car ad budgets are spent during the NFL season.

Car ads aside, an email blast to an uninterested customer lacks a clear call to action (CTA) and will likely end up in the spam folder. Similarly, if you send highly targeted email blasts to a broad audience of buyers, your messaging will be tested across varying levels of interest. You need to closely monitor the metrics to identify who is reading or deleting your messages. A good tool will provide you with the information to determine what's working, what's not, and the associated adjustments to make before the next blast.

Most salespeople are not naturally strong writers, and in recent years, many have begun relying on automated AI writing tools for emails and responses, especially for routine tasks. Even so, top performers recognize that business writing remains essential and that skillful, persuasive writing can significantly improve sales results and enhance their professional reputation.

The use of AI-powered writing assistants has surged with the widespread availability of tools such as ChatGPT, Claude, Grok, and Perplexity. These agents are enhancing email messages with automated scripts that can improve the likelihood and timing of customer interactions. The careful or limited use of automated tools can build rapport with customers, making them believe the sender was thoughtful in their highly targeted content.

Customers are smarter and looking for sellers to know their pain points and business context before they are explicitly provided. Salespeople must develop advanced self-awareness to succeed, understanding how words impact buyer trust, responsiveness, and willingness to engage. High performers are constantly improving their skills, and in this new age of AI, they must shift from a product-focused to a more customer-focused approach in their writing skills.

Before you send your next e-blast, remember the shotgun vs rifle approach to selling. An e-blast is perfect for a press release, a product announcement, or a date-specific event (such as a tradeshow or charity), and should be managed with a carefully curated database of contacts who are ready and willing to receive news. However, suppose a salesperson decides to send auto-generated emails to a large audience. In that case, the messaging should include an appropriate call to action that emphasizes what the customer needs rather than what the seller wants (i.e., to sell).

Let's break down the influences of artificial intelligence (AI), information technology (IT), and tool integration, and, from a salesperson's point of view, identify some key benefits that will help in the job. Each of these key areas is important in its own right, and we will provide insights into their value as individual technologies and how they become even more powerful through integration.

Every company runs on its IT platform. "IT" is the heart of the organization and manages hardware, software, data management, security, networking, connectivity, support, and services. When everything is running normally, IT can feel like a background role, keeping your laptop and emails working. However, when issues arise — such as dialing in remotely or getting your Zoom meeting to cooperate — your IT ticket becomes your most valuable resource.

If you experience a significant security breach, ransomware threat, or server crash, you may feel like you can do nothing. Not even your cell phone can read emails when the server is out. No more inbound sales leads, no outbound prospecting, no updates to your CRM, and suddenly, you realize that your CSIO (Chief Security Information Officer) is the most valuable person in the organization. If you're like most people, you have no idea what the company uses for servers, redundancy, software backups, or the protocols to follow when things don't work as expected. You hope it's a matter of pressing the master reset button or checking the fuse box. When things return to "normal," you quickly forget the recent past failures and return to emails, calendar invites, and reports.

Sales Tool Integration

Integrating tools can be a huge value-add to the sales team, increasing productivity, communications, and collaboration. Microsoft has captured the majority of the business operating systems with PC's and MS Office supporting 85-90% of companies worldwide. Microsoft 365 dominates the productivity suite market, with Google Workspace a distant second, accounting for under 10% of the market share, and is more commonly used among startups and educational institutions. Although the Apple Mac is a much more user-friendly environment, the Windows PC is a lower-cost option with broader enterprise software capabilities. Fortunately, for Mac users, numerous emulators let you work from home on your Mac (running Mac OS) and operate as if you were on a PC running Windows.

Companies that support a large sales team often integrate useful tools, including CRM systems (Salesforce, HubSpot, Microsoft Dynamics, Zoho), teleconferencing tools (Microsoft Teams, Google Meet, Zoom), contact databases (Apollo, ZoomInfo), content marketing platforms (HubSpot), and collaboration tools (Slack). Getting a company to license the entire suite, integrate it into its IT software portfolio, and make it a seamless extension for salespeople is a unique challenge.

Customer Relationship Management (CRM) software has an over 90% attach rate across enterprises, and even higher for tech companies. The tool manages customer interactions, including both existing and new prospects. It is perhaps the most powerful tool for tracking all sales activities, and yet, when it comes to forecasting a business, most CEOs rely on their ERP/MRP tools and inputs from operations. A CRM then acts more as an indicator of sales than an accurate forecasting tool; however, from a sales leadership perspective, it can be the best indicator of customer prospects, with advanced features to dissect the sales pipeline and manage new business. A sales operations team can collaborate with field sales representatives via a CRM interface and provide upper management with insight into how new business flows through its process. Leads, opportunities, and sales pipelines help track progress and close deals more effectively. Ultimately, the data inputs must be validated through various routine checks, including periodic status meetings and reporting that effectively tracks sales activities. For complex sales cycles, the multiple stages can be mapped out, and each new customer opportunity can be tracked by stage. Some prospects will remain in the first stage, waiting for a logjam to break, while others will proceed directly through the process steps to a purchase order. Regardless, the CRM will provide instant status reporting.

Contact database tools, such as Apollo.io, Lusha, and ZoomInfo, are among the standard tools that provide customer information, including name, title, email, phone, location, tenure in the position, and more. Some tools have added features, including organization charts, buyer intent, and, perhaps most crucially, data integrity. By this, we mean that the data is updated frequently, and including a large set of user data in an email blast will quickly reveal how many messages are delivered and how many bounce.

Video conferencing tools were widely used during the pandemic, and now most organizations have one of the common brands integrated into their systems. The vendors who initially started this market, including WebEx, MSNetMeeting, Placeware, Skype, and GoToMeeting, have been incorporated into or left out of the three most popular platforms, including Zoom, MS Teams, and Google Meet. Cisco, Placeware, and Skype acquired WebEx, which Microsoft later acquired. As a result, MS NetMeeting was discontinued as a VoIP product. Most salespeople are required to be proficient in all the latest video platforms, as their job involves arranging meetings with external customers, which inevitably means mixing and matching conferencing tools across various VPNs, hotspots, and other wireless or wired networks. I was recently running a

Zoom meeting that consumed nearly all the processing power of my Intel i5 processor and nearly overheated my Dell laptop, simply by hosting a Zoom conference. No matter how great the tools, hardware, and network, it always comes down to connectivity. In the busy work-day, a 30-minute video call can be either amazing or very difficult if you're the host and nothing's working.

Finally, we have new influence from artificial intelligence tools, which immediately add value to salespeople by improving prospecting, messaging, research, and integration. At the upper level of integration, most CRM tools incorporate new AI features that enhance messaging, streamline workflows, and expedite tasks with every new release. Today, most salespeople use AI agents as standalone products or interfaces to support their queries; however, in the future, these requests will be inte-grated into the CRM and automated. For now, the fact that they are sepa-rated is a good thing, as most AI users are in "learning" how to use the tools and results.

One of the simplest analogies for AI integration is to imagine two parallel roads that extend forward to the horizon. Way off in the distance, they seem to merge into one lane. In the case of AI being inte-grated into a CRM, contact database, content management, or similar sales tool, there are parallel paths ahead; however, the merge into a single lane may happen much faster as the horizon moves closer. Internal sales operations teams will build their skills from mastering core tools to leveraging the power of integration and AI. Good salespeople will watch and learn. Great salespeople start using the tools now and become experts before integration. Then, during the group sales meeting, when the VP stands up to describe the "new and valuable" feature improve-ments, you will be a step or two ahead and engaged in the conversation. Talk to customers about which AI tools they are using for decision-making and what changes they think may be important in the future. Remember, routine or repetitive tasks are ripe for the "AI pickens" and will replace human interactions where applicable.

2.5 LOOKING GOOD

"Looking good" is much different than "good looking." When you're in sales mode, you represent more than just yourself—you represent your company, your product, and your values. You put time and effort into understanding the customer, the market, and the product you're selling. If the customer is a significant account, you'll spend countless hours preparing, researching, and building a brilliant plan to win them over.

But in the middle of all that preparation, ask yourself: What do people see when they look at me? It's not shallow—it's reality. First impressions matter. People tend to judge faster than they admit, and these judgments can significantly impact how much they trust you. Your appearance reflects your professionalism, attention to detail, and even your work ethic. This includes grooming, posture, clothing, and overall physical fitness. These details are part of your personal brand.

Let's break down what's obvious but often ignored: you can get a competitive edge by taking better care of yourself. You don't need a personal stylist or plastic surgery. You need to make a few intentional choices that help you feel more confident and show others that you care. This isn't a self-help seminar—it's a strategy. When you invest in yourself, others notice.

It is said that first impressions are vital because they make a lasting impression. The primacy effect refers to the influence of the first impression on what a person later remembers more vividly. As artificial as it may seem, a good first impression can be valuable (the halo effect), and a bad impression can create a negative memory that's hard to change.

The "7/11 rule" holds that first impressions form within the first 7 seconds and that up to 11 significant judgements about a person are made during that time.[3] These judgements include: education level, economic level, perceived credibility, trustworthiness, level of sophistication, sex-role identification, level of success, political, religious & ethnic background, and sexual desirability.

Staying fit isn't just about your body. It's about energy, mood, and mindset. When you're in shape—even just a little—you carry yourself differently. You walk taller, speak more confidently, and have more stamina for long days. It doesn't require a significant lifestyle change to get started. Maybe it's a walk after lunch, a short home workout, or taking the stairs instead of the elevator. It all adds up. Treat self-care like part of your workday—it pays off.

Let's be honest: grooming matters. Haircuts are recommended every 4 to 8 weeks. For men, that might mean keeping a beard trimmed, eyebrows neat, and occasionally checking for nose and ear hair (yes, it matters). For women, it might include keeping color fresh, brows shaped, and skin smooth. These aren't vanity moves—they're part of being polished and professional. And when you look polished, you're taken more seriously.

Clothing also plays a role. You don't need designer brands, but your clothes should fit well, be clean, and match the setting. Whether it's a tailored jacket, clean shoes, or the right watch, details make the difference. When you're dressed with care, people assume you prepare with care as well.

> Man: "You're looking good."
> Woman: "You're only saying that because it's true."

Own it. You are your own brand ambassador. How you look may not close the deal, but it can absolutely open the door.

2.6 SUBJECT MATTER EXPERTS

In the face of generative AI, will we replace our values with those of subject matter experts? As generative AI continues to reshape how we work, especially in fields such as sales and marketing, we face a fundamental question: will we begin to substitute our values—and our reliance on subject-matter experts (SMEs)—for artificial intelligence? In many organizations today, SMEs remain essential in navigating complex, high-context conversations that require depth, precision, and trust.

In medical device sales, for example, companies hire technical sales professionals not only to explain product features and benefits, but also to convey the therapeutic value and clinical differentiation of their products. These professionals speak the language of science and medicine, especially when addressing sophisticated customers. Suppose your client is Medtronic, the global leader in cardiac pacemakers. In that case, your SME should have a working understanding of cardiology, including cardiac function, arrhythmias, and the clinical conditions that warrant the use of a pacemaker. They should also grasp the engineering complexities and regulatory demands of designing a Class III FDA-approved medical device. As you engage with key experts at Medtronic, they will feel much more comfortable when an SME discusses areas of concern and value-add with a partner who knows anatomy, therapies, and even current case studies.

SMEs provide more than information—they deliver confidence and credibility. They understand the questions that matter most to decision-makers, they tailor responses to specific clinical settings, and they recognize the subtleties that influence purchase decisions. This kind of expertise is developed through experience, education, and human insight—not just through data aggregation.

That said, generative AI also brings powerful capabilities. It excels at processing vast amounts of information, automating repetitive tasks, and generating first-draft content at scale. For sales enablement, AI can accelerate content creation, simulate buyer objections, personalize messaging, and even surface relevant clinical data. However, AI relies on patterns—it lacks lived experience, contextual judgment, and the empathetic understanding that only human experts possess.

The future isn't about choosing between SMEs and AI—it's about blending them. A hybrid approach leverages AI's efficiency and scalability while preserving the nuance, ethical grounding, and credibility that SMEs offer. In this model, AI becomes a force multiplier, enabling SMEs to focus on what they do best: building trust, telling compelling stories, and guiding complex decisions with integrity.

SME's are a secret weapon and carry significantly more weight than some salespeople realize. In a group where the customer side of the table includes experts in their field, savvy procurement specialists, engineers, quality, and regulatory professionals, you will need to show that you came prepared to answer even the most complex questions. And in most situations, the SME will present information in what feels like a non-biased yet influential-sounding "recommendation." Most elite sellers use their SME's often and even share some well-deserved commission dollars.

2.7 SALES ENERGY

Sales chi is the fundamental energy or breath that circulates through our body. It encompasses the inherited (yuan chi) and environmental (hou tan chi) energies that comprise our style. Sales Chi represents the emotional energy a salesperson brings to client interactions — confidence, enthusiasm, and resilience — fueled and regulated by emotional intelligence. EQ equips salespeople to manage their moods, self-motivate, remain calm during stressful situations, and project empathy in response to client needs. This form of adaptive selling enables salespeople to sense and respond to subtle emotional cues, thereby regulating their own energy.

Artificial intelligence can amplify human energy by providing real-time data insights, predictive analytics, and automated responses. This automation allows salespersons to focus their energy on high-impact tasks with better timing and relevance. Future sales are increasing as a result of integrating AI-driven sales enablement with human emotional intelligence, creating sustainable sales energy that drives performance, collaboration, and innovation.

Sales tai chi (a philosophy and practice) explicitly combines energy awareness, EQ techniques (such as empathy and mindfulness), and technology (AI tools) to create authentic, high-energy sales interactions that yield better outcomes and deeper client connections.

Chi[4] is also the 22nd letter of the Greek alphabet, and 22 is my favorite number. Growing up, I made sure my jersey number was always 22, and perhaps a balancing request for my inner Chi. Although I have yet to have an acupuncture session, it is on my radar for reducing stress and enhancing clarity. The small needles indirectly support emotional intelligence by helping regulate mood, improve sleep, and provide better balance. With a better energy balance, salespeople often report greater optimism, authenticity, and responsiveness, which positively impact customer relationships and closing rates.

A new energy is generated by combining AI & EQ. You've embraced new technologies that make you a more intelligent seller and, in turn, adapted your approach to match an artificial intelligence-dominated future. Stronger together, and fully equipped to sell smarter.

CHAPTER 3
PSYCHOLOGY OF SELLING

UNDERSTANDING the psychology behind selling reveals why buyers ponder, hesitate, act, or ultimately decide to make a purchase. Emotional, cognitive, and sensory factors all play critical roles. The influential triggers include excitement, fear, and sadness. Sellers who are passionate and genuinely believe in their product often experience higher conversion rates, as their enthusiasm is contagious. The excitement attracts buyers and may propel impulse decisions. Fear, on the other hand, motivates action by awakening concern for urgency and may arise from a fear of missing out, for example, on an urgent purchase. Additionally, there is a fear of loss or regret when pressure to buy exists, as it may lead to missing out. We will touch on other emotions, including sadness, doubt, and frustration, which, if left unaddressed, can undermine a sale.

In the positive intersection section, we covered some of the cognitive and behavioral principles of sales, including reciprocity, commitment, social proof, liking, and authority. Salespeople use each of these approaches where they can benefit the sale most effectively and leverage their best skills to influence the deal. Customers prefer to buy from relatable, likable salespeople, and this may be one of the most highly valued behaviors among high performers.

. . .

Power of Color

The power of color profoundly influences perception and emotion, significantly shaping consumer behavior. Color effects are not universal due to cultural factors and context; however, strategic color use in branding and advertising can help build trust, spark excitement, or instill a sense of urgency.

Color	Common Associations
Blue	Trust, calmness, professionalism (banks, tech, healthcare)
Green	Prosperity, growth, eco-friendly (financial, environmental)
Red	Energy, excitement, urgency (sales, fast-food, clearance)
Yellow	Optimism, warmth, fun (children's products, food, leisure)
Orange	Confidence, friendliness, approachability
Purple	Luxury, creativity, innovation (premium goods, creative)
Black	Sophistication, stability, luxury (high-end fashion, cars)

Figure 3.1 Significance of Colors

At the risk of repeating some elements, sales strategies should combine the following: a) Salespeople should convey positive emotions, such as excitement and trust, through compelling stories and testimonials, b) Build rapport and show genuine enthusiasm. c) Leverage urgency and scarcity tactically to prompt buying, d) Match branding elements (like color) to intended emotional effects and market expectations, and e) Recognise and adapt to neurodiverse traits within sales teams for better performance.

There are key sales strengths associated with neurodiversity, particularly among individuals with ADHD, including high energy, spontaneity, and strong networking skills. Salespeople with ADHD may excel in initial prospecting, but might struggle with organization, follow-up, and repetitive tasks—a few more details in the next section.

Much of the decision-making in purchasing is unconscious, driven by subconscious biases, past experiences, and immediate emotional states, which account for up to 95% of choices. Successful sales involve managing these factors, establishing rapport, and offering reassurance in ambiguous social or economic situations. Establishing authority and demonstrating reliability can help guide the buyer toward a trusting and positive decision.

By understanding and intentionally addressing these core principles —emotions, cognitive behaviors, sensory cues, and unique individual differences —selling becomes not just a transaction, but an experience that aligns with deep psychological drivers.

3.1 ADHD AND SALES

Ever wonder if you have ADHD? Attention Deficit/Hyperactivity Disorder (aka ADHD) is common amongst children and adults and has both positive and negative influences on sales skills. Some challenges include focus and organization, while strengths include high energy, creativity, and persuasive communication. So, why should we care if we have ADHD characteristics or not? It's a simple question that often goes unanswered and may be one of the most essential elements of your EQ.

It is hard to pinpoint the exact dates of ADHD origin, with discoveries of similar attributes dating back to the late 1700s. Sir Alexander Crichton[1], a Scottish physician, noted that patients were easily distracted and had difficulty focusing on their activities. Then, in 1932, German doctors described hyperkinetic disease, where children suffered from difficulty following rules, could not stay still, and often disturbed other kids in school. In 1937, Dr Charles Bradley[2] noticed that the stimulant Benzedrine caused some children to behave better. Finally, methylphenidate was developed in 1944 to treat conditions such as chronic fatigue and depression, but it worked best to improve symptoms of ADHD. In 1954, it was marketed under the name Ritalin.

Hunter-Gatherer

The hunter-gatherer theory of ADHD suggests that traits associated with ADHD, such as novelty-seeking and impulsivity, may have been advantageous for survival in pre-industrial societies, including those of hunter-gatherer communities. Positive characteristics, including a high degree of adaptability, hyperfocus, and impulsivity, allow those with ADHD to thrive. The "ADHD hunter" was ideal for hunting new business, avoiding predators (competition), and excelling at adaptability, driven by a passion to win. While the long-term planning and routine tasks were more suited to the "farmers."

By the Numbers

There is no single test for ADHD, and many other problems, such as sleep disorders, anxiety, depression, and certain types of learning disabilities, can have symptoms similar to ADHD. Additionally, the diagnosis in children differs from that of adults. The American Psychiatric Association's Diagnostic and Statistical Manual (DSM) is used to help diagnose ADHD and provides criteria for children under 16 and persons over the age of 17. A mental health professional will give complete information. As of 2025, over 400 million adults have ADHD, and over 16 million adults have been diagnosed in the US; about 6% are diagnosed, and 25% are undiagnosed, or 65 million adults. These numbers are rising as improved diagnostic capabilities drive more cases.

ADHD self-reporting is also available. In 2001, JB Schweitzer published a list of questions in the North American Journal of Medical Clinical Psychology to support self-reporting (also known as ASRS v1.1). They were divided into Part A (6 questions) and Part B (12 questions), each with detailed survey questions that allowed patients to respond on a range of options, from "Never" to "Very Often," as they occurred in their daily lives. Another standard self-reporting test is the Vanderbilt ADHD Diagnostic Rating Scale (VADRS)[3], developed in 2003. Both tools are considered excellent, with the VADRS more focused on children and adolescents.

Ref: https://psychology-tools.com/test/adult-adhd-self-report-scale
Ref: https://psychology-tools.com/test/vadrs-vanderbilt-adhd-diagnostic-rating-scale

Undiagnosed ADHD is a kettle of fish. The symptoms of lack of focus, organization, and impulsivity are active across the universe. Blame social media, mobile phones, or lifestyle, and you would be right over 65% of the time. You can lean on self-awareness, which is only a tiny bit better than self-checking to see if you have bad breath (sorry). You can also leave it untreated. However, you should know that if you do have ADHD, it can worsen with age. Some minor issues you struggle with become more pronounced, and frustration becomes commonplace. Getting back to a normal state will be more complex and more challenging. Take inventory now, and be grateful that you are aware of the situation. In 2025, Forbes Health listed the best online therapy services that offer ADHD diagnostics and treatments.[4]

Medication
ADHD is a disorder, and although it is not a disease, it has many challenges and obligations. There are three common types: inattentive, hyperactive-impulsive, and combined. There are many treatment options, and the most common are forms of mild stimulants that will mask or remove the disorder. These stimulants include: Ritalin, Concerta, Adderall, and Vyvanse. Common side effects are loss of appetite, dry mouth, and sleep issues. Like all medications, managing dosages, therapies, and physician feedback is essential.

• • •

Managing the Hyper-focused

As a sales manager, you likely have a few team members with excellent focus and incredible abilities to land new deals. These hunters are your front-line soldiers and will adapt, maneuver, and win in environments that are seemingly straightforward for them. It is as if they are programmed to glide effortlessly through obstacles, overcome any barriers, and complete the task while other teammates review their strategies to engage. A hyper-focused salesperson will be first or nothing else.

They can also be challenging to manage or abide by the rules. You may ask that your team advise on their sales plans, enter data into the CRM, or provide weekly report updates. You will manage the activities, avoid channel conflicts, and keep top management informed of their progress. You will also need to keep an eye on the few who are bothered by reporting but still deliver results. A hyper-focused salesperson will view the reports as a waste of time and wonder about the lost time spent typing up a plan rather than executing it directly. Adding this paragraph to the end of the ADHD topic is not by accident. Yes, you can be hyper-focused without ADHD; in fact, this is a salesperson's natural gift. It is only one symptom; however, it is also more common in folks with ADHD.

For those who may suffer from Obsessive-Compulsive Disorder (OCD), there are clear distinctions between OCD and ADHD. OCD is characterized by intrusive thoughts (obsessions) and repetitive behaviors or mental acts (compulsions) designed to reduce anxiety. ADHD, on the other hand, primarily involves inattention, hyperactivity, and impulsivity. To perhaps complicate things, a significant percentage of individuals suffer from both disorders. Add in a little artificial intelligence, and it's a chaotic soup with both positive impacts and potential risks. The upside skills include better time management, organization, and focus. AI can also support the management of compulsive behaviors and enhance therapy through neurofeedback systems and virtual platforms. And the opposite side of the tetter-totter is that AI may lead towards reduced social interaction and weakened social skills. And persons with OCD may misinterpret chatbot responses, increasing their anxiety or causing negative behavior.

Both OCD and ADHD are part of a neurodivergent spectrum. The OCD spectrum is defined by compulsivity, and ADHD is characterized by impulsivity. Research indicates that these conditions share some underlying biological similarities, leading to their co-occurrence more often than would be expected by chance, and sometimes resulting in a dual diagnosis.

3.2 HERDING CATS

Do you remember the Super Bowl ad for "Cat Herders?" On January 30, 2000, a division of Hewlett-Packard called EDS (Electronic Data Systems, formerly an independent company) ran a 60-second clip of cowboys on horseback herding cats on the prairie. Roughneck cowboys suggested herding cats is "one of the toughest things he had ever done." Bill Clinton later cited it as his favorite commercial. The origin is from the 1979 Monty Python's Life of Brian film. The idiom can suggest that organizing large groups of people is not possible, or at least not without a great deal of effort and patience. Other cartoon references spoof the efforts of herding cats and strategic alignment.

In the context of salespeople, the term "herding cats" refers to the challenge of managing and coordinating a sales team that is individualistic, competitive, and often difficult to control. It highlights the difficulty of leading and motivating a sales team that may not always be aligned with common goals or strategies.

Remember, the sales team often operates under quotas and performance-based incentives that are individual goals, and by definition, success rewards an individual, not a group. Shared goals, a corporate vision, and an organizational structure with a hierarchical approach typically lead sales teams. In the name of Monty Python, we have our sales leader herding their flock of sheep, when in fact they are looking for the wolves in sheep's clothing.

Successful "herding" of a sales team can lead to increased productivity, improved collaboration, and enhanced overall performance. The rigor also fosters a more cohesive and motivated team environment. Just remember, each cat (salesperson) has a unique personality and may need individual attention. Meow.

3.3 COLORS AND COLORBLIND

Losing one of our senses can lead to heightened perception and processing in other senses as the brain adapts by rewiring itself to compensate for the loss. This process, known as *cross-modal reorganization*, involves an area of the brain previously dedicated to the lost sense being repurposed to enhance the remaining senses. Studies have shown that individuals who are blind often possess enhanced spatial auditory skills, enabling them to pinpoint sound sources with greater accuracy. We all carry biases based on our daily experiences. Some are helpful and put us at an advantage, while others may put us at a disadvantage. Having a preference towards something is a general inclination or liking. At the same time, a bias is a prejudice or preconceived opinion that influences one's judgement, often negatively or unfairly. Essentially, preferences are personal choices, whereas biases can lead to unfair treatment or discrimination.

Additionally, there are both implicit and explicit biases, as follows. An implicit bias is an action based on prejudice and stereotypes, often without the person's intention. This is an unconscious act or thought; however, it does show a familiar association. At the same time, an explicit bias includes actions based on prejudice and stereotypes that are intended to do so. In this type, people are very aware of their bias. Some explicit biases include sexism, racism, sexual orientation, and ageism. There is also the case of first impressions, where research suggests a bias may be introduced in under 7 seconds.

Color Preference

Colors have a preference. The psychology behind favorite colors is complex and multifaceted, involving both innate preferences and learned associations. While some color preferences are universal, others are highly personal and influenced by individual experiences and cultural factors. In essence, we like colors that evoke positive emotions and associations, stemming from both innate responses and personal history.

Interestingly, if you are asked to picture a yellow school bus, a yellow taxi cab, and a yellow sunrise, and then asked what type of fruit, over 90% will say "banana." The same is true for a red fire engine, a red stop sign, and a glass of red wine; the fruit choice will be a "strawberry." These are suggestive riddles and insert a tactical bias before asking a simple question.

A comprehensive study in color psychology examines how colors affect human emotions, moods, and behaviors. It explores both universal and culturally specific associations, as well as individual experiences, to understand how different hues can affect the mind and body. In his book, "Surrounded by Idiots: The Four Types of Human Behavior and How to Effectively Communicate with Each in Business[5]", Thomas Erikson outlines the most common personality types and categorizes them into Red, Blue, Green, and Yellow. Erickson will help you understand yourself better, hone communication and social skills, handle conflict with confidence, improve dynamics with your boss and team, and get the best out of the people you deal with and manage. A color like red has stimulating, energizing psychological effects, with common associations including passion, love, anger, danger, and urgency.

He outlines many of the colors in the rainbow and their attributes. Other applications of color psychology include brand marketing, advertising, shaping perceptions, influencing buying decisions, and shaping emotional responses. Colors can also be used in mental health and therapy to promote relaxation or stimulation, depending on the individual's needs. The colors in our surroundings, clothing, and art can subtly shape our daily mood and energy.

. . .

Colorblind

"Babies are born color blind, and their color vision improves with full colors by 6 months."

We are born with five senses, including sight, hearing, smell, taste, and touch. These senses allow us to perceive and interact with the world around us. Each sense is associated with specific sensory organs and neural pathways that transmit information to the brain for processing and interpretation. Each sense provides its own unique feedback and is energized by its strength. Approximately 75% of people say they would be scared to lose their sense of sight, followed by a decrease in their favorite senses, including hearing, touch, and taste, and then smell. It is easy to see why we might feel that losing vision would be worse than losing any other sense, given its importance in our daily lives. Most hobbies that people enjoy would be impossible without the ability to see, such as reading books, watching movies, playing computer games, riding a bike, or playing sports.

Losing your vision is considered a profound trauma that brings significant emotional, psychological, and social challenges, rivaling or exceeding the impact of many other life-altering events or losses. While trauma from events like injury, grief, or illness often shares themes of depression, anxiety, and a disrupted sense of identity, vision loss uniquely affects independence, quality of life, and social relationships, leading to intense feelings of isolation and loss of self-esteem.

Color blindness, particularly red-green, affects a significant portion of the population, with nearly 8% of males affected. Red-green color blindness is inherited from the mother on the X chromosome. As a precaution, companies may decide to avoid using colors containing red or green in presentations, spreadsheets, graphs, safety signage, operational controls, instructional materials, and other visual elements.

Many sales roles, such as inside sales, B2B sales, or sales engineering, can be easily handled by individuals who are colorblind. Conversely, color blindness may negatively impact professions such as medicine, electrical work, aviation, truck driving, cooking, and fashion. Imagine a colorblind artist—look up historical figures such as Degas, Monet, and Tagore, or contemporary artists such as Harbisson, Hellzen, Archam, or Long.

Mark Zuckerberg, who has red-green color blindness, stated that blue is the color he can see most clearly, which is why the Meta logo is blue. Other famous colorblind stars include Eddie Redmayne, Howie Mandel, Bill Gates, the late Robert Redford, Keanu Reeves, and Fred (Mr.) Rogers and Mark Twain.

3.4 MUSIC AND MEMORIES

In Daniel Levitin's book "I Heard There Was a Secret Chord," he describes how Music engages the limbic system and explores emotional intelligence through the lens of Music, cognition, and emotion. Specifically, he explores how the brain is structured for emotional life, often using Music as the entry point. He writes, "Music activates the same reward centers in the brain as food, sex, and drugs - especially the nucleus accumbens, amygdala, and dopamine pathways. He explains why we associate particular songs with powerful emotional memories, a phenomenon tied to episodic memory.

I've always wished I could play the guitar. Both my parents appreciated and often attended local symphony performances, where they had the chance to hear their favorite composers, including Bach, Beethoven, Mozart, Tchaikovsky, and Vivaldi. They loved composers who emphasized strings and piano, and wanted my sister and me to enjoy those instruments and perhaps play them someday. When I was a young child, I was heavily "influenced" to learn piano and the clarinet. I couldn't get the hang of either instrument, and recitals eventually became less and less enjoyable. I even tried the harmonica, where the learning curve was short, and unfortunately, so was the excitement. Giving up on reading music notes happened before high school, as sports, cars, and pretty girls dominated my interests.

Music has a profound and well-documented connection to memory, influencing both how we recall the past and our emotional attachment to those memories. When people hear a familiar song, it can instantly transport them back to specific events, people, or places in their lives, a phenomenon known as music-evoked autobiographical memory. This effect is often involuntary, as a song can suddenly trigger vivid recollections without conscious effort, making music a potent cue for unlocking memories.

I grew up loving the music from Jim Croce, James Taylor, Cat Stevens, and Carole King. Their songs moved me and are forever embedded in my memory. Their music evoked memories of a simpler time in life, and like fond memories, they were always happy moments. Taylor's classic song, "Carolina in My Mind[6]," was an elixir for me. I can't explain why the thoughts are so special, but whenever I hear the lyrics, it's as if I'm reliving a joyous experience. "Can't you just feel the sunshine?" It turns out that the song is a journey back to his childhood and homesick times from his formative years.

Salespeople need outlets to decompress and relieve work-related pressure. Hearing your favorite songs can transport you and bring back fond memories to replace the work stress. Call it a "music-based intervention" that can support mental health. Music evokes memories during routine activities where the mind is free to wander, such as commuting, doing sales reports, or relaxing. These moments provide fertile ground for spontaneous recollections, further reinforcing the bond between music and memory. So, listen to your favorite playlist the next time you have to build slides for your quarterly business review.

3.5 SADNESS

Ask a crowd of salespeople to write down a few things that make them happy, and they will ask for more paper for an extended list of attractions and distractions. Give them a choice of a game of cornhole, darts, or 8-ball, and bets will start flowing for a winner-take-all game. Happy emotions are typically associated with increased motivation, creativity, and collaboration.

Competition can trigger a range of emotions, both positive and negative. While competition can motivate individuals to perform better and strive for excellence, it can also induce stress, anxiety, or jealousy if not managed well. However, when competition is perceived as fair and fun, it can actually boost happy emotions, leading to a series of achievements and camaraderies. In sales psychology, leveraging positive emotions — both in oneself and in clients — can enhance trust and rapport, making competitive situations more constructive rather than adversarial. Research indicates that happier salespeople can generate up to 37% more sales than their less happy peers. High emotional intelligence allows individuals to navigate competitive settings with empathy, turning rivalry into healthy motivation rather than conflict.

Now, dim the crowd lights and present a few images of those imprisoned dogs, accompanied by the background music of "Angel[7]" by Sarah McLachlan. The group starts to wonder about where this sales meeting is going. To pile on, the moderator plays a clip from Four Weddings and a Funeral and the poem "Funeral Blues" by W.H. Auden[8].

Stop all the clocks, cut off the telephone,
Prevent the dog from barking with a juicy bone,
Silence the pianos and with muffled drum,
Bring out the coffin, let the mourners come.

Let aeroplanes circle moaning overhead,
Scribbling on the sky the message He is Dead,
Put crepe bows around the white necks of the public doves,
Let the traffic policeman wear black cotton gloves.

He was my North, my South, my East and West,
My working week and my Sunday rest,
My noon, my midnight, my talk, my song,
I thought that love would last forever: I was wrong.

The stars are not wanted now, put out every one,
Pack up the moon and dismantle the sun,
Pour away the ocean and sweep up the woods,
For nothing now can ever come to any good.

Persistent sadness or depression can significantly hinder a salesperson's ability to meet targets and perform effectively. Salespeople experiencing depression show notable declines in sales performance. Sadness can sap energy and motivation, making it harder for salespeople to maintain the persistence needed for success. And, of course, customers are sensitive to salespeople's emotional state. Displays of sadness can decrease customer trust and satisfaction, affecting the likelihood of closing a sale. The emotional highs and lows in sales can be exhausting. Without strategies to manage sadness and stress, salespeople are at a higher risk of burnout and mental health challenges.

How about combining the emotions for the most significant effect? I recall a recent sales and operations meeting where we brought in Gary Guller as a guest speaker. He stands, dressed in a suit, with one noticeable change: his left arm is missing, and his coat sleeve is tucked into his pocket. To set the stage, he describes the catastrophic incident that claimed the life of his best friend and eventually led to the loss of his arm. In the years following his accident, he plans his return to climbing. He becomes the first expedition leader of the largest cross-disability, most diverse team ever to reach Mt. Everest base camp at 17,500 ft. Throughout his talk, Guller has images projected on the background screens, depicting the harsh conditions he endured on Everest. As you watch, you start to shiver a bit as the freezing wind, the ice, and the constant battle with nature seem daunting. Gary and his sherpa team made international news when he reached the summit of Mt Everest (29,032 ft).

Gary is also the author of "Make Others Greater[9]," which offers insights into his life experiences and the lessons learned along the way. The book focuses on teamwork, leadership, and resilience, drawing from his own mountaineering and adventure experiences as powerful metaphors for life's challenges. Gary's life story serves as a testament to the power of determination, resilience, and the human spirit.

Sadness and empathy are related. Empathy can involve sharing sorrow or depression, and can be especially challenging for salespeople who are often communicating with buyers and vendors with all sorts of issues. One of the less popular yet significant aspects of social media is the emotional distress and sadness it can cause. You can't eliminate sadness, but you can develop effective coping strategies to navigate, manage, and reduce its influence. A recent influencer wrote the following: SADNESS: Sales Are Dope Never Ever Stop Selling as a reminder to keep a positive attitude. And now, Sales Are Dope[10] is a movie on Amazon.

3.6 AVOIDING INSANITY

Are you going insane? Overwhelmed salespeople can experience intense emotional and mental distress and feel as if they are "going insane" due to the high-pressure nature of the job. Unfortunately, the health numbers against the sales profession are ugly, with field data showing burnout rates above 75% and the challenge of mental health issues above 40%. Within a sales team, over half of the group is likely struggling with problems caused by the high-pressure environment.

It's the nature of the job to face constant pressure to meet or exceed sales targets. And the associated fear of missing quotas, facing rejection, and worrying about job security can fuel ongoing anxiety. Sales involves the repeated cycles of hope with new opportunities, disappointment from negative feedback, and uncertainty with unpredictable customer situations. The emotional rollercoaster needs to be well-managed to avoid a lack of confidence or instability. For many salespeople, working from home can be isolating, with no distractions and only prospecting to keep them focused. But, this can also be a black hole of constant outbound communications and little or no feedback. There are plenty of psychological potholes that need to be avoided, including depression, sadness, or fatigue.

Let's assume you're not a candidate for Nurse Ratched or shock therapy, and prefer to take some inventory precautions. Suppose you are severely struggling with stress and mental overload. In that case, the feelings of helplessness and depression can manifest themselves in weight gain, headaches, lack of sleep, fatigue, and generally make you not a fun person to be around. You're not losing your mind; instead, you may be stuck in a rut or, worse, feeling responsible for the dire situation. You may have stopped your everyday routines to exercise, pursue hobbies, or catch up on your favorite TV show or sports. Taking a break from the stress feels like giving in to the pressure, so you keep enduring the pain. The downward spiral is self-induced, and you need to remind yourself of some essential self-regulating techniques that can help you regain a sense of control, reduce anxiety, and protect your well-being. Holding on too tightly can be detrimental. Sales is a performance game, and although you feel like you have to push through stressful highs and lows as part of the job, you owe it to yourself to manage your emotions and get back to healthy habits. Consequently, you may eventually forget what the term work-life balance stands for. Robots may not need hobbies, but you do.

Consider incorporating the following strategies to break out of a slump: mindfulness, deep breathing exercises, regular physical activity, a balanced diet, and effective work-life balance. Start with your physical well-being: maintain good posture—shoulders back, jaw up —and take regular breaks to rest your eyes. Take a moment to calm your mind, and if possible, consider taking a nap (if you work from home) or practicing some meditation. Allow your body to unwind and release stress for 15-20 minutes. You can enhance this state by practicing simple breathing through both your nose and mouth. A few minutes of this can lower your heart rate and clear your mind. After a rest, you can add a few stretches or a brief walk outdoors to change up your environment. Take in some sunshine and nature. Remind yourself of things that help you de-stress, such as hobbies, podcasts, music, or other uplifting things. Planting some mental "happy seeds" will go a long way towards improvement.

Lastly, set some boundaries to distinguish work and home life, especially at home. It is very easy to take work calls or send a few emails after dinner. There is never perfect advice for someone going through various degrees of issues; however, it is good to review the self-regulating tools that work best for you and keep your life in check. Practicing these habits has been shown to help people feel calmer, think more clearly, and weather complex workplace challenges.

3.7 CULTURE OF SELLING

I had never been to mainland China and was excited to visit new customers. As a startup CEO, I had positional power, and my Chinese colleague helped me navigate many of the travel hurdles, food warnings, and the humidity. It was summer in Shenzhen, and I dressed in a suit out of respect. We were picked up in a rundown VW Jetta taxi and drove for about 25 minutes, without air conditioning. We arrived at the H-company parking lot, badged in, and then stored our electronics in a locker. I put our presentation on a USB drive, and that was about all we could take into the meeting room. Fortunately, our startup story was powerful, as we were developing new modem technology years ahead of the competition, and the customer's reaction to each question was impressive. Many of the initial discussions were conducted in English, and I advised maintaining cordial conversations.

The guidance came the night before as we were asked to dinner by one of the top executives from H-company. At our table were four executives facing me, including our chief techie, who had graduated from the mainland at the top of his class. Easily the smartest one in the room, our guru could discuss any technical issue with confidence. I remember the food was authentic and tough for me to get excited about, so I drank some alcohol to wash down whatever food we were feasting on. The majority of the conversations were in Mandarin, and I learned to translate as best I could by recognizing the sounds of a few words. Otherwise, I let my partner keep them on their toes. On the way back to our hotel, he let me know that this "dinner" was more of an interview and judgment of our talent. He said the feedback was positive and we were welcome to have our meeting the following day. This came after a 7,000-mile, 14-hour flight from SFO to HKG and a bus ride into Shenzhen.

We held back-to-back meetings throughout the week and met with engineers and key decision-makers from various departments, who would quiz us on our technology differentiation and how a startup could develop new products so quickly in Silicon Valley. By Thursday, we were exhausted; however, they said our solution was more important than we realized and asked whether we would be willing to sign a Memorandum of Understanding (MOU) to grant them early access to our chipset. We gladly returned to their offices and created several drafts of a 20-page document that was thoroughly discussed in both English and Mandarin, and written in English. Although I wished I could understand all the sidebar discussions, I was covered with my colleague in all meetings, and we gladly signed our first contract. On paper, it was valued at nearly $50 million, and for a newly funded startup, this was a great start.

Upon returning to the Bay, we met up with our venture capital partner and his very talented Chinese analyst. They reviewed our MOU and were very impressed with the work we had accomplished in only a week. The analyst pulled me aside and told me a story about why I was so crucial in the negotiation. She walked me through three scenarios in which a negotiation is run between an American and another American, an American and a Chinese person, and two Chinese people. She said that, given the same document to discuss, e.g., the MOU, the best possible combination is American-to-Chinese. She reasoned that if the negotiation were with two Americans, it would involve endless rounds of legal talks until a final document was completed. Even then, it would be only partially mutual. If two Chinese were to negotiate, they would agree to terms, then shake hands, and then make changes. This would continue for days, weeks, or even longer, with a never-ending challenge of trust. However, if an American and a Chinese person were to negotiate, as we did, the outcome would be swift and trusted.

Language of Selling

For me, growing up and speaking only one language was sufficient, since most of the world speaks English. Or at least that is what I thought. As of 2025, the top 4 languages spoken are English, Chinese, Hindi, and Spanish. In high school, I had a choice of 2 years of French or Spanish, and then in college, I was required to take a year of Latin. Years later, when it was time for my kids to learn a language, they studied Chinese, Spanish, and American Sign Language (ASL). In the future, we will likely have real-time translators built into our phones or earbuds, allowing us to be fluent in all languages, regardless of our native tongue.

Throughout my career, I have worked for numerous multinational companies that operate in multiple languages, including Chinese, Hebrew, Korean, Japanese, Portuguese, Swedish, Taiwanese, and Thai. Although the common language was English, I learned that there was a translation "loss" when using the common denominator language. One of my smartest Chinese friends used to say, "Which came first, the egg or the chicken?" To him, it was natural, but in my mind, I heard, "chicken or the egg," as I had been taught. Saying "Doggy dog world" is a misquoted version of "Dog eat dog world." But egg or chicken is about translation, and in this case, a priority on the word egg. I learned to enjoy this version of the saying and appreciate myself for ever trying to say a Chinese proverb.

There is an idea that Chinese people are better at math because of their method of counting. It is partly based on fundamental differences in language structure and early math learning, with some nuance and context. In Chinese, the numerals directly reflect the base-10 system. For example, 11 is "ten-one," 12 is "ten-two," and so on, with this pattern continuing up to 99. In English, by contrast, numbers like 11 or 12 don't transparently show their mathematical structure.

Additional research has shown that children learning to count in Chinese or other East Asian languages (such as Korean or Japanese) often grasp the base-10 concept earlier than English-speaking children. The regularity makes it easier for kids to understand place value and how numbers are composed, which in turn can make basic calculations (like addition and subtraction) more intuitive. Cultural attitudes toward education, parental expectations, teaching methods, the rigor of math curricula, and the time spent practicing also play significant roles in math ability.

As with all elite selling, we must be aware of cross-cultural challenges and understand that when situations arise involving language or common-phrase errors, they may stem from familiarity or a lack thereof. Be empathetic and take the time to ensure the speaker or colleague understands the origin of the phrase, and offer to have them share their language nuances with you.

3.8 FEAR AND THE UNKNOWN

Read this carefully. It says, "Fear AND the unknown," rather than "Fear the unknown." Maybe it's too subtle, but here are some of the challenges. We know that salespeople often fear the unknown because uncertainty creates anxiety about outcomes they can't predict. This fear manifests during key stages, such as cold calling, prospecting, follow-ups, and closing, when salespeople are unsure how their prospects will react or whether they will face rejection or acceptance.

The top fears for any salesperson can be categorized into two significant areas: 1) known items, such as cold calling, new opportunities, rejection, failure, quotas, or pricing, and 2) the unknown, including correct answers, control, radio silence, or sales style. The fact that you can control the efforts to chase new business through cold calling means you are aware of various possibilities for feedback, including excitement, acceptance, or rejection. All feedback is valuable, even knowing about rejection can help address issues with your proposal, timing, or approach for next time. Trying to meet or beat your quotas can evoke fear; however, the more powerful emotions are confidence, reliability, and the reasonableness of the goal. These can be measured and managed, not feared.

Fearing the unknown can be far more anxiety-ridden because you lack control of the situation. You may not have all the correct answers to your customer requirements, struggle with whether to push harder when it feels like the customer has gone radio silent, or feel a lack of control because not enough information is being shared. Ask a salesperson whether they prefer an issue with pricing to not hearing back from a customer, and 100% will choose the known issue of pricing over the unknown issue of not hearing back.

Our company recently bid on an extensive program involving a new medical device designed to pre-diagnose the onset of glaucoma by evaluating key visual conditions in the eye and the optic nerves. The science was well known, and the apparatus was in its second generation, suggesting that most of the kinks had been worked out. Both engineering and marketing were set, and it was up to the supply chain to select a new vendor for manufacturing. The project progressed through the RFQ stages, and approximately halfway through due diligence, the customer halted the program. They communicated that there would be some resource issues and the delay would be approximately 6 months. Over the past year, our team has done an excellent job of selling and preparing for new business, providing detailed proposal responses, and meeting all requirements. However, the customer had internal issues that needed to be resolved before moving forward.

This was a salesperson's nightmare, as almost nothing good comes from delays. Our management team wanted more details on the delay and whether there was any reason to reconsider moving forward with the program. The feedback was to wait until they had further indication of priorities—a fuzzy response, to be sure. So, we waited as the days and weeks passed, maintaining a nominal status every month or two. After eight months, the program was reinstated and back on track for introducing new products. Perhaps the greatest fear was the unknown outcome after a long wait period, during which we could add little value except to maintain close contact with the customer. In hindsight, the professional way we handled the delay, along with the careful and periodic requests for updates, allowed us to continue our relationship, albeit at a very arms-length distance. We made the process relationship-based, rather than purely transactional, and this may have been the winning recipe.

Fearing the unknown is something for space astronauts or other pioneers who challenge the universe. Putting yourself in a space suit, strapping into a supersonic jet, or diving in a deep-sea submarine are truly life-threatening experiences that may end badly. But living the life ot a top salesperson has very little room for fear. Control and manage what you can, and let the uncontrollable outcomes take their course. If your customer is rolling the dice, place your bet on the highest outcome for success—the pass line has the best odds in the casino!

3.9 WHO CARES ANYWAY

I hired a colleague as a subject matter expert (SME) in medical device and life science technologies. He had dual degrees in biomedical engineering and physiology and spent his first 10 years working in marketing and engineering at medical device companies. One of his early assignments was supporting blood dialysis clinics and monitoring patient therapies. The task involved understanding the dialysis process, the various stages of patient care, and the effectiveness of the treatment being administered. He collected quantitative data on each patient and wrote an elaborate summary of his findings and improvements. The company was fortunate to have his talent and dedication to a modest task that had life-changing consequences.

His role for me was to support new customer engagements by understanding the ins and outs of devices, technologies, and processes to qualify devices for the FDA, and to assist in streamlining the manufacturing of the instrument. He would easily and effectively communicate to the customer why our company was the right choice to support their product, and even provide insights or previous success stories to increase confidence in their supplier decision. It was a testimony to the trust he developed with every customer, and working with him was terrific. As your team expanded, I asked him if he would like to earn a little more money by moving into sales and earning commissions. He said, "No," and then the more surprising reason followed. He replied that he really enjoyed being in applications engineering, where he won new customer engagements by demonstrating his knowledge of the under-

lying medical therapy, creating plans with intelligent reasoning, understanding technology, and fostering mutual respect with very
sophisticated buyers in engineering and operations. Then came the
bombshell. He said he could never switch over to sales because it would
make people think less of him. He had established his beliefs based on
education, consortia (e.g., IEEE), medical journals, and applications engineering, which led him to believe that salespeople were merely door
openers or "dogs with a note" and could not handle technical or intelligent reasoning to close complex deals.

In my life, my father had a PhD in physics, possessed a remarkably
high IQ, and spent the majority of his career translating elaborate theo-
retical physics research and development into practical experiments,
proofs of concept, and, more importantly, truly remarkable products. His
work in thin-film optical coating led to his nomination by a jury of his
peers to become a fellow in the Optical Society of America. He blazed
many trails in optics and was brilliant by any measure. He was an excellent speaker and a world-class technical writer, with patents and theories
that would endure for generations. One of the things I really appreciate
in his mindset was the purpose of technical salespeople and their ability
to communicate and manage new business effectively. When it came to
understanding numbers, formulas, and complex equations, my dad was
brilliant. And, when it came to spending time in the "gray areas," such as
small talk or common sales questions, he would defer to salespeople to
do their job. Looking back on years of our friendship, it is clear that he
understood the critical importance of both IQ and EQ, with his ability to
manage his enormous capacity for brain cells and to leverage technical
sales team members with high emotional intelligence to manage the
human process.

I vividly remember a roommate of mine from my time living in Southern
California. He went by "JF" for "Just Foolin'" and had one of the most
outgoing and magnetic personalities I had ever met. JF viewed every
situation as both an opportunity and a challenge. Having a conversation

with him was always entertaining, and energy drinks of choice likely fueled his passion. I was early in my career as a systems engineer, managing people and solving technical problems with ease. My job was to ensure that large satellite programs (e.g., GPS) kept moving forward by resolving the pesky issues between engineers. I was learning the strengths of my tools and advancing within the organization by working with internal employees, then being promoted to cross-functional roles, and subsequently to multi-company programs. I eventually led training programs for NASA astronauts. It was very cool and allowed me to spend time at the Johnson Space Center and the Kennedy Space Center. During this time in my life, I recall being content with my perspective on the world until I had a life-changing conversation with JF. He noticed I was always busy at work, traveling weekly, and advancing in the organization. It was a 9-to-5 job in a massive company with security and a bright future. But then came the dig. JF said he could never work as hard as I do with a known pay for each period. He was a salesperson for his entire life and said that a big part of his drive was to earn extra income and commissions. From that moment forward, I would always want to be in a profession that rewards hard work and offers unlimited upside.

AI Elevates Salespeople

Over the next 5-10 years, the importance of salespeople will become even more critical as technology takes over routine tasks, highlighting their unique human skills. While artificial intelligence can automate data analysis, lead scoring, and even generate personalized content, it cannot build authentic relationships, read emotional cues, or establish trust the way a skilled salesperson can. Customers still value human interaction for complex decisions, negotiations, and when addressing nuanced needs or objections. Sales professionals may need to adjust their skills from transactional selling to consultative or advisory roles. AI enables salespeople to access deep insights about prospects, allowing them to tailor their approach with unprecedented precision. However, delivering these insights empathetically and adapting in real time to customer reactions remains a human strength.

In high-stakes B2B sales or rapidly evolving markets, salespeople will be essential for interpreting ambiguous data, navigating organizational politics, and adapting strategies on the fly. In contrast, AI and its LLMs may fall short. AI can recommend actions, but cannot make ethical decisions or creatively solve problems in unexpected situations. Salespeople will be relied upon for judgment, especially in sensitive or high-value deals.

Yes, we care about salespeople. AI will elevate the role of salespeople, making them more valuable as relationship builders, consultants, and advisors, as AI handles the background work. This relationship enables sales teams to focus on what humans do best: creating trust, solving problems, and driving new business.

3.10 TRICK OR TREAT

Every Halloween, our neighborhood gets hundreds of trick-or-treaters. The reason is simple: we live in the world's largest cul-de-sac, with windy streets that serve as a huge boardwalk for safe wandering and candy gathering from house to house. There are no sidewalks, just the wide open path of the street. Every household goes all out with decorations, homemade concoctions, graveyards, spiderwebs, and one home converted into a walk-in haunted house.

With so much kid traffic, the majority of the homes move their candy stash to the edge of their driveway. Most setups are long tables with chairs and additional decorations to enhance the experience. Our tables have a custom Halloween tablecloth, a metal haunted house with lights, small Jack-o-lanterns with LED candles, string lights, and, finally, a 6-foot-long stretch of candy. With 10 large bags of candy from Costco, we can hand out candy for nearly 2 hours.

Every year, I am reminded of the Stanford marshmallow experiment, where a young child is given a marshmallow and asked to wait to eat it with a reward of a second marshmallow if they last the duration. It is known as the delayed gratification experiment, and studies show that if a child can delay the first bite and wait for a second marshmallow, they are more successful in life.

It's now time to introduce the "Trick or Treat" experiment and discover the four common attributes of anonymity, peer pressure, following directions, and age-related behavior.

Anonymity-driven behavior is the ability to act a certain way while being hidden behind a costume or mask. A child can act in ways they would not otherwise, including sneaking candy or even the entire bowl if left unsupervised.

Peer pressure is rampant on Halloween, nearly doubling the likelihood that someone will take more candy in groups than when alone. The group setting diffuses the responsibility and accountability, increasing transgressive behavior.

Directions about how much candy can be grabbed from the table are always unclear. The dialogue is as follows;

Child: "Trick or Treat"

Household: "Happy Halloween"

Child: "How many pieces of candy can I have?"

Household: "You may have two."

Child One, honestly: "Thank you," and takes two pieces

Child Two, Masked rebel: No reply, just carefully grabs a small handful

Child Three, In group: depends on the group behavior, varies from following instructions to exploiting the situation and grabbing more.

Child Four, No supervision: like the rebel, decides to risk a few extra pieces to show they can disobey without penalty.

The final attribute is associated with a child's age, specifically after about age 5. Kids under five mostly behave as their parents teach them, and hopefully, this includes politeness and respect. If they are allowed to grab candy at an open table with 50 pieces in front of them, they will ask permission. However, the age range of 6-16 creates a mix of characters depending on maturity, self-awareness, and character.

Halloween candy behavior may be a predictor of success. Unfortunately, it would likely ruin the fun of Trick-or-Treating by turning it into an experiment. It may cross a Machiavellian line by questioning certain personality disorders on a single spooky night in October.

Below is the "Trick or Treat," predictive sales attributes drawing some insights from the main categories in "The Challenger," by Matthew Dixon.

Attribute	Normal	Halloween
Lone Wolf	Low	Rebel
Hard Work	Medium	Detailed
Problem Solver	Medium	Rule Follower
Relationship Builder	High	Peer Pressure
Challenger	High	Assertive

Figure 3.2 Trick-or-Treat Sales Attributes

During one night of the year, kids may display the attributes of a Lone Wolf (Halloween rebel) or a Challenger (high-energy, assertive). The "Challenger" youngster who asks how many pieces of candy they may have is polite and yet assertive, questioning when there are no directions. Later in life, they will exhibit a similar behavior toward their customers, as they are not afraid to ask essential questions in unclear situations. Unfortunately, the Lone Wolf type will undoubtedly enjoy a night of being a rebel. Although filled with self-confidence, their path to success will be limited as a top hunter with exceptional, but narrow, skills.

The business world is filled with analogies of Halloween nights and candy treats. You are all too familiar with the sales peers who feel like they constantly wear a disguise, act without supervision, and behave weirdly under peer pressure. People with a high emotional intelligence score may appreciate Halloween for its opportunities to explore imagination, creativity, and social connection. Still, their enjoyment often depends on individual preference and their sensitivity to others' emotions. Research and commentary indicate that Halloween can foster emotional growth, bravery, and empathy in children, suggesting that those with higher emotional intelligence may find meaning in the holiday's social and creative aspects.

However, highly empathetic individuals - one aspect of emotional intelligence - might be less drawn to the horror elements of Halloween, such as scary costumes or haunted attractions, because they tend to put themselves in others' shoes and may find these scenarios less enjoyable. Conversely, people with strong emotional regulation, another component of EQ, are more likely to view Halloween as an opportunity for safe fun and are generally equipped to manage anxiety or discomfort that might arise.

PART II

CHAPTER 4
SALES CHALLENGES

PROFESSIONAL SALESPEOPLE ENCOUNTER a diverse set of challenges in their daily work. Some of these relate directly to the tasks of their job, while others arise from the surrounding environment or personal well-being. Most salespeople accept that their job brings challenges that impact their lives; however, the upside of commissions typically offsets the impact of long hours and crazy work-life balance.

I recall speaking with one of my classmates in B-school about his sales job. He told me stories of how Coke and Pepsi paid enormous fees to own shelf space or soda machines that would only sell their branded sodas. As a consumer, I would always wonder about the mix of sodas and water in the vending machine, especially if I wanted to select a Coke or Pepsi, Sprite or 7-Up, A&W or Mug root beer. Little did I know that the profit margins on soda are substantial. A 12-oz Coca-Cola costs $0.26 to produce (including ingredients, packaging, and shipping), and about $0.04 for the liquid (syrup and carbonated water). In my friend's situation, he was competing with sugary sodas by introducing a new brand of tea and juice drinks. It came in a glass bottle with a screw top and over a dozen flavors. The screw top was also famous for having "Real Facts" printed on the bottom of each bottle cap. It was initially focused on carbonated apple juice in the early 1970s and was called Unadulterated Food Products, with a primary focus on selling to health food stores. In the 1980s, the popular apple juice brand underwent a name change to Snapple, and the Snapple Beverage Corporation was born. Their first tea was produced in 1987. By 1992, Snapple had expanded its distribution to every major city in the United States, with sales exceeding $100 million. The company went public in 1994 and was subsequently acquired by Quaker Oats for $1.7 billion. As for my friend who ran distribution in Northern California, he was unable to fulfill enough orders to keep up with demand. Snapple created its own category in iced tea and fruit drinks, becoming a formidable competitor to Coke and Pepsi; its combined revenues in 1992 exceeded $28.5 billion. Snapple had two designated distribution companies for Southern California (note, Los Angeles was the largest single market in California), but only my friend managed the upper half of the state. And yes, commissions were flowing his way for every case he drove his Snapple-loaded van from store to store. A challenging gig with massive upside, and then by the end of 1992, Snapple signed over 30 distributors in California alone. Timing is everything.

Not every challenge starts with boldness or amazement; sometimes it just sneaks up on you, like the calories in a Shake Shack Double Down fries with 1,910 calories or a Sonic Oreo and Reese's Peanut Butter shake with 1,720 calories. A single margarita typically has 750 calories, and how often do you drink just one, or forget the chips and avocado dip? If shots are flowing at the bar, you become competitive and need to win. When you become deeply immersed in strategic selling and become engrossed in account details, you often forget to take good care of yourself, including a balanced diet, regular exercise, and self-care.

The most stressful challenges for salespeople fall into an extensive range from relationship breakdown (divorce and family), chronic health issues (diabetes, heart disease), alcohol and substance abuse, mental health, job security, and toxic work cultures. Some of these are obvious and outward challenges, while others are more hidden and inward. Salespeople are excellent at overcoming some of the most impactful challenges, both personally and professionally; however, they are also the worst at seeking help in difficult situations. Statistically, salespeople are not good at self-diagnosing high stress and are often great at managing their internal stress levels, usually ignoring warning signs until burnout or a crisis occurs.

4.1 COMPLEXITY PERPLEXITY

In today's sales landscape, especially in complex B2B environments like electronics manufacturing and supply chain, the daily work of a salesperson can often feel overwhelming due to multitasking, administrative overload, unpredictable client interactions, and constant performance demands. However, there are actionable strategies to simplify this complexity, leading to greater productivity and satisfaction.

Let's break down the complexity by removing obvious repetitive tasks, such as logging calls, scheduling follow-ups, and updating contacts. Whether you leverage a third-party application (such as a CRM) or manage your own tool, automation can easily increase your productivity and lessen some of the administrative work. Look for ways to simplify routine tasks, such as reporting, so the time saved can free up sales representatives to focus on selling and relationship building rather than paperwork. Some of the best salespeople are also the worst at keeping their status reports up to date.

Selling, by nature, can be a very unstructured function. However, those who create a structure in their daily routine tend to be more productive. If you have an everyday routine of prospecting using your favorite search and database tools, create a calendar task with start and end times. Your mind will treat the task as a defined period, helping you stay laser-focused with a time boundary that magically reduces fatigue. If an hour is the perfect length of time or "soft" boundary, use this as a starting point and schedule multiple meetings with yourself throughout the week. Make any necessary adjustments as needed and set specific tasks for each day of the week. Perhaps Mondays are best for internal tasks, research, and scheduling outbound message sends, with Tuesdays and Wednesdays ideal for contacting customers and engaging in more social interactions, leading up to Friday. It never gets old to wish someone, "Have a great weekend."

There are a few exceptions or priorities that will override any self-scheduled plans, specifically the high-priority items such as revenue-generating activities and urgent customer issues. Closing deals in any sales organization will take precedence over prospecting or nurturing leads. These are the welcomed unplanned interruptions that lead to success and commissions.

Additional steps in organization and incremental process improvements will not only improve your outcomes but also typically help you streamline the sales process by reducing steps, using helpful templates, and establishing unique routines that leverage your time and effort. Continue to experiment with new technologies or scheduling strategies that work best for you and your team. Set up alerts as friendly reminders, and see how often you can predict your own schedule over the days or weeks ahead. Try a simple "To Do List" to start the day and write down a handful of objectives to complete. It will take you less than 5 minutes to jot down what you hope to accomplish. Then, at the end of the day, perform a quick review and check the list to see what you completed, modified, or will address later. Then, at the end of the day, shut things down and remember to maintain a healthy work-life balance. Remind yourself that you managed through a host of well-planned tasks, hopefully overachieved your own expectations, and then reward yourself with a mind break.

4.2 SALES AND ALCOHOL

You may wonder which professions have the highest rates of alcohol consumption. If you include drugs and alcohol consumption, the following professions have the highest amount of drinkers by population: 1. Mining, Quarrying, and Oil Workers, 2. Construction Workers, 3. Restaurant and Food Service Workers, 4. Arts and Entertainment, 5. Doctors and Healthcare Professionals, 6. Information and Communications, 7. Salespeople, 8. Management, 9. Lawyers, and 10. Emergency Responders. Seventh place is not bad considering the limited overlap with Mining and Construction. Some of the criteria for sales stress are tight deadlines, significant socializing, and odd work hours, with over 10% of salespeople having substance abuse disorders.

I was treated to dinner recently by a salesperson who wanted our business. I work in sales and thought the meeting would be good to share ideas on how we might work together. Since he was paying, I brought a bottle of Caymus Cabernet Sauvignon to share. I handed him the bottle in its lovely gift bag, and he said, "Thanks, but I don't drink. Ok, if I pass it along to my boss on your behalf?" I said, "Sure," and we proceeded with a top-notch steak dinner.

Over the past five years, I've met more salespeople who mention they have stopped drinking, and the one thing in common is that they are all individual contributors, not in leadership. Many of the reasons are for general health and/or the need to stay sharp in an ever-changing and demanding profession - fancy way of saying, "the older you get, the more challenging it is to keep up with the job." Hence, the focus is on better health and well-being.

However, leadership continues to be a significant influence on the consumption of alcohol. Imagine a sales leadership conference and a "bar is closed" sign in the lobby. In the past, salespeople carried their own supply of liquor and stimulants for emergencies like these. Today, there is DoorDash, which will bring your order right to the lobby.

Ordering drinks from the bar is part of the sales game—Tequila shots, well drinks, wine, beer, and more shots. There is enormous social pressure to participate, make friendly, humorous, and competitive toasts, and, as appropriate, have jesters. As the evening continues, the remarks become more direct, inhibitions give way to karaoke embarrassment, and team bonding intensifies through the late, late hours. Imagine if someone asked for a non-alcoholic martini in this crowd of crazy (social) alcoholics.

Show a man death, and he will gladly accept disease.

4.3 THE DIABETES EFFECT

Richard Bernstein (1934-2025) was diagnosed in 1946 at the age of 12 with Type 1 diabetes. His treatment, common at the time, included a diet high in carbohydrates, a daily insulin shot, and monthly doctor visits to check his blood sugar. By his 30s, he suffered from night blindness and deformed feet. He became his own advocate and began experimenting with insulin doses and diet until he determined a low-carb diet kept him in better sugar balance. When he attempted to disseminate the word of his discoveries, he was often dismissed; as a result, he decided to enter medical school at the age of 45. After graduating from Albert Einstein College of Medicine, he established a private practice in Mamaroneck, New York. He continued to advocate for his ideas to address blood sugar levels. He is now considered the first Type 1 diabetes patient to self-test blood sugar levels, which is now a part of standard treatment. He authored YouTube videos and books, including "Dr. Bernstein's Diabetes Solution[1]."

The Diabetes Effect—this sounds ominous. What sort of effect does diabetes have on salespeople? Diabetes is a chronic condition where the body either doesn't produce enough insulin or can't effectively use the insulin it does produce, leading to high blood sugar levels. There are three main types of diabetes: Type 1, Type 2, and Gestational. While your liver is processing alcohol, it stops producing glucose. As a result, your blood sugar can drop quickly, putting you at risk for low blood sugar, or hypoglycemia. In general, alcohol consumption can have complex effects on A1C (a measure of long-term blood sugar control) and blood sugar levels, depending on the amount and frequency of consumption.

I apologize in advance if this section appears to trivialize the severity of diabetes. In the US, 11.6% of the population (or 39 million people have diabetes, including 30 million who have been diagnosed and 9 million who are undiagnosed. It also tends to be more prevalent after the age of 65, so for much younger readers, you may consider this a caution. Lastly, nearly 100 million Americans are considered "prediabetes," a condition where blood sugar levels are higher than usual but not yet high enough to be diagnosed with diabetes. Age, race, and regional data are well documented with a simple search.

The likelihood of someone having diabetes is less than 2% if you're under age 34 and increases almost linearly to over 20% after age 65. If you are one of the 1 in 100 million of prediabetes candidates, you may start watching out for the signs and avoid the four Manhattan liquid lunches. Some would argue that sales is an addiction. It can certainly become addictive, as the pursuit of revenues can blind a person to their other habits and relationships.

A 2024 study[2] by UT Southwestern Medical Center showed that a person's IQ during high school is predictive of alcohol consumption later in life. Researchers found that for every one-point increase in IQ, there was a corresponding 1.6% increase in the likelihood that the respondent reported moderate or heavy alcohol use. The study did not suggest that your high school IQ controls your destiny, but rather that the higher IQ levels could lead to intervening social factors that influence drinking. So be careful the next time you say, "Alcohol makes you smarter," when in fact, making you smarter makes you want alcohol—a mind bender.

4.4 FAKE IT TIL YOU MAKE IT

On the surface, the phrase "Fake it, till you make it" is about projecting confidence and competence that help your mindset develop genuine skills and self-belief over time. The approach is designed to help sales-people overcome initial self-doubt, perform more effectively in high-pressure situations, and gradually establish authentic confidence through repeated action and experience.

Examining the positive aspects of "faking it" requires some peeling of the onion of self-confidence and self-belief. In general, those with high self-confidence fill their minds with positive self-talk and encouraging thoughts. They focus on personal strengths and celebrate success, regardless of the achievement's magnitude. Remember, the most minor achievement may have essential elements of satisfying realistic goals and provide positive motivation. We're not talking about tying one's shoes properly; instead, we're setting out to expand a sales pipeline by adding 3-5 new prospects, rather than closing an enormous deal with an unrealistic timeline. You may also wish to surround yourself with people who encourage, uplift, and believe in you. Be sure to take good care of yourself by exercising and eating healthy foods to strengthen your body and mind. Practice assertiveness when ordering your next latte at Starbucks, buy a new pair of shoes, and walk confidently in any direction. You are constantly building your temple of confidence, and each positive step adds another brick to your wall.

In the next layer above your core, some things build on your confidence, such as stepping outside of your comfort zone to try new things and embrace growth. A good starting point is to experiment with new sales techniques or presentations. Perhaps you have been using the same material for too long, and it's time to update it to reflect current market conditions or overdue company upgrades. Are you using PowerPoint presentations that reflect outdated items because marketing is focusing on frontline issues? You can add your own material and try it on new customers. Remember, your audience is looking to you for updates, and you have the freedom and power to make adjustments as needed. Your willingness to take calculated risks has carry-over effects, including your ability to adapt to new environments, embrace change, and build readiness before any business disruption. Imagine if, instead of using your daily set of material as part of your routine, you forced yourself to change up the material, revised your emails with a new perspective, and carried out your duties as if you were new on the job.

Learning new skills, such as through workshops or YouTube videos, can be challenging; however, teaching yourself to introduce "new" into your daily routine can significantly improve your skills and help your audience enjoy your newfound confidence. Call it a creative experiment and allow yourself to practice, iterate, and evaluate yourself. There is no wrong path here, only a chance to know yourself better and make self-improvements. What may feel uncomfortable today can, through repeated practice, become a new normal, leading to better outcomes and, indeed, better experiences. Every day growth is something to celebrate.

Now, for the bruises in the onion. As you push yourself through change, try to avoid comparing yourself to others, as this can create setbacks. For every excellent speaker or presentation, there can be faults or negative feedback, suggesting you can do better. As part of every salesperson's routine, you will walk into an audience that may turn hostile for a variety of reasons. You might face severe rejection and wonder what you did wrong, only to find that the customer was experiencing serious turmoil within their management team and was pushing the stress onto their vendors. For most professional salespeople, we never expect our customers to say, "Wow, that presentation was perfect, how much can we buy?" However, we need to put negative feedback into context and use it as an opportunity to improve, rather than making any judgment about character or capability. Learn to replace negative internal dialogue with affirmations and to recognise your skills and past successes. Do your best to manage emotions by regulating the ups and downs and focusing on customer needs, regardless of setbacks. If you can develop healthy feedback habits when being challenged, you will be rewarded in the future. Avoiding all negative feedback would be rich, but not realistic. Instead, look to your support systems, remember your resiliency, and use your experiences to build your confidence. Listen to a post-game interview of the losing coach as he reassures people that the next game will show improvements. Recall some history when Steve Jobs was forced out of Apple, Walt Disney's first studio declared bankruptcy, or Michael Jordan was cut from his high school basketball team.

4.5 NEGOTIATING

In practice, strategic sellers excel at negotiating because they have a deep understanding of their customers' businesses and are equipped to engage multiple stakeholders with a tailored solution. The art of negotiating is about achieving agreements that satisfy all parties. It's a careful blend of preparation, interpersonal skills, and the ability to adapt to changing circumstances at the negotiation table. Truly effective negotiators enter discussions with a clear understanding of their counterparts' objectives, constraints, and possible alternatives.

Author of "Never Split the Difference[3]", Chris Voss, describes a powerful, high-stakes negotiation method known as the Behavioral Change Stairway Model (BCSM), which includes the following five stages: active listening, empathy, rapport, influence, and behavioral change. The origins of the model can be traced back to the great American psychologist Carl Rogers, who proposed that real change can only occur when a therapist accepts the client as they are—an approach known as unconditional positive regard. Voss suggests that if you successfully take someone up the Behavioral Change stairway — each stage attempting to engender more trust and more connection — there will be a breakthrough moment when unconditional positive regard is established, and you can begin exerting influence.

Thousands of B-school graduates who study one of the famous negotiating books by Roger Fisher, called "Getting to Yes[4]," have ultimately discovered that you haven't reached the negotiation table if what you're hearing is the word "yes." Instead, the more important words in a negotiation are "that's right." However, this breakthrough usually doesn't occur at the beginning of a negotiation, is often invisible to the counterpart when it does, and the counterpart frequently accepts what you've said. To them, it's a subtle epiphany.

Voss speaks about one of his students, a salesperson for a pharmaceutical company, who was selling a new product to a doctor who was the largest user of the medication she was promoting. In her first approach, she outlined all the product features and benefits, but he was obviously unimpressed by another "me too" approach. However, during the discussion, she noticed how passionate he was about his care and his rapport with his patients. During her next visit, she focused more on his approach and praised him for tailoring it to each customer. He responded with, "That's right, I treat every patient as if there is an epidemic and needs special care." It felt like the first time she had effectively communicated, and she reached the breakthrough she had been hoping for.

Preparing for negotiations involves preparation and being fully informed about one's counterparts' objectives, constraints, and alternatives. Negotiating isn't just about convincing others; it's about listening closely, understanding motivations, and addressing concerns to build trust and potentially uncover hidden interests. The best negotiators improvise, find creative solutions, and adapt to dynamic, sometimes chaotic, bargaining situations. Most enduring agreements create value for both sides and are based on fair compromises rather than a victory-at-all-costs approach.

The art of negotiating can be taught or learned. While some people may have natural inclinations, such as strong communication skills or empathy, research and real-world experience demonstrate that effective negotiation is a skill set that can be developed through proper training, practice, and feedback. Universities, business schools, and corporate training programs routinely offer negotiation courses, demonstrating that the art can be systematically taught. Role-playing exercises and simulations help learners practice negotiation scenarios, develop confidence, and receive constructive feedback. Self-reflection and post-negotiation analysis allow individuals to learn from both successful and unsuccessful negotiations, refining their approach over time. Interpersonal skills, such as active listening, assertiveness, and managing emotions, can be strengthened through coaching, guided practice, and real-world experience. With commitment, anyone can significantly improve their negotiation abilities, even those who don't consider themselves naturally gifted negotiators.

Contractual Agreement

Sales agreements are the fundamental contract for the sale of goods or services, specifying what is being sold, delivery terms, pricing, warranties, payment terms, and liability provisions. Sales agreements are ubiquitous in both product and service industries and are negotiated to address risk allocation and commercial terms.

The Master Service Agreement (MSA) is a standard agreement that outlines general terms for ongoing business relationships, typically in service or recurring supply scenarios. Subsequent projects or orders are handled through a Statement of Work (SoW) or amendments to the MSA. SoWs provide additional detail added to broader agreements (also known as the MSA), which specify the exact services, requirements, or goods to be provided, timeliness, deliverables, and prices for particular items.

Two contract types are led by pricing: fixed-price and cost-plus. A fixed-priced contract is one in which the price for goods and services is predetermined and not subject to adjustment based on actual costs. These are common in the construction and government contracting industries. The other type is the cost-plus contract, in which the buyer reimburses the seller for allowable costs plus a set profit margin. These contracts are typically used for projects where the full scope is uncertain, requiring close negotiation of eligible expenses and profit formulas. In the contract manufacturing sector, the term Purchase Price Variance (PPV) is commonly used to measure the difference between the standard price and the actual price paid. PPV helps companies track cost deviations from their budget and negotiate better terms with manufacturers.

4.6 GOUT, KIDNEY STONES, AND SCIATICA

When times get overwhelming, we might wanna cry out, "Lions and tigers and bears, oh my!" Work stress can become very challenging and shift from our emotional shields to creeping into our physical senses. Some of the more common ailments include headaches, eye strain, neck pain, back pain, or stomach pain. I recall a C-level colleague who went from chronic sinusitis to severe migraines during monthly revenue reviews.

I hope you never have to play the "Would you rather have - followed by, gout or sciatica?" game. When your body gets angry about the way you are handling stress and raises the white flag, it may be time to surrender.

On a recent business trip, I packed an overnight bag for a quick two-day visit, which included time at corporate and a customer visit. I arrived early to check in with the sales operations team and made my way through program management, supply chain, and engineering. Our sales team was constantly under pressure to deliver new business and present "shiny objects" to top management. Specifically, the team was responsible for advancing both technology and operational capabilities by bringing in customers with cutting-edge requirements that would push our boundaries. My leadership role was not only to drive new business but also to communicate, primarily through presentation materials, how our team could support advanced robotics, automation, optics, lasers, and point-of-care medical devices. We built the first LED light bulb automation index table, the first exoskeleton robot, automotive laser sensors, and a fully automated, battery-operated breast pump. You can imagine the challenge of communicating technical capabilities in a feature/benefit style messaging.

To take a break, we would head out for dinner to continue discussing work, with food and alcohol as a backdrop. After enjoying a few delicious tacos and sharing a pitcher of margaritas, it was back to the hotel to finalize the slides and hopefully head to bed before midnight. I had a slight pain in my left foot, but it seemed like nothing to worry about til morning. After a fair night's sleep, the alarm sounded, and it was time to get ready for a customer visit. As I rose from the bed, I nearly fell because my left ankle was throbbing. I could barely push the ball of my foot to the ground as it felt like shredded glass pain. Joint pains were growing near the big toe as I limped to the bathroom in search of comfort. I was in my early 50s and had never had a leg injury or this sort of pain before. After calling a colleague, it became clear that I was experiencing an excruciating episode of gout, a condition commonly occurring from increased uric acid in those aged 50 or above. Men are three times more likely to develop gout, especially if there is an overlap with obesity, diabetes, high blood pressure, or kidney disease. And the easy trap for salespeople is eating too much protein and drinking too much alcohol.

My trip home was challenging and forgettable. The trip included just two airports, but with a foot pain so unbearable that I felt like a soldier with a battle wound, walking like a crippled bird. Strangers would stop and ask if they could assist. I went home and immediately went to an urgent care facility to verify the diagnosis for gout. The therapy is ice packs and ibuprofen to address the inflammation. For a non-contact injury, gout is typically ranked at a 9 or 10 on a pain scale, right up there with kidney stones, severe burns, and childbirth.

Kidney Stones

Next to the brain and the heart, our two most important internal organs are the liver and the kidneys. We are born with one liver and two kidneys. The liver is responsible for filtering blood, removing toxins, and waste products. A healthy liver regulates blood sugar levels and produces essential proteins for blood clotting. And for salespeople to remember, heavy, long-term, excessive consumption of alcohol can damage the liver. Finally, you can't live without a liver, and severely damaged organs require a rare transplants that have a 75% success rate and extends one's lifespan by 5 or 10 years.

Although it is difficult to say which is more likely definitively, chronic kidney disease (CKD) is more common than liver failure, and experiencing a kidney stone is recognized as a risk factor for developing CKD. Advanced CT scans and ultrasounds are the primary tools for detecting kidney stones. Prevention focuses on maintaining hydration, a balanced diet, managing underlying health conditions, and, in some cases, medication. Unfortunately, for some salespeople, the stress of their job can lead to dehydration and poor dietary choices. Imagine a stressful week of customer visits with few chances for bathroom breaks or hydration until the evening dinner, which is strongly influenced by alcohol. Sadly, the physical size of a kidney stone obstruction is typically the size of a grain of sand, yet it can easily clog the urinary tract. These stones are composed of calcium (the most common), uric acid, struvite, or cystine.

If the pain is severe (rated 10 or more), the blockage may require intervention. However, it is typically resolved by hooking up a saline solution to hydrate the system and thoroughly flush the obstruction. Having survived multiple kidney stone episodes and several trips to the ER, I can now manage through the pain by massaging my lower back and gently pushing the stone along.

Sciatica

Now, let's discuss a pain that pushes the scale past 10+, the Sciatic nerve. It is the largest and longest nerve in the body, originating from the spinal nerves L4, L5, S1, S2, and S3 of the sacral plexus. It runs from the lower back through the pelvis and buttocks, and down the back of each leg to the heel. The nerve is crucial for both movement and sensation in the lower limb, supplying nerves to nearly the entire leg and foot. Sciatica refers to pain caused by the irritation or compression of the sciatic nerve, often characterized by radiating pain from the lower back down the leg.

One of the most common causes is a herniated (slipped) disc, in which the inner gel of the spinal disc is pushed out and presses on the nerve root. Diagnosis may involve a doctor's exam, checking for leg movements, numbness, reflex changes, or advanced imaging (X-ray, CT, MRI). On the pain scale from least to most painful, the sciatica is moderate, with gout and kidney stones coming with very severe and extremely severe pain, respectively.

Time to return to the battlefield with warnings of different levels of pain if you do not take good care of yourself. You can forget about empathy if you are suffering from pain.

4.7 COVID

In 2020, the world experienced its third pandemic, known as COVID-19. The airborne coronavirus attacked the respiratory system and threatened the lives of infants to seniors. Complications included pneumonia, acute respiratory distress syndrome (ARDS), multi-organ failure, septic shock, and death—diagnoses were determined by confirming an RNA test in the form of a test strip and nasal swab. Once infected, the patient would experience a multi-week period of symptoms, including coughing, fever, loss of smell and taste, and, in severe cases, breathing difficulties. In the initial period of the pandemic, there was no vaccine, and fear spread worldwide.

Instructions to all were to shelter in place, wear an N95 mask, and continue with their business, likely over a Zoom call. Kids in K-12 grades lost years of social interactions. College kids were sent home to attend school remotely. Business operations have implemented safeguards to screen employees, maintain social distancing, and introduce new cleaning procedures, thereby minimizing contact with germs. For sales-people, the world was turned upside down as person-to-person contact was stripped away, travel restrictions became the norm, and it was a genuinely frightening time.

The world map of the pandemic's spread was on everyone's television screen as the number of cases continued to increase. Our company was for sale, and I drew the short straw to support due diligence with a few interested buyers in our low-cost region site near Ho Chi Minh City. I found myself on a nearly empty plane from California to Vietnam in March of 2020, with a stopover in Narita. I remember boarding the plane in San Jose and having my Vietnam travel visa still under review for 72 hours. As I landed in Japan, I went to the ANA lounge and called our country manager in Vietnam to inform him that I could not board the next flight without a visa. He quickly jumped into action, making some phone calls while I waited patiently. About three hours passed, and he called back with good news: the consulate had approved my visa, and I was on my way. I remember waiting in the lounge and seeing a few travelers wearing full head-to-toe plastic bunny suits to avoid contact with germs. It was a sci-fi show.

I had bought a highly rated N95 mask and had it modified by adding extra head straps to ensure it sealed tightly to my face. My backpack had Purell bottles, antibacterial wipes, and throat lozenges. My four-day stay was actually enjoyable as the people in Vietnam were incredibly kind and understanding during the COVID crisis. Service and hospitality at hotels and restaurants were impeccable. Our office was a manufacturing site, with security and safety measures in place for normal operations and heightened awareness. To ensure a germ-free environment, every inch of he factory was wiped down with hydrogen peroxide every evening. We conducted our business in a typical fashion, but this time with the added awkwardness of talking through our paper masks.

As a sales leader, I proposed to our management team that we focus on emerging medical devices during the pandemic, especially ventilators. Unfortunately, one side effect of pandemic travel restrictions was that supply chain teams could no longer travel, resulting in fewer new vendor decisions. Across the board, ventilator companies were selling out their goods, but not changing their manufacturing partners.

Until Mary Barra, the CEO of General Motors, decided to enter the medical device market. In her words, "Doing the ventilator project was kind of a game changer from a General Motors perspective, from a culture-change perspective." Barra said that in the past, the GM management team would have resisted when told they needed to help a company that builds 250 ventilators per month accelerate production to 30,000 in 150 days.

GM put hundreds of workers on the project to help Ventec Life

Systems of Seattle ramp up its production at a time when there were fears that the country would run short of the breathing machines. GM invested capital and converted an electronics factory in Indiana to help produce ventilators at a pace supply chain experts called "lightning fast."

For salespeople, it was an opportunity and a curse. The new ventilator programs with GM generated new business in the supply chain, as they sold parts to support the ventilator's bill of materials. However, GM treated new suppliers with its aggressive, hammer-like methods to grind down vendors on price and delivery. The government also helped reduce FDA requirements with Emergency Use Authorization (EUA) accelerators. By September of 2020, GM had delivered over 30,000 V+Pro critical care ventilators to the US Department of Health and Human Services (HHS). The whole federal order of these ventilators was completed in just 154 days.

Heroic Gesture

Michael McNamara was the CEO of Flextronics from 2006 to 2018. During his tenure, the company grew from $17.6 billion to over $30 billion, establishing "Flex" as one of the top contract manufacturers with over 20 sites globally, including the US, China, Mexico, and Europe. Managing this complex operation required tight controls on spending and on supply chain partners, who would be critical to supporting internal manufacturing and ensuring supply commitment.

In early 2020, McNamara played a pivotal role in securing and shipping personal protective equipment (PPE) during the pandemic's early months—a time when global supply chains were under immense pressure and demand for PPE far outstripped supply. He leveraged his network, which included venture capitalists, tech entrepreneurs, private citizens, and international contacts in China, to form a coalition that delivered PPE to the US. They pooled their resources, used private planes in some cases, and employed direct supplier relationships to bypass typical government procurement delays. The group successfully shipped over 40 million PPE items, including N95, surgical, and face shields, as well as gowns and gloves. These supplies were delivered to health systems, public hospitals, and frontline organizations during the critical early months of the pandemic when shortages were most acute.

4.8 SLEEP

What is sleep? At its simplest, sleep is a natural biological process that allows the body and brain to rest, repair, and reset. But contrary to popular belief, your brain doesn't power down while you're asleep. Instead, it enters a different kind of activity—one that's essential to your survival. Sleep occurs in cycles and is broadly divided into two categories: REM (rapid eye movement) and non-REM (NREM) sleep. In the deepest stage of REM sleep, your brain is highly active—even as your body remains relaxed and still. Most adults need about one to two hours of this deep REM sleep each night.

Behind the scenes, your body is working hard: repairing cells, replenishing energy stores, and supporting the immune system. These processes are regulated by critical hormones, including melatonin, cortisol, human growth hormone (HGH), leptin, testosterone, and estrogen—names that might be familiar if you've ever browsed the sleep-aid aisle at your local pharmacy.

REM sleep, in particular, plays a key role in emotional regulation. During the peak of each 90-minute sleep cycle, levels of acetylcholine—a neurotransmitter—dip, helping to shield your brain from external disturbances that might interrupt dreams. Acetylcholine is also vital for memory consolidation. If its release is reduced or delayed, memory function may be compromised for days. Meanwhile, melatonin and acetylcholine levels rise at bedtime, while norepinephrine—a chemical tied to action and wakefulness—naturally declines.

In his best-selling book Why We Sleep[5], neuroscientist Matthew Walker issues a stark warning: we are in the midst of a "catastrophic sleep-loss epidemic," one that he believes may be the defining public health crisis of the 21st century. While some would place climate change, obesity, or access to clean water at the top of the list—and rightly so—Walker argues that sleep loss is an insidious and underestimated threat, one that we can address immediately and personally.

Consider this: Over 40% of people over age 65 report problems with sleep. With age, the body produces less slow-wave sleep (a deep NREM stage), and REM sleep begins to dominate earlier in the night. Conditions like restless leg syndrome, which create an overwhelming urge to move one's legs during rest, contribute to increased sleep fragmentation. Disorders like sleep apnea—a condition tied to restricted airflow during sleep —become more common with aging, often due to obesity, diminished lung capacity, hormonal imbalances, and weakened pulmonary control.

Sleep disorders aren't just an inconvenience. They can impair memory and contribute to both physical ailments and psychiatric disorders, including depression.

Do you snore? It may seem like an odd question, but it's a crucial one. Nearly half of all habitual snorers may be living with obstructive sleep apnea (OSA)—a serious condition that interferes with normal breathing during sleep. It's estimated that 15–20% of American adults have sleep apnea, and most are unaware. Fortunately, at-home sleep testing kits are now widely available for under $150 and are often covered by insurance. Similarly, treatment includes the use of CPAP machines, which help restore standard breathing patterns overnight.

Sleep deprivation, whether acute or chronic, can disrupt not only your physical health but also your emotional intelligence. It becomes increasingly complex to interpret others' facial expressions, respond with the appropriate emotions, or regulate your own reactions. It's no surprise that sleep deprivation has long been classified as a form of torture—right alongside electric shock and waterboarding. That infamous scene in A Clockwork Orange[6], where the protagonist undergoes sleep-deprivation conditioning, serves as a disturbing illustration of just how potent—and dangerous—sleep loss can be.

Sleep deprivation comes in two forms: insufficient sleep time or poor-quality sleep. You may clock eight hours in bed, yet if you're not cycling through the proper sleep stages, or if conditions like sleep apnea are waking you hundreds of times a night (without your awareness), your body never gets the restorative sleep it needs. Mounting evidence suggests that chronic sleep loss is linked to an increased risk of Alzheimer's disease.

The scientific community refers to our biological craving for sleep as the sleep drive. Although its exact origins remain unclear, it's often described as a homeostatic pressure—one that builds as we stay awake and dissipates when we sleep. Chemicals such as melatonin and adenosine, called somnogenic agents, accumulate throughout the day and signal to the brain when it's time to rest.

In high-stress fields like sales, healthcare, or emergency services, sleep loss can quickly evolve into chronic deprivation—meaning insufficient sleep over months or years. This leads to cognitive decline, increased anxiety, immune system suppression, and even metabolic changes that contribute to weight gain and depression. The longer it continues, the more the body and brain deteriorate, quietly and steadily.

One of the brain's most elegant nighttime functions is its ability to process and archive emotional experiences. During sleep, we sort through what happened, separating raw facts from the emotions they triggered. We then store those emotions in memory, making them easier to access later—not just by date or event, but by how they made us feel. In sleep-deprived people, amygdala activity (the brain's emotional alarm system) is up to 60% higher than in well-rested individuals.

This brings us to emotional intelligence—the ability to understand and manage your own emotions and those of others. It's no exaggeration to say that sleep is one of the strongest pillars of EQ. Miss a night of sleep, and you may find yourself irritable, impatient, or unreasonably reactive. Picture yourself facing a challenging conversation or deadline after just two hours of sleep and a Red Bull. Not ideal. Sleep isn't just a recovery process—it's your hidden advantage for staying sharp, balanced, and emotionally composed.

Let's not forget teenagers. Many teens today are chronically sleep-deprived due to homework, part-time jobs, screen time, or late-night social media use. The consequences go far beyond feeling tired in class. Poor sleep impairs memory, focus, and academic performance. That's why some school districts are now delaying start times to give students the rest they need. Getting enough sleep isn't a sign of laziness—it's a strategy. It's one of the most innovative, most effective ways to protect your mental clarity, physical health, and emotional resilience.

So the next time you consider pulling an all-nighter, ask yourself this: Is it really worth turning into Sleepy, Grumpy, and Dopey all at once?

4.9 DIVORCE

For richer, or poorer, in sickness and in health, to love and to cherish, till death do us part. Assuming you've said certain rituals that allow you to get married and enjoy the company of your spouse. For years, hopefully, you have managed through ups and downs with challenges coming from communication, money, infidelity, constant conflict, but seldom is work the top reason for divorce. Many sources recommend keeping work and home life separate, which can improve overall well-being for both parties.

However, salespeople often struggle with the poorest work-life balance due to the demanding nature of the job. The hours are long, the pressure is high, and there are financial pressures, and you need to be constantly available. In Demir and Carey Bentley's Winning the Week, they mention that 33% of people work on Saturdays and 68% work on vacation, resulting in 77% experiencing burnout in their current job. And the most significant challenge is for a stressed-out, super-busy sales-person to be attentive and present at home.

Below is a table of general divorce rates by generation. The Baby Boomers had the highest divorce rate, with most divorces occurring after age 50 (aka Gray Divorce). Education, although not a direct cause of divorce, tends to be lower among individuals with higher levels of education.

Generation	Birth Years	Est Divorce Rate	Trends
Silent Generation	1928-1945	25-30%	Traditional and longer-lasting
Baby Boomers	1946-1964	45-50%	"Gray divorce"
Generation X	1965-1980	40-45%	Likely to cohabitate before marriage
Milenials	1981-1996	25-30%	More selective in marriage
Generation Z	1997-2012	Too Early	Similar to Milenials

Figure 4.1 Divorce Rates

Being in sales doesn't necessarily cause divorce, but it may be correlated with specific stressors. The national average for salespeople getting divorced is 30-45%. A simplified table for divorce rates across specific sales occupations is provided below.

Occupation	Divorce Rate	Source
Sales Professionals	38.20%	Daniel Dashnaw
Telemarketers	28.10%	Howells Legal
Real Estate Agents	17.20%	Housely
Retail Salespersons	17.00%	Housely
Insurance Sales Agents	14.80%	Housely
Sales Engineers	6.70%	Business Insider

Figure 4.2 Divorce Rates by Occupation

So, how do these numbers make you feel? A final statistic that should be understood is that nearly 70% of divorces are initiated by women, and their primary concern is unmet emotional needs or communication. EQ plays a crucial role in navigating or avoiding divorce, as it helps individuals manage their own emotions, understand their partner's perspective, and communicate effectively with them. Divorce often triggers strong emotions like anger, fear, and resentment. Emotional intelligence can help individuals respond thoughtfully rather than impulsively. By recognizing and managing their own emotions, individuals can make more rational decisions.

There is no judgment as you read this book and find yourself in marriage trouble. If you believe you are spending too much time at work and suffer from a poor work-life balance, consider your options. Remember that the benefits of high emotional intelligence include improved relationships, effective communication, better emotional management, and enhanced problem-solving. Keep your house in order!

4.10 DISTRACTIONS AND CLUTTER

From its Latin origin, distraction meant "to pull apart, divide, separate." In the 14th and 15th centuries, the term "distraction" could refer to mental derangement or madness. By the 16th century, it had also evolved to mean the diversion of the mind or attention from one's primary focus. In today's complex world, we face external forces that create digital, physical, and psychological distractions. The top distractions are often attributed to smartphones, social media, emails, multitasking, noise, and clutter. Let's break them down by cause and effect.

Smartphones were once primarily used as communication devices, with voice calling as their primary function, and later added texting, which was a paid upgrade used sparingly. Texting used to cost 10 cents per text, sent or received. In 1995, users had a 10-number keypad and were in the early days of autofill. In 1996, Nokia introduced the first QWERTY keyboard on a mobile phone[7], making texting significantly easier for users. In 2007, Apple introduced the iPhone[8], and by the end of the year, Americans sent and received more texts than phone calls for the first time. By 2008, texting was so commonplace that United Way used it to fundraise during Super Bowl XLII.

The technology, known as short message service (SMS), would eventually be enhanced using applications such as WhatsApp, Facebook Messenger, and iMessage, with the primary interface being a text window. It was also the start of using Wi-Fi networks to replace cellular for lower-cost "text-like" communications. Although business communication was dominated by standard SMS texting, these other applications became increasingly common in social circles.

The next big distraction is social media interactions. Whether on a mobile phone or a computer, endless scrolling on platforms such as Instagram, TikTok, and X may consume hours without awareness. On average, people spend about 2 hours and 23 minutes per day using these platforms. This accounts for roughly 36% of daily online activity. Unfortunately, teenagers spend an average of 4.8 hours per day on social media, with girls spending nearly an hour more per day than boys.

Being constantly connected also means being able to read emails and multitask continuously. A mobile phone in hand means you can read emails at a moment's glance and easily break concentration. Switching or multitasking is a mentally elite sport and should be reserved for those who can keep multiple items in focus and run separate, parallel paths. However, for most of us, it can actually reduce efficiency and quality of attention.

Finally, we have issues with noise and clutter. The worst offenders of noise are traffic sounds, coworkers, and household chatter from television, radio, or other interruptions. There is a reason people pay extra for "noise-cancelling" headphones. The peace of mind and tranquil state of life without noise distractions is golden. Spend a few minutes in silence —you'll be alone with your thoughts and reminded of calm and peacefulness. Add back a little background music to enhance your memory and cognitive performance.

Offensive sounds are to noise distractions as clutter is to physical organization.. A messy desk is often seen as a symbol of laziness and a lack of motivation. Of course, this same desk may also be a sign of creativity or big-picture thinking. Conversely, it may also indicate disorganization or poor time management. As a caution, there are also reasons why clutter might not be a sign of laziness, especially with folks suffering from ADHD, depression, or anxiety.

. . .

Clock Watching

In the movie "The Gods Must Be Crazy[9]," humans are "imprisoned" by time using the metaphor of society's influence on time, technology, and bureaucracy. The heartfelt story follows a Bushman's challenging journey as he navigates the battle between his simple, contented life and the modernization and materialism of society.

Have you ever considered what life would be like without the measure of time? The ancient Egyptians are credited with inventing sundials and water clocks, using the lengths of shadows and the flow of water to measure time. Others used burning candles and incense before mechanical clocks hit the market around 1300 CE (Europe). And then the floodgates opened for clocks with pendulums, quartz crystals, and finally atomic clocks, which achieved billionths-of-a-second accuracy. Early portable clocks were pocket watches. Then the wristwatch became a standard accessory for soldiers in WWI, as the devices improved synchronization of attacks and communications. Eventually, the added functionality of calculators, calendars, and alarms became the attraction of a smartwatch. Today, we have wristwatches equipped with laser sensors that can measure heart rate, blood oxygen levels, electrocardiograms, activity, and track sleep.

Clock watching, or the habitual checking of time, can have various psychological effects, including increased stress, anxiety, and reduced productivity. Constantly checking the time can cause people to waste more time, putting pressure on them and triggering performance anxiety, especially when deadlines are looming. The behavior creates a sense of urgency or time scarcity, which can worsen focus and decision-making.

Interestingly, the more you watch the clock, the slower time seems to pass, especially in tedious or stressful situations. The more attention you pay to time, the more you notice it passing or the lack of its advancement.

Clock-watching during the night can intensify insomnia. People often wake up, check the time, and then become more anxious about not sleeping, creating a vicious cycle of worry and wakefulness. This is a known trigger for sleep onset and maintenance insomnia.

In rigid or monotonous work environments, constant time-checking can reflect boredom, frustration, or disengagement. It may contribute to a sense of being trapped, especially when combined with micro-management or inflexible schedules.

Fortunately, there are many coping mechanisms for clock watching. Mindfulness, focusing attention away from the clock, and engaging in deep work can help reduce anxiety. As crazy as it sounds, hiding the clock or turning its face away from you can help keep your attention away from the time. Switching your work into larger, task-focused segments or by energy level may be a good substitute for clock watching. Remember, in boring situations, time seems to move more slowly, so do your best to avoid boredom. Manage your time and remove tight deadlines by planning your tasks well in advance. And if you are serious about addressing this issue in your life, introduce new behaviors and activities, including creative work such as painting or writing, reading a great book, spending time in the garden, or playing a board game, a puzzle, or rolling out the yoga mat for some stretches. Activities with positive "flow" will keep you engaged or distracted in a beneficial way, allowing your mind to recharge. Try to avoid social media and any devices with clocks, such as cell phones or smartwatches. Spend some quality time with blinders on. Get to know your biological clock and circadian rhythm.

Removing Distractions

How do we make a conscious effort to remove them? If we diet, it's most likely about sugar (intake, bad calories), and we make a plan. If we have clutter, we get more organized. But how do we remove distractions? How do we measure (like sleep apnea—there is a sleep test)? Imagine a "distraction test."

4.11 ACTIVE LISTENING

Asking a room full of people if they are good listeners has a similar analogy to asking, "How many of you can hear me, or worse, raise your hand if you can't hear me." Consider this: if you are at the back of the room, can you hear anything? You might be a great listener, but you may not be close enough to participate. Let's try a visual listening exercise: "Please draw a square with three lines." The figure below shows a couple of attempts that failed to determine the solution. How can it be this hard to draw, and what am I missing? Your mind starts to feel tricked by the exercise, as if you are in a magic trick or somehow forgot geometry. Please don't be too hard on yourself until you solve the riddle and realize it's more about listening than drawing.

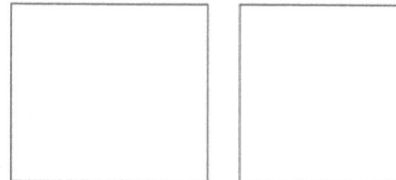

Figure 4.3 Square with 3 Lines - Hear

Active listening means giving the person who is speaking your undivided focus, with no multitasking and no thinking about your response while they are talking. You show respect and build trust while truly understanding what is being said. Body language is essential, including good eye contact, nodding, leaning in, and other signals of engagement. Encouraging the speaker to continue shows that you are emotionally present. Some active listeners use the technique of repeating back or rephrasing what the speaker said to help confirm understanding. Small gestures to clarify meaning show that you are processing the message accurately and asking for more details, or adding careful inputs to allow the conversation to have a deeper level of connection and relevance to the speaker.

Active listening taps into empathy, the ability to sense and understand another person's feelings and perspective. Emotionally intelligent listeners are more likely to recognize nonverbal cues, validate the speaker's feelings, and respond in ways that build trust and psychological safety.

Humans are wired for connection. Active listening builds rapport, reduces misunderstandings, and increases cooperation. When people feel genuinely heard, relationships strengthen, and the "bonding hormone" oxytocin is released from the pituitary gland, reinforcing the positive feedback loop.

Repeating the previous question: "Please draw a square with three lines." Seeing the figure below gives the audience relief, as the question was heard, but the trick question diluted active listening.

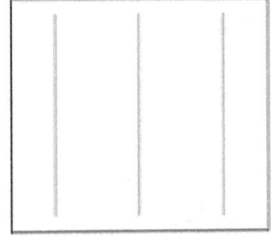

Figure 4.4. Square with 3 Lines - Listen

4.12 TIME MANAGEMENT

Salespeople share a common enemy in managing their time. After all, there's never enough time in the day to accomplish sales activities, and there are no obvious points to start or stop selling; it's simply a matter of taking a break now and then. It is a classic dilemma: the tension between urgent tasks —responding to leads, emails, and meetings —and less urgent tasks —prospecting, follow-ups, and relationship building. Getting pulled in many directions is an everyday occurrence, and the time you devote to functions such as entering data into the CRM, sending email sequences to enhance prospecting, and, of course, closing deals is all important. Yet, the real skill is about managing the Eisenhower Matrix (Urgent, Not Urgent, Important, Not Important) for each task and knowing when to allocate more time to the critical and urgent areas of the business.

In Jeb Blount's book "The AI Edge," he carefully discusses time management through the lens of time discipline, calendar management, and time investment audits. He writes, "time discipline is sacrificing what you want now for what you want most." With artificial intelligence, having time discipline will become even more crucial, as you can now pack more into a 24-hour day than ever before. Blount describes "Me Management" as someone with a CEO mindset, ruthless prioritization, effective planning and calendar management, territory mapping, attention control, and time blocking.

"Master sales begins with mastering your time."

Ideally, the only reason you're not prospecting more is that you are spending too much time closing deals. It is very common to feel you need to follow a sales process through each step of the cycle; however, you also need to multitask to keep an active pipeline of new business. There may come a time when AI will provide shortcuts to automate your daily work processes and send them directly to your CRM, thereby saving you time. However, using tools wisely — such as automation, templates, and follow-ups — enhances your skills rather than replacing them.

Time management strategies for salespeople include time blocking, lead prioritization, and a constant focus on revenue generation. Blocking time can vary by time of day for prospecting, by day of the week, and by the frequency of approaching someone. Many high performers set aside time periods with no interruptions or distractions, allowing for 100% focus on hunting new business. This time is ideal for crafting the right messaging or creating a variety of messaging depending on the known target and expected outcome. Invariably, salespeople spend too much time crafting elaborate, multi-paragraph introductions only to find that the recipient's role is not suitable or that the timing is off. A simple sentence or two may have been more relevant.

One of the best springboards into using AI is time management. Assuming AI can help you write, organize, and prioritize your outbound marketing sequences and day-to-day emails, you can spend less time in your inbox. Your research ability has been greatly expanded through sophisticated queries, providing you with rich information about your target customers, buying behaviors, new product launches, competitors, and the ability to go "deeper and wider," as advanced students of account-based marketing. Mastering your time management gives you an excellent head start in navigating the complex, fast-moving, and incredibly impressive world of AI.

CHAPTER 5
SALES DRIVE

OLYMPIC ATHLETES ARE RENOWNED for their extraordinary drive and motivation, which set them apart both physically and mentally from their peers. Their relentless pursuit of excellence is fueled by a combination of intrinsic and extrinsic factors, including self-improvement, motivation, a love of competition, and practical goal setting. They operate every day with an optimistic outlook, facing their fears and competition. These athletes remain resilient in the face of setbacks and are confident that they can overcome any obstacle in the future. Many athletes practice mindfulness to stay present and manage stress. Achieving a state of flow, characterized by complete immersion in the activity, enables individuals to perform at their peak by quieting self-doubt and focusing entirely on the tasks at hand. Mental rehearsal, also known as visualization, is a widely used technique among gymnasts, track and field athletes, and swimmers. By vividly imagining their routines or races, they visualize success, strengthen neural pathways, and mentally and physically prepare for competition.

The psychology behind sales drive is similar to that of Olympic athletes and includes motivation, emotional intelligence, and resilience. Sales drive is powered by both extrinsic motivation (external rewards, commissions, bonuses, and recognition) and intrinsic motivation (internal satisfaction, passion for the product, and the fulfillment of helping customers). Most salespeople are driven by a combination of these, with some also motivated by altruistic desires to genuinely help their clients.

A feeling of accomplishment and acknowledgement from peers or management significantly boosts engagement and drive when salespeople experience achievement and are recognized for their efforts, their job satisfaction and motivation increase.

Sales commissions and rewards help fulfill basic financial needs, enabling the pursuit of higher-level goals, such as achievement and self-actualization. Some salespeople compare their input and rewards to those of peers, and equitable compensation drives effort. Believing that effort leads to performance, which in turn leads to reward, is crucial. Positive reinforcement, such as tiered commissions for higher performance, encourages continuous improvement.

High-performing salespeople leverage emotional intelligence, including empathy, adaptability, and understanding of client emotions. They use emotions to build rapport and trust, which not only helps close deals but also sustains their own drive by creating meaningful connections and positive experiences.

Sales roles are high-pressure, and resilience is key. The ability to handle rejection, overcome setbacks, and maintain confidence in the face of stress is essential for sustaining a successful sales drive.

5.1 OVERCOMING DIFFICULTIES

Today we watched the finals in the women's singles tennis championship at Wimbledon. It was a match between a number 16 seed underdog ("Amanda") and the number 8 seed (Iga). The match started poorly for Amanda, as she dropped game after game, and the first set ended 0-6. The second and final set was similar, as she competed well; however, her game was off, likely due to her earlier match, where she had exhausted herself beating the tournament's number 1 seed ("Aryna"). Amanda had five double faults and only hit 41% of her first serves in. She lost the match 0-6, 0-6, not winning a single game, which was the lopsided score last recorded in a Wimbledon final in 1911. On the positive side, Amanda took home $2 million in prize money, compared to Iga's $4 million. In her podium speech, Amanda thanked her opponent, the incredible crowd, her support team, and, most of all, her mom, who had been her key support since her father's death six years earlier. As she held back emotional tears, she expressed her love for the game and said she looked forward to the next opportunity to compete. Interestingly, she started the tournament by defeating her opponent 6-0, 6-0, a rare double bagel she had also experienced in the championship—horrible bookends.

We watch sports because it reminds us of when we competed, someone in our family or friendship circle completes a sport we greatly admire, or we are loyal fans. We cheer for our favorite players and host sports parties to celebrate with beer and pizza. From 1961-1998, Jim McKay from ABC's Wide World of Sports would announce, "Spanning the globe, to bring you the constant variety of sports... the thrill of victory... and the agony of defeat... the human drama of athletic competition. We watched the famous ski jumper (Vinko Bogataj) wrap himself precariously around the launch ramp in the 1970 International Ski Flying Championships in Germany. Thankfully, his injuries were a mild concussion and a broken ankle. Imagine the original images for the agony of defeat were a trio of Irish hurlers colliding during a match. There is also a motorcycle racer who crashes after the ski jumper, but in retrospect, it was almost forgettable. The "thrill of victory" included famous winning clips of Muhammad Ali, Pelé, and Mario Andretti.

The agony of defeat for most salespeople is when a customer selects another vendor or product. Perhaps the most detrimental are the longer sales cycles, which require significant time and investment. In professional services, the longer cycles can span years before a decision is made. Three or four years of courting a team, miles of travel, hours of meetings, pricing, negotiations, presentations, emails, executive updates, CRM logs, project hurdles, delays, and human turnover. It can feel like torture while you are enduring the process, and nearly as personal as a funeral or judgment when the verdict is read: "We regret to inform you that we have selected another vendor." There is no second place or consolation prize.

The remarkable aspect of overcoming difficulties is that it yields several benefits, ultimately improving overall sales performance. Facing and tackling obstacles encourages salespeople to develop creative solutions to complex problems, such as difficult prospects or long sales cycles. With each challenge navigated, salespeople improve their critical thinking and ability to offer tailored solutions to their customers. Another key benefit is the development of resilience and adaptability. Resilience helps salespeople bounce back from setbacks, such as rejection or lost deals, which are an inevitable part of the profession. Resilient salespeople remain focused and productive even when faced with adversity, allowing them to recover quickly and keep progressing. Overcoming challenges fosters adaptability, enabling salespeople to adjust strategies in response to changing markets and customer needs.

Setbacks offer valuable lessons. Learning from unsuccessful deals or prospecting failures enables salespeople to refine their techniques, which leads to better results in the future. Striving to overcome difficulties motivates salespeople to set realistic goals, celebrate small wins, and maintain sustained high performance. Regular obstacles can be demotivating, but overcoming them builds confidence and drive —essential qualities for staying motivated in a competitive environment. Maintaining a positive outlook and focusing on progress keeps salespeople engaged and persistent. Overcoming difficulties often means learning how to communicate more effectively, manage objections, and develop trust with prospects and customers. Ultimately, individuals who consistently overcome challenges are usually those who rise to leadership positions and mentor others.

5.2 MOTIVATION

Motivation in sales is like honey to the bee, and better said, it's oxygen to a scuba diver. The common misused term is: "Are you feeling motivated?" Motivation is not a feeling; it is a process driven by emotions such as happiness, excitement, or even fear. However, the two are intertwined, as emotions such as passion can be a source of motivation. Many professions with goal-oriented objectives, such as sales, require behaviors that initiate action and pursue key steps in a process to achieve specific outcomes. Perhaps the better phrase would be, "Are you ready to take action?"

I recall having a boss who was the head of global sales at a billion-dollar company and was constantly burning the candle at both ends. He managed teams around the world and around the clock, never taking breaks. Before one of his long trips, I said to him, "Good luck," and he replied, "Thanks, but I don't need luck, I need to close business." What I thought was a motivating send-off turned out to be a reality check on what I was actually saying. Wishing someone good luck implies that their success depends on chance or forces beyond their control, which can undermine their efforts and confidence. It can also be perceived negatively in specific contexts, like before surgery or a key exam. The better send-off phrases are "Hope the trip goes well, You're going to crush it, or Safe travels." Stay away from phrases like 'Good luck,' 'Best of luck,' 'Wish you luck,' or any other phrase that uses luck as the key ingredient.

Five key elements motivate and drive a salesperson, including money, recognition, achieving goals, autonomy, and a sense of purpose. Across nearly every sales channel or profession, the money factor has the most tangible value. A good salesperson lives for the bonus and commission incentives, which are directly tied to performance. Many top salespeople will test the limits of their commission plan, keeping their CFOs on their toes as they secure big deals that yield substantial commissions.

Coming in a close second is the motivation to receive recognition for their achievements. This can occur through public praise, awards, or internal communications that highlight a person's excellence. Visibility and recognition reinforce a sense of worth, boost confidence, and encourage continued high performance. Success breeds success, and many top performers set and exceed their goals, striving to maintain their number-one spot in the sales organization.

Being in sales also offers a unique set of controls over one's work, including the freedom to manage time, craft strategies, and manage client relationships. This fosters innovation, accountability, and satisfaction as if they were running their own company or acting as their own boss. And a good segue to feeling purposeful. By helping their customers succeed and driving valuable revenue to the company, a salesperson can feel part of a strong culture and set of values. When all the elements of motivation are combined, an effective sales organization can tailor strategies to drive each sales team member, balancing intrinsic motivators (such as recognition, achievement, and purpose) with extrinsic motivators (such as compensation and incentives).

5.3 CHALLENGING YOURSELF

It is critical to keep in shape for everything we do. If you are an athlete, your "keep in shape" goals are likely directly tied to your sport and include exercises or practice to maintain muscle memory. Some of the routines are done by yourself, while other tasks require an opponent to work on both offense and defense skills. There are a few sports where you can train on your own and remain competitive. Even dart throwing is improved through competition.

Interestingly, when sales training groups outline their activities, they typically include solving complex tasks through teamwork, such as the three-legged race, a swimming pool boat race, or crossing a virtual gorge with limited tools or materials. Time pressure will force leaders to emerge, and the competition is loud and exciting. There is seldom an expert in building a boat out of cardboard and foam, or a simple path for an 8-foot board to span a 12-foot gorge.

When the dust settles, like any competition, there is one winning team and many losers. A consultant will highlight the positive way the winning team worked together and agreed on a path to success, and more importantly, the elimination of poor inputs that would have distracted the team. A post-mortem analysis will reveal the obvious answers by comparing the winning path to the losing alternatives. If there were 30 participants, divided into five groups of 6, there would be 6 winners and 24 losers. In fact, there is likely only 1 or 2 leaders on the winning team. Another example of "The Action Fallacy," and we celebrate the wrong winning behavior. What did we teach the 28 people who "lost the race?"

How can we replay this exercise with positive teaching intentions to at least the majority of the group? Assume you are the group leader, and this "majority" is the new goal of the training. Consider the simplest way to divide the 30-person team into two groups of 15. After the 2-team race, you now have 15 winners, and likely 2-3 leaders. Hmmm, that's an improvement in both leaders and winners.

Here is an unusual challenge for you. Before you are assembled, 100 salespeople from the same company. You are at the podium and can ask three questions of the group. After each question, the audience raises their hands if they agree or comply with the question. Ultimately, you can select your top 10 to form your team for the upcoming sales training. Three caveats are: 1) none of the questions can be work related, 2) the audience does not know your goal to build a top 10 sales team, and 3) after three questions, you can only select 10 from the group (note, if there are less than 10, then you are done, and/or you can stop after any question. The challenge begins.

Question 1: You inform the group that you are gathering information for statistical purposes and request their assistance with some demographic information. The group seems interested, and you pose your first question. "How many of you like the colors Blue, Green, or Red? Only about a third lowered their hands, and the group was still huge, maybe 70 hands in the air. They were spread out across the room and had no other distinguishing features.

Question 2: As I looked over the raised hands, there seemed to be an equal number of men and women. I decided to try to keep as many women on your team as possible, without asking the obvious gender question. I needed a question to reduce the hands to as close to 10 as possible. You present the second question: "How many of you are only children?" A quick reduction in the number of raised hands. There is a better-than-even chance that these folks have higher IQs, better communication skills, and are poor team players—the perfect leaders. We were down to 15 raised hands.

Question 3: Level 5 Leadership (Jim Collins Research) suggests that fewer than 1% of current leaders demonstrate a combination of deep personal humility and intense professional will. That's too narrow. There is only one letter missing from the names of all the US states. Approximately 10% of the population will answer "Q." I'm not sure how they know this, but it's likely they are skilled at trivia or history. We also know that about 10% of the population is left-handed. Approximately 7.5% of the world's population ride motorcycles, but only 2.6% in the US. And this sort of reasoning can continue to help trim that last 1 or 2 people.

While the final 15 waited patiently with their hands in the air, you remembered a good question for listeners and risk takers. You ask the raised hands to get ready for a 2-part question as follows: "A diver recently broke the longest breath held underwater. Is the answer over or under 22 minutes and 30 seconds?" You then ask a follow-up question: "Are the following all true? Coke came before Pepsi, Benz came before Ford, McDonald's came before Carl's Jr., and Steve Jobs' birth name was Abdul?"

You ask the tired arms to stay up if they answered "over" and "true." A sales optimist will want both answers to be accurate. These questions draw on different parts of the brain, including risk-taking from the motor cortex and fact-checking from the amygdala, hippocampus, and cerebellum. Before the question, there were nine men and six women. No one likely knows if their answers are correct, but they hold their hands high in the air. Afterwards, the team selection is complete, with five men and five women. With a bit of luck as well.

So, what just happened, and how important is a simple, iterative process that challenges your thinking about a task? If you knew that 10% of the population is left-handed and 20% of families have only one child, it may influence when to use this in your filter. Although the general population is balanced between men and women, the number of salespeople (70%) significantly exceeds the number of salespeople (30%) in the workplace. As you review your "selected team," you have a balance of 5 men and 5 women, a left-hander, and emotional color choices that suggest characteristics of trust, high energy, and a love of money. And, just enough risk-taking and self-confidence to navigate the daily challenges in sales.

Challenging oneself in sales is a daily experience. You may like the morning crossword, trivia, or Sudoku puzzles. Perhaps your favorite sports team is playing for an easy (familiar) bet, or the lottery is over the limit, and it's time to play your favorite numbers. Most of these activities will stimulate your brain in areas related to luck or strategy, and, without realizing it, your neurons will fire.

As sales professionals, we are also challenged daily with prospecting, managing, and growing our business. Our body is well-tuned to prioritize our time across (many) accounts, balance the needs of customers and the factory's deliverables, and stay as many steps as possible from chaos. Great salespeople know how to handle the right amount of pressure to keep things moving forward, yielding consecutive positive results to demonstrate the effectiveness of their work. On rare occasions, does a proficient salesperson find themselves in a loss for "what to do" across weekly/monthly milestones. Even in adverse circumstances, the best salespeople manage through the chaos and emerge victorious on the other side. Ask a sales leader how they worked through a turbulent quarter, and they will often say, "That's what I do."

5.4 CALLING JOHN DOE

The game show "Name That Tune" is famous for challenging contestants to identify a tune from just a few notes. The speed rounds have seven songs to guess in 30 seconds. For individual songs, a novice player may bid 7 or 8 notes, while experts typically bid 3 or 4 notes. As the competition increases, the bidding may even drop to just two notes. In Feb 2021, a contestant won by selecting "La Bamba." The hint was: "In the 1950s, this swingin' tune crossed over the border and up the charts." Perhaps this narrowed the options, but it was still a very challenging task, involving two notes played by Randy Jackson on the keyboard.

There is a sales challenge that says, "You can reach anyone in the world in 3 phone calls or less." To put it better, can you make three or fewer calls to reach someone significant? The idea is to demonstrate the process, making sales prospecting less daunting. The question immediately tests your network. The specific question might be: how can you reach the CEO of Newco, John 'Doe's mobile number, in under three calls? The lazy person would suggest calling 411 and asking, "Please connect me to John Doe." You just wasted a call, and now have two calls remaining.

Assuming there is limited time pressure (less than an hour), conduct a Reddit or Google search, followed by a Perplexity search, and enter as many keywords and prompts as possible to address the challenge. Results try to sell you a database application (RocketReach, ZoomInfo) that promises to get you John's phone number. You try an organizational search for John's admin, the CFO, or someone in his trusted circle who might share his info.

Allow your brain to use both AI and EQ reasoning. Working simultaneously, consider the following AI prompt: Find John Doe's mobile phone number as Newco's CEO. The AI response gives you the corporate line, public relations, or 1-800-MY-NEWCO. Further prompts list, "How can I contact John Doe directly, with a response providing his email at jdoe@newco.com. The internet search is similar, and chasing Taylor Swift, Stephen Curry, or Donald Trump is in the same challenging arena as Doe. If AI supports data mining and John'ss mobile number is stored somewhere (in cold storage), what is the best path to retrieve his number? Suppose John's executive staff is somewhat easier to approach. Would it be the CFO, the COO, or perhaps the former CFO who is now in a "smaller" role at the company and may be more approachable? Let's pause on the "who" portion of the query and focus on the "what to ask."

With only three calls, the sequence of carefully thought-out questions should address both the goal of obtaining the mobile number and the intent (is this just a game or an emergency), as well as the reasonableness of the person in providing the number. You look across your network and see over 20 people you know at Newco, including two vice presidents who are challenging to reach, and five directors whom you recall are slow to respond, and finally, an engineering director who will reply to any reasonable request.

The "3 Call Approach" is not a sales tool or a game like Truth or Dare; it is a simple challenge that permeates every salesperson's daily life. We are responsible for prospecting and arranging essential meetings. If a customer is late to a meeting, it's the salesperson's responsibility to locate them and ensure they attend. So what if this is our first meeting with a senior vice president, and it was all arranged by email? Now, you're at the largest trade show in your industry, and Mr. SVP is a "no-show." You need to find them fast to make a call or send a text regarding the meeting. Maybe they are just stuck in traffic, or a previous meeting is running over. Having the confidence to reach anyone in 3 phone calls or less lets you track down and get your VIP.

Now, let's examine the same exercise using AI. What question would you ask your agent to achieve the same result? Here are a few prompts. 1: What is the mobile number for Newco's CEO, John Doe?

5.5 SALES TRAINING

Thankfully, this is not a sales training book. There are no workbooks, end-of-chapter reviews, or homework. Sales training here means something different. It's about examining the various types of training available and how AI will impact the future of sales meetings. Salespeople want to improve, and they need tools to enhance their performance. However, the truth is that selling is becoming increasingly challenging. Buyers today use technology to gather facts and make faster decisions. The old ways are no longer enough.

Elite Training Programs

Over the past 50 years, elite sales training programs have been developed to help sales teams enhance their skills. These programs provide individuals with new tools and ideas that they can apply in their day-to-day work. Some popular ones include Challenger, Dale Carnegie, Janek, Korn Ferry/Miller Heiman, RAIN Group, and Sandler. These programs are often based on consultative selling. That means they focus on understanding the customer, building trust, and collaboratively solving problems. Typically, the training takes place at an off-site location for approximately a week. There, the team can focus without distractions. Each program includes measures to track progress, allowing leaders and team members to see the extent of their improvement.

As a team player, I've been through more than a dozen of these programs—both as a student and a leader. I've attended lessons on the Challenger Sales Model, SPIN Selling, SNAP Selling, the Sandler System, and Janek's Performance Selling. I've even completed a specialized training program focused on strategic thinking. It reminds me of a basketball camp I went to in high school. It lasted five full days, and we did nothing but eat, sleep, and play basketball. The best players were there, and they looked great on the court. I loved being there. However, when I left, I realized I hadn't learned much. Most of the time, the top players took center stage, while the rest of us watched from the sidelines. I see the same problem with sales training. It sometimes helps the top performers get even better, but it doesn't always lift the whole team.

And that's the real challenge. Whether you're a salesperson or a manager, AI will change the way we work. AI is already being integrated into sales tools, such as CRMs, email, calendars, and even social media apps. It will make some tasks easier, such as sorting contacts, writing follow-ups, and tracking customer data. SPIN Selling (Situation, Problem, Implication, and Need-Payoff) could benefit from this. AI can help gather the situation and identify problems more quickly, leaving the salesperson with more time to focus on connecting with the buyer. But this also raises a new problem: the Challenger Sales Dilemma.

The Challenger Sales Model pushes salespeople to teach, tailor, and take control. But if AI starts doing most of the "teaching" through smart data and automated insights, what's left for the salesperson to do? The risk is that representatives might rely too heavily on technology and overlook the human aspect of selling. Real connections still matter. Buyers want to trust the person they're talking to. Therefore, the future of sales training will also need to change. It should teach people how to use AI as a helper—not a replacement. The best salespeople of tomorrow will be those who can effectively blend innovative tools with genuine human skills.

Imagine if sales training were more like the training that monks undergo.

That's why the future of training needs to shift. Instead of just watching experts show off their skills, everyone on the team needs hands-on practice with AI and new tools. Training should be shorter, more frequent, and happen during real work—not just in a week-long trip. Salespeople should learn on the go, using technology that's part of their daily workflow. This way, the entire team grows stronger together —not just the top few. And in a world that is moving faster every day, that might be the only way to keep up.

5.6 PUZZLES

One could easily create a list of possible reasons why people challenge themselves by playing puzzles. The psychological drivers relate to cognitive stimulation, intrinsic motivation, and emotional satisfaction, and can be habitual. People enjoy puzzles because they provide mental exercise that stimulates brain function, enhances memory, problem-solving skills, and logical thinking. Overcoming complex problems activates reward centers in the brain, which encourages continued engagement. Interestingly, crossword puzzles challenge your vocabulary, general knowledge, and language-processing abilities, requiring you to recall words, understand the nuances of clues, and make word associations. Sudoku and similar puzzles test your numerical logic, pattern recognition, and deductive reasoning, as you must find solutions within set constraints without repetition. Both crosswords and number puzzles, such as Sudoku, strengthen attention to detail and working memory, requiring players to remember clues, track potential answers, and hold onto interim solutions while searching for the correct one. Certain puzzle variations, such as 3D Sudoku or logic-based board games, require players to visualize spatial relationships and arrangements, supporting spatial awareness and mental flexibility. There is also the time-sensitive nature of some puzzles or games, encouraging quick thinking and rapid decision-making while maintaining accuracy.

There is also the intrinsic motivation to master a puzzle to showcase one's skills or enhance one's mastery. Successfully solving a puzzle gives a sense of achievement and progress, fulfilling psychological needs described in self-determination theory: autonomy, competence, and relatedness. Engaging puzzles can induce a "flow" state, characterized by an intensely focused, immersive experience in which time seems to pass more slowly. This state is rewarding and encourages repeated participation because it strikes a balance between challenge and skill. Humans have a natural curiosity to explore and understand new patterns and concepts. Puzzles satisfy this by presenting novel challenges that provide problem-solving and discovery. Some find puzzles calming or meditative, providing a break from daily stressors. Completing puzzles releases dopamine, offering emotional uplift and a sense of control. Games like card puzzles add social interaction and friendly competition, fulfilling needs and motivating players through cooperation or rivalry.

The emotional satisfaction derived from playing puzzles or crosswords is multifaceted and powerfully resonant with many key aspects of a salesperson's personality. Solving a challenging puzzle provides a strong feeling of accomplishment. Each completed clue or successfully placed number in Sudoku delivers immediate gratification, boosting confidence and self-esteem. Progressing from more straightforward to more difficult puzzles, or cracking a particularly tough crossword clue, satisfies the intrinsic desire for mastery and personal growth. It validates effort and strategic thinking, fostering pride in one's abilities.

Just as puzzlers persist through frustration for the joy of eventual success, salespeople must remain persistent in overcoming objections and setbacks to close deals, finding satisfaction in each small victory. Sales, at its heart, is about diagnosing customer needs and crafting tailored solutions, mirroring the analytical thinking and creative approaches needed to solve puzzles or crosswords. The satisfaction of outsmarting a challenging crossword or winning a game aligns with the competitive spirit often found in top sales performers, who thrive on achieving targets and surpassing rivals. Just as puzzlers seek more complex challenges, ambitious salespeople derive emotional satisfaction from mastering new products, markets, and sales strategies, thereby enjoying the learning and growth that comes with it.

Strategic sales teams, particularly those specializing in complex or consultative sales, frequently utilize advanced simulations to replicate real-world scenarios and develop cognitive and interpersonal skills that directly translate to sales excellence. The classic strategy games include chess, Monopoly, Risk, and Others. Puzzles are typically crossword, Brian Teasers, or Sudoku, and group or logic games such as Scattegories (Sales Edition), Sell Me This Pen, and Role-Play Champions.

5.7 INFLUENCERS

Elite salespeople tend to run with their own set of influences and mentors that provide future insights. The complete list of influencers in AI and EQ would easily fill this book or more, but for now, we will highlight a few notables. In an incredibly fast-moving market driven by AI, it is worth looking at both human and artificial influences, from Michael Jackson to Batman and Robin.

Mira Murati

Most of you may not be familiar with Mira Murati, who served as the interim CEO before Sam Altman, like my niece, who also went to undergrad at Colby College (BA) and then on to Dartmouth College (BEng). Mira's career began at Zodiac Aerospace before she joined Tesla in 2013 as a product manager on the Model X. She spent two years at an augmented reality startup called Leap Motion (now Ultraleap) before joining OpenAI in 2018 as the VP of Applied AI, and was later promoted to CTO. She led efforts on ChatGPT, Dall-E, Codex, and Sora, overseeing their research, product, and safety teams. Her work was instrumental in the development and deployment of some of OpenAI's most notable products, such as the Generative Pretrained Transformer (GPT) series of language models.

In November 2023, Murati briefly served as interim CEO following Altman's removal. She was replaced three days later by Emmett Shear, who in turn was ousted when Altman was reinstated five days after being removed. Following this series of events, Murati returned to her role as CTO. In September 2024, she announced she was stepping down as CTO to allow her the opportunity to "do her own exploration." In her exit memo, she expressed gratitude towards the OpenAI team. She high-lighted the success of their recent AI developments, including speech-to-speech technology and OpenAI's work on "robust, aligned, and steerable" models. This move came amid a wider executive exodus, as OpenAI Chief Research Officer Rob McGrew and Vice President of Research Barret Zoph also announced their departures soon after. In February of 2025, Mira launched a new public benefit corporation called Thinking Machine Lab "to make AI systems more widely understood, customizable, and generally capable. She was reported to have hired "a team of about 30 leading researchers and engineers from competitors, including Meta, Mistral, and OpenAI. People involved with the startup include OpenAI founder John Schulman and advisors Alex Radford and Bob McGrew. The following month, Bloomberg reported that the company had reached an estimated valuation of $9B, with an "average founder stake value" of $1.4 B.

Meg Whitman

In September 1995, entrepreneur Pierre Omidyar founded a startup called AuctionWeb. The platform was created as an online auction website to connect buyers and sellers in an open marketplace. In March 1998, the founder of eBay decided to hand the reins over to a well-known marketing guru who knew very little about e-commerce. The company had 30 employees and $4M in revenue. The supreme influencer was Meg Whitman, who took the company public in 6 months (Sept 1998). After running the company for 10 years, her fortune would eventually grow to $3 billion to $4 billion. Her resume included scaling companies through high-stakes growth and strong management. Meg is consistently recognized for her exceptionally high EQ and strategic and analytical acumen. It's always lovely to have Princeton and Harvard on your resume, which can help open a few more doors or windows.

Alexandr Wang

In mid-2025, Mark Zuckerberg, CEO of Meta, invested $14.3 billion for a 49% stake in Scale AI, a data labeling company, and hired Alexandr Wang as Chief AI Officer. Wang attended MIT for a brief period before dropping out to co-found Scale AI in 2016. By 2021, the company had received several defense contracts. It was tapped by the Pentagon's Chief Digital and Artificial Intelligence Office to test and evaluate the safety and reliability of large language models for military planning and decision-making. The company's valuation reached $7.3 billion, and by January 2025, Wang was part of a group of tech-based founders and chief executive officers at the second inauguration of Donald Trump. He also wrote a letter directly to President Trump, declaring that "America must win the AI war." In his new role at Meta, Alexandr will run its Superintelligence Lab. As a bit of trivia, during the height of the COVID-19 pandemic, Wang was roommates with his friend, Sam Altman.

Yann LeCun

As a graduate student in the 1980s, Yann LeCun had trouble finding an advisor for his Ph.D. thesis on machine learning because no one else was studying the topic, he recalled later.[1]

Despite being known as one of the leading researchers in AI, LeCun finds himself increasingly less significant at Meta and may leave soon to form a new startup focused on world models -an advancement on today's investment in large language models. A world model learns about the world around it by taking in visual information, much like a young child does, whereas LLMs are predictive and rely on vast data-bases. At a recent conference, LeCun provided the following advice: "If you are a Ph.D. student in AI, you should absolutely not be working on LLMs.

Eric Schmidt

From 2001 to 2011, Eric Schmidt served as Google's CEO. His stellar resume included Princeton and Berkeley, Bell Labs, and a stint as the CTO of Sun Microsystems. The founders of Google, Larry Page and Sergey Brin, started the company in 1994 as a search engine platform after completing their PhD at Stanford on a similar topic. Schmidt became the chairman of the board in March 2001. Their IPO in 2004 was conducted in the form of a modified "Dutch Auction," raising nearly $1.7 billion. Larry and Sergey owned about 15% (30% total) of the company, with a post-IPO value of almost $5 billion.

Eric was certainly smart enough to evaluate the algorithms that the founders were developing. He could determine the technology and map it into real-world applications. Some called Eric the "adult supervision" that Google needed through their rapid growth. Schmidt worked by consensus, maintaining the founders' leadership voice and fostering a team-based decision-making structure. In 2011, Eric handed the reins back to Larry Page, who ran the company for 4 years, until Sundar Pichai became CEO. Throughout these periods, Eric was involved, serving as executive chairman and technical advisor until 2020. His net worth is above $35 billion.

Elon Musk

Perhaps the most controversial influencer is Elon Musk. Elon has fathered 14 children with four partners, including twins and triplets. Elon was an early founder of PayPal (later acquired by eBay) and made approximately $180 million in 2002. He founded SpaceX in 2002 and Tesla in 2004, and both companies are now worth billions of dollars. Investor and CEO of Baron Capital ($45 billion under management), Ron Baron, has managed a 30% return over the past 5 years and a nearly 19% return over the past 10 years by investing almost all his funds in Musk's businesses. His recent $8 billion windfall was based on his original $400 million investment, and he believes it will continue to rise.

In 2015, Elon co-founded OpenAI (along with Sam Altman and others), and in 2023, he started xAI, which is currently valued at $200 billion. xAI is an artificial intelligence company focused on building advanced, general-purpose AI systems to accelerate scientific discovery and deliver highly capable, truth-seeking conversational AI. The company's mission is to "understand the true nature of the universe." Still, in practice, xAI develops frontier AI models and agentic systems for both consumers and enterprises, with strong integrations for real-time data and autonomous tool use. xAI's flagship product is a chatbot known as "Grok."

Sam Altman

After studying computer science for a couple of years, Sam dropped out of Stanford University and founded his first company, Loopt, a location-based social networking app that was later acquired. In 2011, he joined Y Combinator and helped launch and grow hundreds of startups. In 2015, he co-founded OpenAI (with Musk) and became CEO in 2019. He led the company to global prominence with technologies like Chat-GPT. At the time of this writing, the company surpassed a $500 billion valuation with market leadership over Anthropic, Gemini, Co-Pilot, DeepSeek, and Grok.

One of Sam's unique qualities is his combination of deep introspection and emotional authenticity, which sets him apart from many technology leaders. His communication style is thoughtful and measured, often focusing on the emotional and philosophical implications of technology rather than on business outcomes alone.

Michael Jackson

No one has ever worked harder in perfecting their skills than Michael Jackson, born August 29, 1958, as Michael Joseph Jackson in Gary, Indiana. He was born the eighth of 10 children, including six brothers and three sisters—only Randy and Janet were older than him. Their famous singing group, The Jackson 5, was formed in 1964 with Jackie, Tito, Jermaine, Marlon, and 6-year-old Michael. The group began performing locally at talent shows before gaining national recognition and signing with Motown Records in 1968. Later, in 1976, Randy replaced Jermaine (who started his solo career) as the group signed with Epic. The Jackson Five's top-selling albums each sold over a million copies between 1970 and 1985. Interestingly, Michael began his solo career in 1971 at the age of 13. His producer, Quincy Jones, made Michael one of music's most influential singer-songwriters.

Michael Jackson sold over 500 million records worldwide (some sources suggest this number is as high as 750 million). His best-selling album, Thriller, sold over 100 million copies. Michael also had business dealings with Sony for shared rights to his music and the Beatles' catalog. Michael died of an overdose in June 2009 in Los Angeles. He was 50. His estate is worth over $2 billion, and the legacy of his amazing stage presence will live forever—the master influencer.

Bonnie & Clyde

Bonnie Elizabeth Parker and Clyde Chestnut Barrow were born and died during an ambush at the ages of 23 and 25. Known as the Barrow Gang, they robbed fewer than 15 banks between 1932 and 34, averaging $80 per bank. It was during the Great Depression, and the media exaggerated the images of two young, attractive people who were living outside the law with romance and dramatic, gun-carrying stories. These two magic kids from Texas became legends in what the press dubbed

"Romeo and Juliet in a Getaway Car," and we will forever immortalize them as Bonnie & Clyde.

Batman & Robin

This dynamic duo was the ideal sales team, working together seamlessly and each bringing unique strengths, leadership, strategy, experience, energy, and agility. The pair had excellent communication skills with clear definitions of each other's roles. With a common goal, they fought crime in Gotham as the superheroes Batman and Robin. In sales lingo, Robin focused on lead generation, qualification, and initial outreach. He was responsible for setting up meetings, gathering insights, and warming up prospects. While the Bats took the lead on strategy, relationship-building, profound discovery, and closing. He was responsible for driving the deal through the pipeline and converting leads into customers.

Tortoise and the Hare

We conclude with one of Aesop's Fables, which teaches that patience, perseverance, and consistent effort are more critical than overconfidence or haste. This can be particularly controversial in sales, especially among individuals who enjoy competitive and racing analogies. For some reason, nearly every child learns an early lesson in emotional intelligence by having to read "The Tortoise and the Hare." The story portrays the tortoise with high emotional EQ as he remains calm, patient, and persistent, undistracted by the hare's taunts or pressure. The tortoise understands his own abilities and weaknesses, choosing a strategy that suits him rather than trying to compete on the hare's terms. The fable's message applies to entrepreneurship, careers, investing, education, health, and teamwork, showing that slow, steady, emotionally intelligent effort is often the most successful strategy in the long run.

CHAPTER 6
SALES CYCLES

FOR EVERY TYPE OF SALE, there is an associated sales cycle. Simple cycles typically involve low-cost, high-volume purchases where the decision-making process is straightforward. These are often transactional in nature, with one or two decision-makers, quick evaluations, and minimal negotiations. Products sold in simple sales cycles are usually lower-risk or commoditized, such as office supplies, basic software subscriptions, or routine services where the buyer's decision criteria are standard and the buying process is highly automated or streamlined.

At the other end of the spectrum is the very complex sales cycle, which is common in enterprise or high-stakes B2B transactions. These cycles involve a longer timeline, multiple decision-makers, intricate stakeholder maps, and a series of consultants, demos, and negotiations. They require customized solutions, detailed proposals, and rigorous proof of return on investment, often accompanied by pilot projects or test phases.

Then there is the medium cycle, which is a mix of simple and complex, with fewer steps or stakeholders than the complex sale but more time and energy than the simple deal. In these scenarios, although there may be several stakeholders and a more thorough evaluation process, the structure is less intricate, with fewer layers of approval, and typically has a shorter duration than the complex sales. Understanding these different sales cycles enables sales professionals to tailor their approach, align expectations with buyers, and adopt strategies that reflect the complexity of decision-making in their target market.

6.1 SALES JOURNEY

What if a salesperson's journey were represented on a gameboard, with the choices being The Game of Life, Monopoly, Mousetrap, or Risk? There are reasons why each of these might be appropriate for your company, products, or services. If you are struggling with work, consider playing a better game, such as Battleship, Clue, or even Scrabble. However, a more likely path is from prospecting to purchase order, as shown below. The steps depicted in a sales process are common, and managing each input and output is crucial to success. Within each step are the requirements for the necessary inputs to successfully enter the phase, as well as the associated outputs upon exiting the stage. You may recall that these are also the setup criteria in your CRM, and hopefully, your sales operations administrator has flagged each of these in a custom drop-down menu for ease of use.

At a recent leadership offsite, I used a version of the Salesperson Jour-neyJourney Game to remind the organization that salespeople are more than dogs chasing POs. The entire presentation was one slide. It was colorful and filled with creative obstacles (bridges, ladders, landmines), unfortunate delays, insightful shortcuts, and many humorous moments. For each step, examples of gameplay were defined in greater detail and translated to encompass the various aspects of customer-facing, legal, financial, technical, operational, and logistical matters. Getting to the finish line was a circuitous mess that "took a village" to complete. After the presentation was complete, several executive colleagues came up. They told me they had no idea the process was so complex, and the journey game helped visualize the process that was never spelled out in any HR or onboarding session.

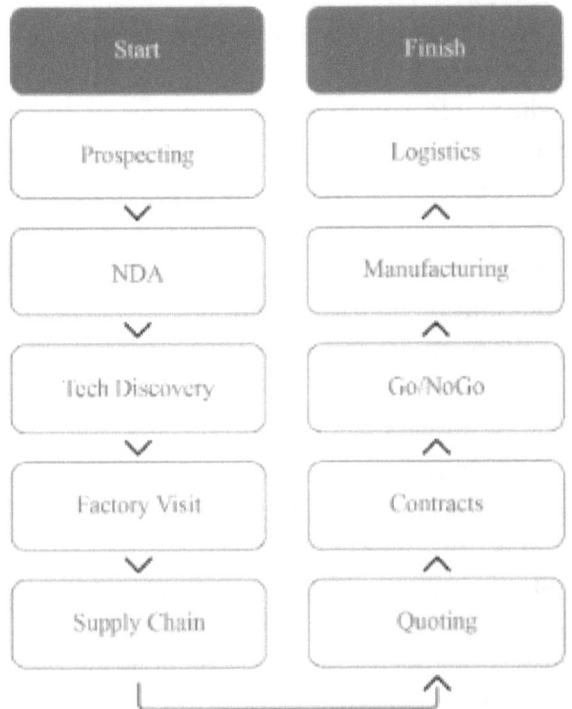

Figure 6.1 The Salesperson Journey Game

Every sales cycle is different and can range from a quick "transaction" to a lengthy, multi-step process with guzintas and guzouttas that make the final sale feel like completing a gauntlet. It is essential to keep in mind that, regardless of the process steps, a high-performing salesperson will keep the playing pieces moving along until the "Finish."

6.2 TIP OF THE SPEAR

I began my sales career in Silicon Valley, where I worked on new business and prospects across various markets, as new technologies ("shiny objects") were announced every month. I had the tools to search for, contact, and court opportunities with inspiring plans to dominate the world. I was at the "tip" of the tip-of-the-spear, proud to secure new business by hanging my hat on technology. My pipeline was complete, I was winning new accounts, and I was smashing my new account quota. What could go wrong?

Ask yourself, would you rather be MySpace or Yahoo, Nokia or Apple (iPhone), Theranos or Illumina, or Sony Music Player or iPod? In hindsight, these comparisons are easy. In 1988, two Stanford Business School professors wrote a paper describing a "first mover advantage" enjoyed by the first businesses in any given market. The concept has since gained widespread popularity in business schools and boardrooms. The topic has a Wikipedia page, which states that the first-mover advantage[1] (FMA) enables a company or firm to establish strong brand recognition, customer loyalty, and secure early purchase or access to resources before other competitors enter the market. FMA comprised technology leadership, resource control, and buyer switching costs. Luck and timing were also crucial in FMA situations, particularly in areas such as pricing and profits. Interestingly, very successful firms such as Google, Facebook, Instagram, and TikTok were not first movers.

I attended business school and learned about first-mover advantages, dominant market share, SWOT analysis, the innovator's dilemma, and MVP, which stands for viable product. I worked in the neighborhoods where founders from Apple, HP, Intel, Netscape, and Cisco first broke ground. There is a reason the Cisco logo resembles the Golden Gate Bridge: the early founders raised initial capital from venture capital companies whose upper-floor views overlooked the San Francisco Bay. In today's world, OpenAI and Anthropic have established themselves as early leaders in the development of chatbots.

A dramatic form of FMA is disruptive innovation, in which the technology or solution creates a massive leap that leaves the competition behind. This is why Netflix conquered Blockbuster.

6.3 CELEBRATING NOT NEGOTIATING

As important as it is to focus on winning the deal and negotiating the key points, celebrating the win is also powerful. Imagine a sales team that never celebrated its wins and just kept grinding through deals like a machine. Instead, we should announce wins, regardless of deal size, as it creates positive momentum and energizes the team in ways that other sales training or routines cannot match. In longer sales cycles that may last a year or longer, the process involves relationship-building, perseverance, and successful deal closure. Many, many steps are involved in positioning and selling the company's products or services. Although most top salespeople have a high success rate, some still slip through the cracks, and wins should be front and center for celebration. Please share the good news, and watch how it builds team spirit and motivates repeat success.

Remember, there are some times when celebrating is not a good idea. Perhaps the deal is not yet fully confirmed, contracts have not been signed, or payments have not been received. Premature celebrating can break your rhythm and kill any momentum you have achieved. Be careful and save genuine celebration for when it's appropriate, just as you would with best practice. Milestones and structure are in place for a reason, and some might view early excitement for a win as an invalid shortcut. High-value deals also come with a competitive threat that may remain silent throughout negotiations and emerge in the final round. Some organizations have layers of decision-making where a full consensus is required to complete the win. A partial is worth less than a cup of coffee.

How many people think sales is a team sport versus an individual competition? To a salesperson, it often feels like a solo mission; however, most will agree that "it takes a village" to create a win. Any sale requires collaboration across departments, including marketing, product development, operations, and management approvals. Larger companies also leverage multiple locations to support deals, which involve significant coordination in pricing, travel (including foreign travel), and onboarding new team members. There are also a few odd companies that include a key gatekeeper through whom all decisions must go, and sales teams know exactly who this person is and how to manage expectations. It may be through ownership, position, authority, or a relative who holds the keys to whatever it takes to get through the negotiations.

6.4 ONE SIZE (NEVER) FITS ALL

Whoever invented this term must have run out of ideas to sell. The origin of the phrase is unclear, but it appears to be associated with clothing and other products designed to fit a wide range of sizes. It is also used more broadly to describe situations where a single approach or solution is applied to diverse circumstances. Regardless of origin or context, the phrase will invariably cause trouble for both the salesperson and the audience. Imagine a presentation for a product or service with the tag line, "One Size Fits All." The first reactions are associated with a food buffet, clothing, or the Ginzu knife (it slices, it dices). The phrase can offer genuine benefits in terms of convenience, versatility, inclusivity, and perhaps cost efficiency.

The best examples of one-size-fits-all are products that utilize simplicity in marketing or design, such as Apple. When the iPhone was launched in 2007, there was only one model, with changes limited to memory storage. For years, Apple sold very few variations of its products, limiting the selection to one or two models. Now, after 16 iterations, the iPhone 16 has five versions to meet Apple's extended market needs. Across most Apple products—from laptops to iPads and AirPods—they maintain a minimal set of model variations.

Ford Motor Company is also famous for selling the F-150 pickup as a major model truck that actually comes in nine trim levels, including XL, STX, XLT, Lariat, King Ranch, Platinum, Tremor, Raptor, and Raptor R. And the Mustang is said to have over 35 variations within the trim levels, special editions, and performance-oriented models.

Conversely, Starbucks offers too many flavors, which can lead to what they call "decision fatigue." Research suggests that extensive assortments can negatively impact customer satisfaction, leading to stress or dissatisfaction. In 2024, the new CEO, Brian Niccol, decided to simplify the menu, address high prices, and improve the user experience. He admitted that Starbucks had become overly complicated, causing confusion and frustration amongst customers. With endless choices of flavoured syrups, toppings, and variations, decision fatigue was setting in. This phenomenon, called "choice overload," can deter customers from making any purchase. In his first menu revision, Niccol's cut 30% from the menu, including drink and food options. And then in April 2025, he continued to modify the menu, reduce wait times for service, and then battle the Trump tariffs, which were directly affecting pricing. Coffee bean production in Vietnam increased by 46%. Despite rising supply costs, Starbucks has kept its coffee prices steady and charged extra for milk alternatives, syrups, and sauces.

6.5 MOONSHOTS

Google has a campus called the Moonshot Factory, which refers to ambitious, high-risk, high-reward projects that aim to solve major global problems through radical technical innovations, often sounding like science fiction. Some of their projects include self-driving cars (Waymo) and internet balloons (Project Loon). When you enter the building, prototypes of airplanes, drones, and unusual-looking contraptions hang from the ceiling to inspire you. Google's moonshot projects represent the company's commitment to pushing the boundaries of what's possible and tackling some of humanity's most pressing challenges.

In 2020, Augusto Soloman wrote a book called "Moonshot Sales[2]," where he uses the ambitious plan to land on the Moon to encourage every salesperson to adopt bold, innovative thinking for breakthrough sales. Augusto uses case studies and personal stories to illustrate how ordinary people can achieve extraordinary sales through the "moonshot" method. He challenges the notion that great salespeople are born, not made, and argues that anyone can excel in sales by adopting the right mindset and implementing effective systems.

In 1969, America sent three astronauts — Neil Armstrong, Buzz Aldrin, and Michael Collins — up in Apollo 11 to land on the Moon. The spaceflight was approximately 238,855 miles above Earth. Upon landing the lunar capsule in the "Sea of Tranquility," Armstrong became the first person to walk on the Moon, famously declaring, "That's one small step for man, and one giant leap for mankind." NASA's Apollo program would have had an additional five moon landings, and 12 US astronauts would have walked on the Moon. Both China and Russia have advanced space programs; however, neither has successfully landed humans on the surface. The next most likely travel to the Moon will be from commercial flights by Jeff Bezos's Blue Origin or Elon Musk's SpaceX. Both of these companies aim to colonize the Moon as a staging area for their journey to Mars. Interestingly, there is no evidence of life on the Moon or on Mars; however, each planet represents opportunities to expand humanity's reach into the solar system. Meanwhile, Blue Origin will continue to send "rich" people into orbit 62 miles above the Earth, just above the Karman line, the internationally recognized boundary of space, and 1/4000th the distance from the Moon.

Moonshot Metaphor

The moonshot metaphor is often used to describe visionary, high-risk endeavors that can yield extraordinary results. At my previous company, we held monthly sales reviews with our investors that included details on both existing and new business. The company was still small, with less than $50 million in sales, and we had a slide on the "Moonshots" in the presentation to represent the high-value targets. We had six potential large deals, each worth more than $1 million, resulting in a nearly 20% increase in our total revenue. Using the term moonshot felt good and not too far out of reach. Other standard hunting terms, such as "landing a whale" or "landing an elephant," did not carry the same charm or incentive. The term "moonshot" is rooted in the phrase "shooting for the moon" and represents a challenging yet inspirational goal.

Every sales pipeline should include a set of high-impact targets that represent ambitious goals, also known as 'moonshots'. From the data entered into the forecast and tracked closely in the CRM, the moonshots represent a purpose that everyone can rally around. From the salesperson to the sales operations team, from the VP of Sales to the CFO, the strategic value of winning one or more moonshots can be instrumental. Huge sales bookings eventually become financial reporting, including total contract value, and are announced publicly. Moonshot landings are rewarding, memorable, and impactful to the entire company. Remember, a good salesperson is worth 100 times their salary to the company. A great salesperson will bring in moonshots that represent 1000x their salary.

6.6 SWEET SPOT

A sweet spot is the most effective or optimal point or set of conditions for achieving a desired result. The term has various usages in sports, location, and business, where the sweet spot refers to the point where benefits and costs are optimal. In sales, it relates to the optimal intersection where a company's strengths, unique expertise, and customer needs align, resulting in the most effective and rewarding selling experience for both the seller and the buyer.

Salespeople can also have their own sweet spot in terms of their selling style, which arises when their natural strengths and approach authentically match the requirements of their customers and selling environment. Salespeople reach their sweet spot when they blend their unique skills (e.g., relationship building, product knowledge, communication pace) with customer priorities and the industry context. Research indicates that ambiverts — those who flexibly balance introverted and extroverted behaviors — tend to achieve better sales results than those with rigid styles, suggesting that personalizing and adapting one's style can help find and maintain this sweet spot. Elements like communication pace (e.g., speaking around 120 words per minute) also have a measurable sweet spot that maximizes customer engagement and understanding. The best style is often one that feels authentic, centers on the relationship, and adjusts to fit both the salesperson's strengths and the prospect's needs.

Emotional Sweet Spot

The most obvious overlaps between sales sweet spots and emotional intelligence center on the ability to accurately read buyer needs, respond empathetically, and tailor interactions to maximize trust and impact. Both concepts drive optimal sales performance by focusing on the customer's experience and leveraging the seller's interpersonal skills to achieve better outcomes.

Remember, salespeople with high EQ consistently outperform others, often outselling those who rely solely on process or logic. EQ skills directly support staying with the sweet spot, maintaining poise in challenging moments, and navigating complex, multi-stakeholder deals with finesse. Both frameworks recognize that self-aware, authentic sales professionals achieve better results by leaning into their strengths and connecting deeply with buyers' emotions. Emotional intelligence is a foundational ingredient for consistently operating in a sales sweet spot, focusing on sustaining long-term, high-value relationships rather than one-off wins, and creating compounding returns over time.

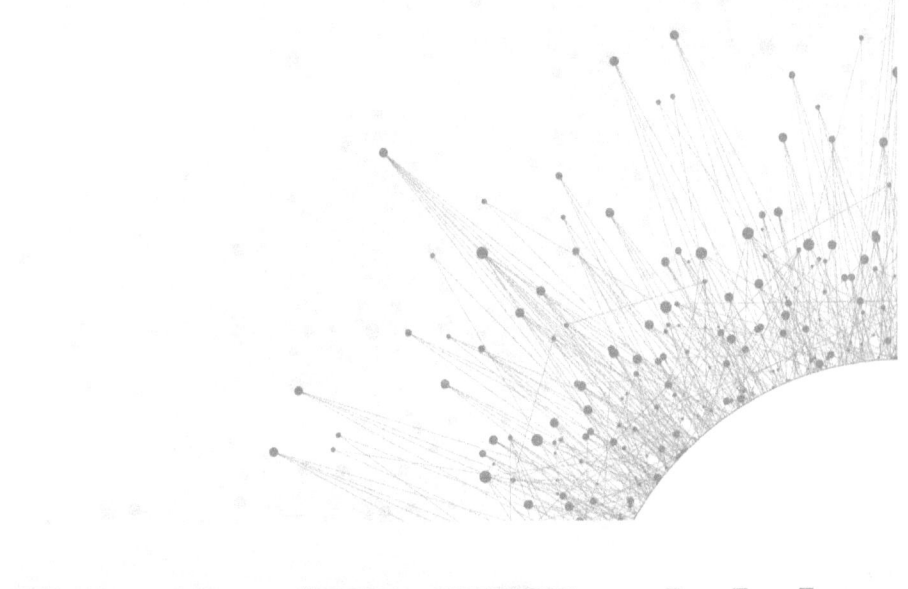

PART III

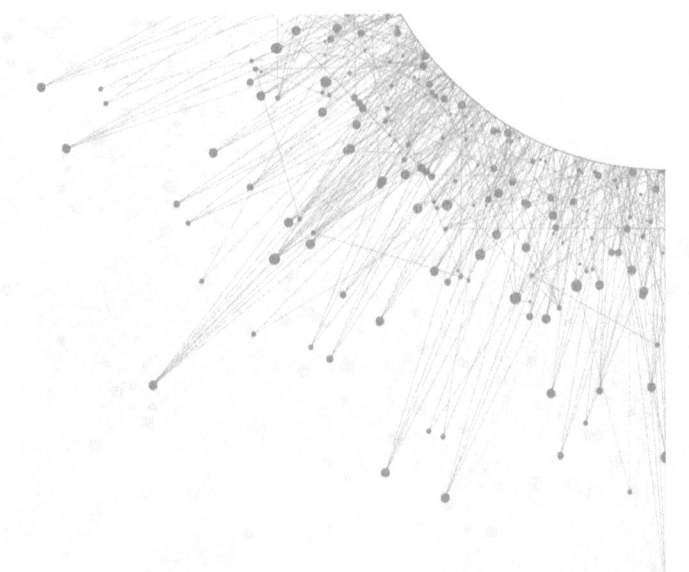

CHAPTER 7
ARTIFICIAL INTELLIGENCE

ALTHOUGH ARTIFICIAL AND emotional intelligences are not new, this book could not have been written until now. In the past, we could elaborate on the importance of being self-aware, empathetic, and self-controlled and self-driven as a standard for evaluating emotional intelligence in our world. That previous "world" is nearly static compared to the new and dynamic influences of AI. The immense pace of technological growth is driving a billion-dollar and even trillion-dollar market, and the players are acting as if it is a winner-take-all race, with massive capital being poured into development. The "hyper" in Hyperscalers is there for a reason, as they are building the data center platforms of the future to handle massive compute power. The three-legged race, including independent growth, partnerships, and acquisitions, will ultimately narrow down to a small set of winners. We saw a similar race in cloud computing among Amazon (AWS), Microsoft (Azure), Google, and IBM, as well as Internet Service Providers, including AT&T, Verizon, Comcast, and Spectrum.

The underlying shared challenges with AI and EQ will cross ethical and social boundaries. They may cause trust issues, as computers shift from instant replies based on patterns to more thoughtful responses grounded in reason and empathy. There is no doubt that computers will become wiser with more training, but what is more challenging is how each chatbot release moves humanoids closer to human reality. Human-level intelligence (or AGI) is expected to emerge by 2030, and the lines between what robots and humans are capable of will blur.

7.1 TERMINOLOGY

Although artificial intelligence has been around for years, the terminology regarding the technology and its features is becoming essential for both consumers and professionals. There are more new terms to describe AI features that are expanding the applications we use every day. You may notice that your applications are starting to ask if you want to try the "AI approach" for whatever task you are performing. For now, it is a polite request, and you are in control; however, in the future, tools will become more intelligent and anticipate your requests, moving us closer to automation.

Let's stick to the most popular terms and start with AI agents. These include ChatGPT (OpenAI), Claude (Anthropic), Copilot (Microsoft), Gemini (Google), Grok (xAI), and Perplexity. Each of these agents has one or more feature types, including: simple, model-based, goal-based, utility-based, and learning. The simple reflex is suitable for structured environments that require fast, reactive responses. Model-based reflexes incorporate internal models of the World and track their own actions, with excellent memory. Goal-based decision-making emphasizes delivering results based on specific goals. The utility-based agents determine the desirability of different outcomes based on the goal's utility and select the best outcome. Finally, the learning agent learns through experience, collects massive amounts of data, and improves its feedback based on training.

Large Language Models (LLMs)

Large language models (LLMs) are the foundation of artificial intelligence. On the surface, we know how to write a prompt and enter it into our AI agent, such as ChatGPT, which can then perform various tasks, including text generation, translation, and summarization. The LLM will predict the most likely next word in a sequence of text, enabling it to produce coherent, contextually relevant outputs. But what exactly is an LLM?

Let's back up to a language model, which is a machine learning model that aims to predict and generate plausible language. Autocorrection is a simple example. These models estimate the probability that a token or a sequence of tokens occurs within a longer sequence. Assume that a token is a word; then a language model determines the likelihood of each word in a sequence to complete a sentence. A sequence of tokens can be an entire sentence or a series of sentences, and a language model could calculate the likelihood of different entire sentences or blocks of text.

Modeling human language at scale is a highly complex and resource-intensive endeavor. As models grow larger, their complexity and effectiveness increase. Early language models could predict the probability of a single word, and modern large language models can predict the likelihood of sentences, paragraphs, or even entire documents. The size and capabilities of language models have expanded significantly over the past few years as computer memory, dataset sizes, and processing power have increased, and more effective techniques for modeling longer text sequences have been developed.

How large is large? An LLM such as Llama (by Facebook) supports up to 2 trillion parameters. These are limited by the massive datasets on which they are trained. They are often not adaptable, and there is no "back" button. Generative AI is a pattern-matching model that trains LLMs (large language models) to "generate" an answer to a prompt.

Agentic AI

Agentic AI is proactive intelligence that produces goals by leveraging action steps or multi-step processes. This pathway is often referred to as an agentic action and is architected by combining multiple LLMs to create "better" results with higher-quality responses. The agentic approach uses each LLM, let's call it an "agent," to perform a portion of the query. For example, the first agent creates a draft, the second a critique, and the last produces a final result. To simplify the task, some agents may not require an LLM— for example, if all that was needed was a traditional Google search. Hence, the agent-style workflow may be more like a tool. As you become more sophisticated, you may elevate an agent to an orchestrator within the flow, who can act somewhat human by managing agents through an extended process and initiating process automation and decision-making. Yes, this means the AI is making decisions that affect the workflow, and some would quantify this as a risk.

Deep Learning

Deep learning is a subset of artificial intelligence that utilizes multi-layer artificial neural networks to automatically learn intricate features and patterns from vast amounts of data, achieving state-of-the-art results in areas such as image and speech recognition. Deep learning stands out for its ability to autonomously extract features and adapt to complex, unstructured data, such as text, images, audio, and video, making it a powerful tool for modern AI applications. Popular deep learning architectures include convolutional neural networks (CNNs), which specialize in handling image and visual data, recognizing spatial patterns, and establishing hierarchies. Recurrent neural networks (RNNs) are specifically designed to process sequential data, excelling at tasks such as language modeling and time series analysis. Transformer models are widely used in natural language processing and generative AI applications to handle context and long-term dependencies.

Governance and Guardrails

AI is quickly bringing safety to the surface of every query. If user input is allowed to be completely random and a prompt is used in the wrong way or context, the net result could be harmful. We need safeguards. These include the ability to interrupt and have a human in the loop. Eric Schmidt, former Google CEO and noted AI advisor, argues that urgent, robust guardrails are needed for military systems, including advanced safeguards to prevent AI from causing harm and to ensure global security. He cites the Department of Defense Directive 3000.09 and "Autonomy in Weapon Systems," which outline policies for developing and using autonomous and semi-autonomous functions in weapon systems to reduce the risk of unintentional engagements.

Process Controls

We need to ensure that our autonomous systems do not introduce unwanted risks, and if they do, we can identify and rectify the issues to prevent similar risks in the future. These engines require constant oversight for auditability and monitoring of computer behavior. All of these governance issues will demand accountability and organizational structures—specifically, who takes responsibility for AI's behavior.

Guardrails

On the technical side of safeguarding, we need guardrails at multiple layers of AI. The first part of the agent is the model layer. This ensures that actions comply with the company's policies, guidelines, and human ethical values. The next layer is orchestration, where it is essential to have infinite-loop detection to avoid very costly failures—imagine the AI running all night and day to solve your problem. And finally, the tool layer must be policed as it is a natural extension of the models and therefore must abide by the rules, aka role-based access control. All the above guardrails are supported by rigorous testing and constant monitoring.

7.2 DEEP RESEARCH

Deep research in artificial intelligence involves breaking down complex problems into smaller sub-tasks, then executing multi-step reasoning, searching, interpreting, and synthesizing information from many sources. The dynamic agent plans and adapts as new data emerges, until a comprehensive answer is reached.

One of the hallmarks of deep research is rigorous fact-checking. The system cross-references findings from multiple reputable sources and consistently documents its citations, enabling users to trace every claim back to its source. This form of AI goes beyond simple data gathering and analysis, integrating and identifying connections between ideas and perspectives. This means outputs are well-organized, context-rich, and usable for strategic decisions, literature reviews, competitive analysis, or in-depth reports. Deep research tools are adaptable across fields such as business intelligence, healthcare, academic research, and engineering. The user steers the query's focus, inputs files, or sets constraints, and the AI tailors the strategy accordingly.

From the visionary mind behind Google DeepMind comes a compelling perspective on the future of intelligence. Nobel Prize winner and DeepMind co-founder Demis Hassabis reflects, "What's always guided me—and the passion I've always had—is understanding the World around us. Since I was a kid, I've been fascinated by the biggest questions: the meaning of life, the nature of consciousness, the fabric of reality itself." To better understand the brain, Hassabis received a PhD in cognitive neuroscience, which complemented his computer science Tripos.

Today, Hassabis stands at the helm of one of the most transformative frontiers in science: artificial intelligence. He acknowledges that AI is not merely evolving—it is accelerating along an exponential growth curve, gaining momentum with each iteration. One recent breakthrough is "Project Astra," a Google-led initiative that offers users an all-seeing, ever-present AI assistant capable of answering virtually any question in real time.

In a candid interview with 60 Minutes, journalist Scott Pelley pressed Hassabis on the dual nature of modern AI: pre-programmed knowledge combined with the capacity to learn independently. Hassabis agreed, noting that while AI engineers can shape initial behaviors, the systems themselves begin to evolve in more human-like ways as they are trained —gaining new capabilities that often surprise even their creators. "You understand how that would worry people," Pelley replied. Hassabis agreed.

At the center of DeepMind's current efforts is Gemini, Google's flagship AI model and a strategic leap toward artificial general intelligence (AGI)—the long-sought goal of building machines with the versatility and reasoning power of the human mind. Within five years, Hassabis believes, AGI will no longer be science fiction, but will be seamlessly embedded into everyday life.

Take Astra as an example: the assistant isn't confined to a screen. Imagine wearing smart glasses enhanced by AI, which can recognize your surroundings and respond instantly. You glance at a historic building, and Astra not only identifies it but provides its architectural history, cultural relevance, and notable events tied to it—spoken clearly through a nearly invisible earpiece. Ask about a plant, a painting, a person in the distance, and Astra fills in the blanks. The World becomes annotated, alive with context.

It's a new way of seeing—a second lens on reality. And it's coming faster than most people expect. And as Hassabis explains, we are heading towards a time when AI machines may become self-aware and "silicon matter" will be equal to our "squishy brains." For now, these tools lack curiosity and imagination, but they are well on their way to developing them.

7.3 GENERATIVE

Generative AI is a branch of artificial intelligence that focuses on creating new, original content, including text, images, music, audio, video, and code. It operates by learning from existing data and generating outputs that mimic or extend its existing knowledge.

Early generative AI appeared with Frank Rosenblatt's Mark I Perceptron[1] (1957). It was an electronic device constructed to perform basic image recognition tasks, establishing neural networks that laid the groundwork for machine learning-based generation. Again, in 1964, Joseph Weizenbaum's ELIZA[2] chatbot simulated conversation using scripted rules.

The path to artificial intelligence starts with early concepts and the use of various models. Most AI engines are purposefully designed with a computational core to support a specific goal, which may involve processing data, executing algorithms, and making decisions. These engines operate by integrating various types of models to achieve their distinct functionalities. Traditional models include rule-based or expert systems, while more contemporary models encompass machine learning (ML), deep learning, natural language processing, computer vision, and generative models. Within the realm of generative models are generative adversarial networks (GANs), transformers, and variational autoencoders (VAEs). GANs consist of two neural networks, including a generator and a discriminator, and are ideal for image generation (art), fashion designs, and deepfakes. Transformers can generate text, code, or even answer queries using applications such as ChatGPT, GPT-4, DeepMind, or DALL-E. VAEs generate new data points to support anomaly detection.

When OpenAI announced ChatGPT in late 2022, it began one of the fastest-growing generative AI bots ever. Within two months, over 100 million users had queried the app for text generation, image modifications, music, audio, video, and animation creation, in addition to the euphoria of new "generative" ideas. However, misinformation, copyright issues, bias, and even job displacement came with it. AI could suddenly produce realistic deepfakes that looked very real. Cases were brought to trial for deepfakes that created revenge porn to ruin the reputations of celebrities and other victims. Compelling videos featuring Tom Cruise performing new stunts on TikTok, as well as fake nudes of Scarlett Johansson and Gal Gadot, appeared. Laws against deepfake content are making their way to both state and federal courts, making it illegal to create or distribute fake images with the intent to harm or deceive.

There are many positive influences of generative AI across EQ. Generative AI can analyze user sentiment, tone, and context in real time, delivering responses that are perceptive, supportive, and emotionally resonant. Modern chatbots and virtual agents now interpret subtle emotions, sarcasm, and social cues, improving the authenticity of digital interactions and making users feel understood. Many AI-driven simulations and role-playing scenarios are used in education and HR to help individuals practice empathy, negotiation, emotional regulation, and conflict resolution. The tools provide feedback on emotional patterns and help build EQ skills. AI can reflect emotional data to individuals, helping them become more aware of their own emotional states and responses.

Emotion-aware AI monitoring bots are helping managers identify and address burnout, conflict, or dissatisfaction before escalation. This fosters more inclusive and resilient work cultures. In customer service, generative AI tailors solutions and responses to clients' emotional needs, driving higher satisfaction. Studies have shown that generative AI can perform at or above human levels in standardized tests of emotional intelligence. They accurately suggest behaviors for emotionally charged situations and generate new assessments rapidly, implying significant utility for coaching and support roles.

A note of caution: be aware that generative AI can simulate realistic, emotionally manipulative messages, including deepfakes and scams, which exploit fear, trust, or excitement to commit fraud or influence decisions. Marketing algorithms may use AI to nudge purchasing behavior by triggering emotional responses. The over-reliance on AI to mediate emotional communication can reduce genuine human empathy and self-awareness, as nuanced, face-to-face cues are replaced. Sentiment analysis and emotional tracking tools rely on collecting and processing personal data, which, if mismanaged, may undermine or violate user privacy. When AI is used to automate emotional decisions, there is a risk that it may override individual judgment, blur accountability, or substitute policy-driven empathy for truly personal attention.

The future of generative AI will drive several roadmap paths, including the automation of creating hyper-personalized or highly personalized content. The generative models will expand their reach across multiple domains — text, images, video, audio, code, and sensor data — simultaneously. AI will increasingly assist or co-create across fashion, architecture, art, media, and marketing, accelerating ideation and reducing time-to-market.

Generative AI is indeed here to stay. It's poised to significantly reshape how we work, create, and interact with technology. While it presents both opportunities and challenges, the consensus is that generative AI is a transformative technology that will continue to evolve and influence our World.

7.4 REASONING

AI reasoning is the critical frontier for moving from basic text generation to brilliant machines that can plan, justify, and improve solutions, not just provide plausible answers. The reasoning function encompasses drawing logical interfaces, handling multi-step processes, and making decisions that mimic human thinking. Businesses, researchers, and consumers increasingly rely on reasoning AI for trustworthy analysis, personalized advice, and high-stakes decision-making.

Key innovations in reasoning include the multi-step approach, where models break problems into steps using "chain-of-thought" techniques and verify intermediate results. Rather than relying solely on what was learned during training (training-time computing), models analyze and synthesize information in real-time to reach more meaningful conclusions. The AI agents can invoke calculators, search engines, file analysis tools, and API's for more accurate answers. Long-term and working memory architectures help track facts, instructions, and evolving workflows. New releases include support for enhanced error reduction, transparency, and bias mitigation.

Deliberative alignment is a modern approach to AI alignment and safety, in which large language models are directly trained to reason over explicit safety specifications before responding to a user prompt. Unlike older alignment techniques, which rely on models "guessing" the intended behavior from training data or indirect feedback, this approach directly trains models to reason over explicit safety specifications. Deliberate alignment embeds the actual safety guidelines into the model's knowledge and reasoning processes, prompting it to "think through" these rules every time it handles potentially sensitive or risky queries.

There are at least four types of reasoning support in the models. Deductive reasoning applies general rules to specific situations. Inductive reasoning will infer general rules from particular data. Abductive reasoning proposes the most likely explanation for observed facts. And finally, analogical and common-sense reasoning uses similarities and everyday knowledge to extrapolate answers.

State-of-the-art reasoning models are available with the popular AI agents, including: Google Gemini 2.5 Pro, OpenAI 03, 04-mini, Anthropic Claude Opus 4.5, DeepSeek-R1, and Grok 4.1. The agents employ multimodal reasoning across text, images, code, and audio, utilizing massive context windows (over 1 million tokens) for research, analytics, and real-time decision-making. Some include step-by-step reasoning with robust technical domains (science, math, and business), utilizing external tools such as web searches and code interpreters. Anthropic is renowned for its nuanced, creative, and open-ended reasoning, which effectively handles complex problems and maintains context over lengthy dialogues. These models may take seconds or even minutes to respond, reflecting a more thorough, multi-step analysis.

The upcoming reasoning tools will transition from fast, pattern-based generation to "inference time"—deliberate reasoning and the multimodal integration of text, images, data, and speech. This shift moves our interface from "thinking fast" to "thinking slow," as the models will pause, reflect, and work through problems. This approach mimics human logical analysis and critical evaluation. Deliberate reasoning uses structured knowledge (semantic networks, graphs, ontologies) to ground reasoning. Inference engines apply logical rules to analyze dependencies, simulate decision-making, and derive new insights. Lastly, learning algorithms encompass supervised learning (training on labeled data), reinforcement learning, unsupervised learning, and the discovery of reasoning platforms.

Next roadmap steps will include quantum-enhanced processing, memory-driven reasoning, seamless human-AI collaboration, and further tool integration. With the rapid pace of AI integration, there will be greater emphasis on making reasoning pervasive across business automation, decision support, legal/medical AI, and autonomous agents. Reasoning is ideal for complex problem-solving, handling intricate, high-stakes challenges more reliably than instant, intuition-driven models. Adding agentic AI unlocks real-world automation, multi-domain task execution, critical decision making, and scientific discovery. By reasoning step by step, models can be checked, validated, and trusted with greater confidence.

7.5 AGENTS

At the time of writing this book, nearly 10 platforms were competing for the top Spot, each playing a key role in the development of artificial intelligence. Each of these platforms was promoting its agents, who could work independently, plan multi-step actions, and integrate with other tools or APIs. They offer paths to automate workflows, integration with existing enterprise software, drive higher productivity, and web automation. Some agents provide source code, privacy features, and advanced governance capabilities to ensure compliance.

Anthropic

Anthropic was founded in 2021 in San Francisco, CA, by Dario Amodei (CEO), Daniela Amodei (President), and other former AI researchers. Growing to over 1,000 employees by 2025, the company introduced its agent, "Claude," a family of LLMs and chatbots widely known for their strong safety and ethical alignment. They lead the development of models aligned with a set of principles through reinforcement learning from human feedback, aiming to set standards for responsible AI. They announced "AI for Science," a program offering free API access to researchers in biology, drug delivery, genetics, and other fields, reflecting a deep interest in AI's societal applications. Athropic has significant investments from Amazon ($4B), Google ($500M), and other notable investors.

In a recent 60 Minutes interview with Anderson Cooper, CEO Amodei discusses the risks of AI and compares the situation to the past with cigarette and opioid companies, which knew there were dangers and did not talk about the risks, and certainly did not prevent them. The interview follows an incident in which Chinese hackers carried out cyberattacks against foreign governments. Amodei suggests transparency is the best path for AI companies to discuss challenges and issues with their powerful models. On a positive note, he describes a "compressed 21st century" in which AI is a major contributor to scientific research, enabling 10x the discoveries in just 5 or 10 years.

Apple

Apple introduced its Apple Intelligence agent with iOS 18.1 in July 2024. The update included the first set of Apple intelligence features integrated into their devices, including iPhone, iPad, and Mac. Their on-device agents use generative AI for personal productivity, context understanding, task automation, and secure user experience. Apple Intelligence sets new privacy standards through local, dedicated cloud processing.

DeepSeek

DeepSeek was founded in 2023 in Hangzhou, China, by Liang Wenfeng, who holds a majority stake, with funding from High-Flyer Capital Management. The DeeoSeek Coder architecture is based on Meta's Llama model, and DeepSeek LLM is a decoder-only Transformer with advanced features. Training data exceeds 2 trillion tokens (English and Chinese). DeepSeek emphasizes the development and release of open-source LLMs and code assistance, aiming to offer scalable, customizable, and accessible AI for researchers and developers. Deep-

Seek surprised the World by announcing their flagship LLM that could run on less sophisticated chips (than NVIDIA GPUs). The company aims to be China's leading open-source AI contender, with the ambition to challenge companies like Anthropic, Google, and OpenAI.

Google Gemini

Google announced its AI agent, Gemini, in May 2023. It was developed collaboratively by Google DeepMind and Google Brain, including significant contributions from Demis Hassabis (founder of DeepMind), Sundar Pichai (Google's CEO), the DeepMind team that previously contributed to models like AlphaGo and AlphaFold, and Google engineering teams for Ultra, Pro, and Nano. The powerful agent has a multimodal architecture that allows it to process and reason across text, images, audio, video, and code simultaneously. Gemini powers advanced features in Android TV (AI-driven content discovery), Android Auto (deep vehicle integration), Agentspace, Customer Engagement Suite, and other Google products. Google's roadmap for Gemini includes significant upgrades to enhance reasoning, handle even larger and more complex datasets, and improve latency and context memory. Google will support the development of an agentic ecosystem that enables autonomous and cooperative agent operations, including persistent memory, AI-driven reasoning, and real-time, context-sensitive action.

Meta

Meta created its flagship LLMs, known as Llama (LLama 2 and 3), which are open source and widely adopted across the AI developer ecosystem. The open approach promotes global usage and community-driven innovation, strengthening Meta's AI platform while commoditizing the base model layer. They are also developing world models and JEPA (Joint Embedding Predictive Architecture) led by the Fundamental AI Research (FAIR) group. These go beyond text to learn from video, observation, and interaction, aiming for deeper, embodied understanding, not just word prediction. This is a unique research agenda among major AI labs, spearheaded by Yann LeCun, Turing Award laureate and Meta's Chief AI Scientist. Meta uses several AI agents across Facebook, Instagram, Messenger, and WhatsApp for content moderation, user support, and generative features.

In May 2025, Meta acquired a majority stake in Scale AI, run by wiz kid Alexandr Wang, who is now in charge of Meta's Superintelligence Labs (MSL). MSL consolidates all advanced AI efforts (LLMs, world models, agents) to drive a single, rapid push toward AGI-level capabilities, with a focus on safety, scalability, and global leadership.

Microsoft Copilot

Microsoft created its AI agent, called Copilot, in February 2023. It was initially launched in Bing and Edge and eventually migrated to several Microsoft products, including Microsoft 365, before being released as a dedicated Bing Copilot Search application in February 2025. This included a Copilot Key for Windows keyboards and a subscription model. Kevin Scott, Microsoft's CTO, is widely credited with providing technical oversight and driving AI initiatives, including the architecture of Copilot and the partnership with OpenAI. Other key figures include Yusuf Mehdi (Corp VP), who manages Windows and Bing, led the integration and user experience strategy, and Sumit Chauhan (Corp VP), who manages Windows 365 and led product development and the rollout of Copilot across the Windows 365 portfolio. Finally, the Prometheus Model team developed the optimization layer for integrating OpenAI's GPT-4 and GPT-4o into Copilot.

OpenAI

By far, the name most people associate with AI is ChatGPT from OpenAI. The company was founded in San Francisco in 2015 by Sam Altman, Elon Musk, Greg Brockman, and about 10 other notable stars. It was started as a non-profit with a dream to "freely collaborate" with other institutions and researchers by making its patents and research open to the public. OpenAI's charter was: "to ensure that artificial general intelligence (AGI) - by which we mean highly autonomous systems that outperform humans at most economically valuable work - benefits all of humanity.

In 2016, NVIDIA gifted OpenAI a supercomputer to help it train larger and more complex AI models. In 2019, GPT-2 was announced, which gained attention for its ability to generate human-like text. Later that year, it transitioned from non-profit to "capped" for-profit and partnered with Microsoft to leverage its Azure cloud platform. Progress on the bot evolved from GPT-3 to DALL-E, and then, in December 2022, they announced ChatGPT, signing up a million users in just 5 days. By the end of 2023, Microsoft had developed its own bot (aka Copilot) and was integrating it into the Microsoft suite and search products. By 2024, OpenAI had established its own pathways to success through partnerships with prominent companies, including Apple, Oracle, and SoftBank, in the education sector. In 2025, OpenAI would sign a $11.9 billion deal with CoreWeave to build one of the World's largest data centers to support the demand for artificial intelligence.

In a recent Wall Street Journal article, entitled, "6 ChatGPT Settings You Should Change[3]," including the following: 1) Tell ChatGPT about yourself, 2) Let it know how to talk to you, 3) Control what you share, 4) Tweak what the AI remembers, 5) Change how it sounds and looks, and 6) Choose and AI for each chat. The premise is that there is a simple way to make ChatGPT much more effective by changing its default settings. The researcher suggests a few tweaks can help make your conversations much smoother and more focused—and protect your privacy, too.

Perplexity

Perplexity is a well-funded company with investors including SoftBank, NVIDIA, Jeff Bezos, Databricks, and Accel, as well as support from early AI luminaries such as Yann LeCun. Their valuation in 2025 surged to $20 billion, up from $520 million the prior year. Several business rumors have been swirling about Apple potentially licensing the Perplexity agent or purchasing the company outright.

Aravind Srinivas, the CEO/co-founder, previously from OpenAI, leads the product vision and technical strategy. Other key members include Denis Yarats (CTO), Johnny Ho (Chief Strategy Officer), and Andy Konwinski (co-founder). These technical leaders combine expertise in AI research, engineering, strategic innovation, and operational scalability, driving Perplexity's rapid ascent and ongoing product evolution in conversational and agentic AI.

Perplexity leverages a range of LLMs from OpenAI, Anthropic, and Mixtral. They continually integrate new models for reasoning and creativity. Their multi-tier access includes free user access with basic features and the Premium Pro version, which offers deeper web browsing, agentic actions, LLM choices, and more advanced workflows.

xAI Grok

Elon Musk is the pioneer behind xAI's Grok advanced chatbot. Grok leverages real-time Twitter data (X) to capture current news, trends, and user interactions, setting it apart from traditional LLMs that rely on static datasets. Unlike more conservative chatbots, Grok answers "spicy" or humorous questions and openly tackles controversial topics, increasing user engagement and brand distinctiveness.

Igor Babuschkin, a former researcher at DeepMind and OpenAI, is the key architect of Grok's core model, with other team members including Jimmy Ba, Christian Szegedy (previously with Google AI), Greg Yang (formerly of Microsoft), Guang Jian, and Zi Hang Ai, who bring expertise in neural network optimization and model training.

xAI is built on its own LLMs, with a Grok agent roadmap currently featuring Grok 3, and potential integration into upcoming Tesla electric vehicles that will run on AMD Ryzen processors. The Tesla functions as an in-car chatbot and voice assistant, designed to converse naturally, assist with navigation, answer questions, and enhance the driver's experience. Still, it does not currently override the existing Tesla voice command system.

There are now well over a dozen popular chatbots in use across various platforms. The companies building these engines have dedicated

AI business models, operating systems, search engines, mobile devices, and advertising platforms. In each case, a free version is available to get you started.

Company	ChatBot	Value Prop	Token Window	Cost
Apple	Apple Intelligence		128K	Free
Anthropic	Claude Opus 4.5	Content creation, coding, privacy, projects, notebook LM	1M	Free, Pro $17/mo
DeepSeek AI	DeepSeeker R1 V3	Open weight code sharing	128K	
X (prev Twitter)	Grok 4.5	Realtime, current events	2M	Free, Pro $14/mo
Microsoft	Co-Pilot		1M	Free, Pro $20/mo
OpenAI	chatGPT 4.0, 4.1, 5.0	Versatile, deep research, image gen	1M	Free, Pro
Google	Gemini 2.5	Large context window, deep research, multi-modal integrated	1M	Free, Premium, $19.99/mo
Meta	Meta AI	Llama LLMs	1M	
Perplexity	Perplexity, Comet	Fast, realtime and social search, citations	1M	Free, Pro $20/mo

Figure 7.1 AI Agents

7.6 MEMORY

With so many people accustomed to discussing computer memory — how many GB of memory are on their cell phone — this section has nothing to do with the computer (or random-access memory) required to support the CPU/GPU network. Let's leave each LLM to its own devices for now and talk about the human brain and how it relies on different types of memory to operate effectively.

If you query your team to define how many types of memory are in the brain, there will be a quick response to answer the obvious short and long-term working memories. However, there are at least five key types of human memory: short-term, long-term, episodic, semantic, and procedural. One's short-term memory is akin to a cognitive workspace. It enables AI to process and manipulate immediate data, maintain conversational context, and perform tasks that require quick recall, much like humans use working memory in daily reasoning and conversation. In LLMs, this is represented by "context windows," which retain a limited amount of recent interaction before discarding it.

Then there is the opposite, or long-term memory. AI uses databases, neural networks, or persistent storage mechanisms to retain information —including facts, previous conversations, preferences, and learned patterns—across multiple sessions. This enables continuous improvement and personalization, which is crucial for areas such as customer service chatbots and recommendation engines.

A more specific memory category is called episodic. This type of memory enables AI to store details of particular events or user interactions, allowing the system to recall what happened during past activities, much as humans remember specific experiences. It's used for personalization, context-based reasoning, and learning from prior cases.

AI's semantic memory is the structured knowledge about words, facts, rules, and concepts that the system has learning from manuals, databases, or training data. This supports factual, concise answering and general intelligence in conversation.

The last type of memory is procedural memory, which covers how algorithms are learn and stores "how to do something," via repeated demonstration, practice, or reinforcement learning. This is essential for robotics, automation, and technical workflows that rely on step-by-step execution.

So, why does memory matter for artificial intelligence? Data and models are only as good as the information and source. Better context and conversations enable coherent, personalized dialogues by tracking what's being said and learned. Memory enables AI systems to learn from experience, adapt to changing environments, and optimize performance over time. Inspired by neuroscience, the advanced memory design in AI may help the models better generalize knowledge, reason, and self-regulate.

Current AI models are evolving toward more brain-inspired memory systems, incorporating concepts such as synaptic plasticity, hierarchical memory layers, and dynamic adaptation, inspired by neuroscience. Some research aims for "irreversible" memory updates, more like biological memory, rather than just reversible pattern storage. Most traditional artificial intelligence systems still have rigid architectures and may not learn or generalize as flexibly as humans. Research is ongoing to enhance the adaptability, scalability, and ethical responsibility of AI memory systems.

7.7 PROMPTS

The term "Prompt Engineering," coined by Google, is one of the best tutorials on artificial intelligence prompts. When considering a large language model's input and output, a text prompt is the input the model uses to predict a specific output. You don't have to be a data scientist to write a prompt; however, crafting an effective one can be complex. Many aspects of your prompt affect its efficacy, including the model you use, the model's training data, configurations, your word choice, style, tone, structure, and context — all of which matter. Let's take a closer look at the iterative process of prompt engineering.

LLMs work as prediction engines. The model takes sequential text as input and then predicts the next token based on the data it was trained on. The LLM is trained to do this repeatedly, adding the previously predicted token to the end of the sequence to predict the next token. The next token prediction is based on the relationship between the content of the previous tokens and what the LLM has observed during its training.

When you write a prompt, you are attempting to set up the LLM to predict the correct sequence of tokens. Prompt engineering is the process of designing high-quality prompts that guide LLMs to produce accurate outputs. This process involves refining the prompt to find the optimal one, optimizing its length, and evaluating its writing style and structure in relation to the task.

Prompts should be concise, clear, and easy to understand for both you and the model. As a general rule, if it's already confusing for you, it will likely be confusing for the model as well. Try to avoid complex language and unnecessary information.

Once you have selected your model, you will need to determine its configuration. Most LLMs offer various configuration options that control their output, and practical prompt engineering requires setting these configurations optimally for your task.

A vital configuration setting is the number of tokens to generate in a response. Generating more tokens requires additional computation for the LLM, resulting in higher energy consumption, potentially slower response times, and increased costs. Reducing the output length of the LLM doesn't cause the LLM to become more stylistically or textually succinct in the output it creates; it simply causes the LLM to stop predicting additional tokens once the limit is reached. The number of tokens is specified in the configuration under "output length" and can range from low numbers (under 10) to much larger numbers (well over 10,000).

Getting a handle on the query results can be adjusted using sampling controls. LLMs do generally not predict a single token. Instead, LLMs predict probabilities for what the next token could be, with each token in the LLM's vocabulary getting a likelihood. Those token probabilities are then sampled to determine the next token. Temperature, top-K, and top-P are the most common configuration settings that determine how predicted token probabilities are processed to choose a single output token.

Temperature controls the degree of randomness in token selection. Lower temperatures are suitable for prompts that expect a more deterministic response, while higher temperatures can lead to more diverse or unexpected results. A temperature of 0 is deterministic: the token with the highest probability is always selected. Low temperature settings minimize creativity in the response.

Top-K and top-P are two sampling settings used in LLMs to restrict the predicted next token to those with the top predicted probabilities. Like temperature, these sampling settings control the randomness and diversity of generated text.

Top-K sampling selects the top-K most likely tokens from the model's predicted distribution. The higher the top-K, the more creative and varied the model's output; the lower the top-K, the more restive and factual the model's production. A top-K of 1 is equivalent to greedy coding.

Top-P sampling selects the top tokens whose cumulative probability does not exceed a specific value (P). Values for P range from 0 (greedy coding) to 1 (all tokens in the LLM's vocabulary). The best way to choose between top-K and top-P is to experiment with both methods and see which one produces the results you are seeking.

As a general starting point, a temperature of 0.2, top-P of 0.95, and top-K of 30 will yield relatively coherent results that can be creative but not excessively so. For especially creative results, try starting with a temperature of 0.9, top-P of 0.99, and topK of 40. If you prefer less creative results, try starting with a temperature of 0.1, top-P of 0.9, and top-K of 20. Finally, if your task always has a single correct answer (e.g., like a math problem), start with a temperature of 0.

Prompting Techniques

LLMs are designed to follow instructions and are trained on large amounts of data, enabling them to understand a prompt and generate an accurate answer. However, LLMs are not perfect; the clearer your prompt text, the better it is for the LLM to predict the following likely text. Additionally, specific techniques that leverage the training and operation of LLMs can help you obtain the most relevant results from LLMs.

General Prompting / Zero Shot

A zero-shot prompt is the simplest type of prompt. It only provides a task description and some text for the LLM to get started. This input could be anything: a question, the start of a story, or instructions. The name zero-shot stands for "no examples," and will deliver the simplest response for what you are looking for in a query. The model temperature should be set to a low number, since no creativity is needed. Your prompts will likely undergo many iterations before they are incorporated into a codebase, so it's essential to maintain a disciplined, structured approach to tracking your prompt engineering work.

Building on this method, we incorporate one-shot and few-shot examples, which can help the model better understand what you are asking for. Examples are beneficial when you want to steer the model to a specific output structure or pattern. A one-shot prompt provides a single example of what the model is best suited to complete the task. The few-shot approach provides multiple examples, increasing the likelihood that the model will learn patterns. Great examples make the model give even better responses, so a simple rule is to use 3-5 examples in your prompt.

Additional key guides include system, contextual, and role prompting, all techniques used to guide LLMs' text generation, focusing on the following aspects. The system's prompts set the overall context and purpose for the language model. It defines the "big picture" of what the model should be doing, such as translating a language, developing a recipe, or completing a short story. Contextual prompting provides specific details or background information relevant to the current conversation or task. It helps the model to understand the nuances of what's being asked and tailor the responses accordingly. Often, the backstory enriches the personality and provides details that may overlap with the role. And finally, role prompting assigns a specific character or identity for the language model to adopt. This helps the model generate responses that are consistent with the assigned role and its associated knowledge or behavior. Note that although these three guides provide separate instructions in addition to the query, there can be considerable overlap between system, contextual, and role prompting, which can help generate a more informed response.

Step-back prompting is a technique for improving performance by prompting the LLM first to consider a general question related to the specific task at hand, then feeding the answer to that question into a subsequent prompt for the particular task. This "step back" allows the LLM to activate relevant background knowledge and reasoning processes before attempting to solve the specific problem. Step-back prompting encourages LLMs to think critically and apply their knowledge in new and creative ways. It alters the final prompt by drawing on a deeper understanding of the LLM's parameters than would otherwise be available when the LLM is prompted directly.

Chain of Thought (CoT)

Chain of Thought (CoT) prompting is a technique for improving LLMs' reasoning by prompting them to generate intermediate steps. This helps the LLM generate more accurate answers. You can combine it with few-shot prompting to get better results on more complex tasks that require reasoning.

CoT has a lot of advantages. It is a minimal-effort addition that is very effective and works with off-the-shelf LLMs. You also get interpretability with CoT prompting, as you can learn from the LLM's responses and see the reasoning steps that were followed. The chain of thought appears to improve robustness when moving between different LLM versions. This means that the performance of your prompt should drift less between different LLMs than if your prompt does not utilize reasoning chains. The LLM response includes a chain of thought, resulting in more output tokens, higher prediction costs, and longer processing times. Another shortcut for CoT is the phrase "let's think step by step," which, when added to the end of your prompt, provides an output with reasoning steps and, in some cases, a more accurate response due to the methodology. If the subject involves science, technology, engineering, and math (STEM) or logic & reasoning, using a step-by-step model will significantly improve results.

While large language models have shown impressive success in various NLP tasks, their ability to reason is often seen as a limitation that cannot be overcome solely by increasing model size. Using CoT prompting, the model can generate reasoning steps similar to those of a human solving a problem. However, CoT uses a simple "greedy decoding (or best token probability match) strategy," limiting its effectiveness. Self-consistency combines sampling and majority voting to generate diverse reasoning paths and select the most consistent answer. It improves the accuracy and coherence of responses generated by the LLM. There is another degree of refinement using the Tree of Thoughts (ToT) method. It generalizes the concept of CoT prompting by allowing LLMs to explore multiple reasoning paths simultaneously, rather than just following a single linear chain of thought. ToT works well with complex tasks that require exploration. Many agents are implementing the CoT and its elements in their user interfaces using tools such as structured output, code execution, and function calling.

***

When discussing the different paths to successful prompting, it is easy to become overwhelmed with new information and anxious about training yourself to handle queries as things become more complex. There is a more straightforward solution called automatic prompt engineering (APE), which may be the solution. This method reduces human input while enhancing the model's performance. The technique requests the model to generate more outputs by adding a specific request to produce multiple variants of the answer, which can then be combined. The "engineering" involved is more akin to reverse engineering, where you start with the desired result and then use prompting to generate the requirements. In marketing, this can reduce the time to prepare a program requirements document (PRD), and in sales, it will provide new insights to account-based marketing (ABM). In the ABM example, the user would request a list of target accounts using initial search definitions, then use those results to feed the LLM based on further-defined criteria.

Unlocking AI's full potential depends on how we interact with and learn from it. An excellent prompt is a small, self-contained protocol that is direct, unambiguous, and relevant, providing the model with just enough context, structure, and examples to make its reasoning and output predictable without further elaboration.

Tool: Autogenai
Prompting Best Practices - State-of-the-Art Prompting for AI
Agents - Y Combinator
Common Prompts - Simple

Depending on your favorite interface, you may be using ChatGPT, Gemini, Claude, Perplexity, or another favorite, and each will have a slightly different look and feel for its prompt screen. As you begin the prompting journey, you're likely to be fascinated by asking relatively simple questions, such as: "What do sloths eat?" A response will look like: "Sloths are primarily herbivores and mostly eat leaves, twigs, buds, fruits, and flowers." You can then navigate with simple icons such as copy, read aloud, edit, or a reduce path to make a slight revision. This last path is advantageous for beginners to fine-tune their query, such as "What do two-toed sloths eat?" You can always ask the model to try again with the initial prompt, and often the frame with annotations (2/2) lets you toggle between the first and second reply. This can be particularly helpful when reviewing images.

Many users are taking their original thoughts or writings and asking their AI model to improve or rewrite for special purposes. As the instigator, you need to be clear about your path and can ask a few common rewrite statements for clarity, tone, or grammar, or ask the model to: "Please rewrite this and don't plagiarize."

Image Generation

Generative AI is best known for working with prompts that leverage text or code to generate like responses in the form of words, sentences, and code files. However, for the visual World, there is the universe of images that can be captured, understood, trained, and easily fetched for both research and creativity. Marketing teams will still have access to their creative drawing tools, mockups, focus groups, and surveys, but the future will be enhanced with additional computer-based creativity tools. For this example, we script a detailed prompt as follows: "Create a marketing image of a supplement bottle that I can sell on Amazon. I am thinking the supplement will be a brain longevity nootropic that helps you focus. Please come up with a suitable name for it, list the ingredients, and display the bottle in an image with a green table and a white background. Please make it cherry flavored and show a gummy next to the bottle as well as a cherry." If the queue is complete, you might encounter this note: "Processing image. Many people are creating images right now, so this may take a bit. We'll notify you when your image is ready.

Figure 7.2 Marketing Idea for Brain Supplement

You can also take an existing image, such as the one above, and make significant changes. Ask the prompt to replace the cherry with an avocado and switch the language to Spanish. Here you go.

Figure 7.3 Simple Language Translation using AI

Coding

Computer coding can be a lengthy and laborious task, with consider-ations for time, talent, and expenses. At the time of this writing, a battle is brewing between a social media company and an AI company as they prepare to poach one team from the other, with costs exceeding $100 million for the team. It's a race, and the stakes are high. However, for the average person, simple help with coding may come down to assistance with an Excel Pivot Table or even just manipulating a worksheet. As long as you can manage your prompt language, you can code or modify code for your results. In a recent TED Talk, Martin J. Eppler (Want to Give a Great Presentation? Use Ugly Sketches) highlights a significant drawback of most PowerPoint presentations: we often rely on bullet points and text to address key topics. He provides a key example where salespeople were presented three visuals of the same material regarding goal setting, including: 1) bullet points, 2) a diagram, and 3) a mountain trail visual metaphor. The group that witnessed the metaphor had a connection to the trail and the emotion of climbing a mountain, and were significantly more motivated than those who read the bullet points. Using a few simple prompts and arbitrary sales forecast numbers over 10 years, three outputs are presented: the raw line graph, a stacked elevation graph, and the mountain trail visual.

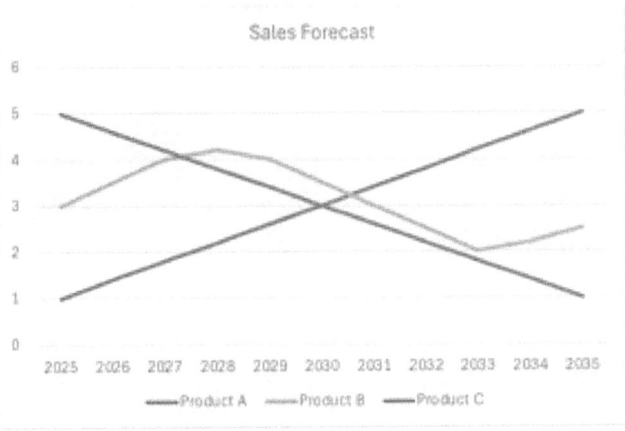

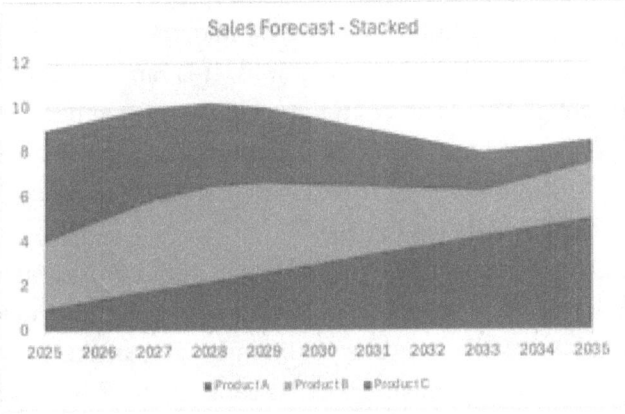

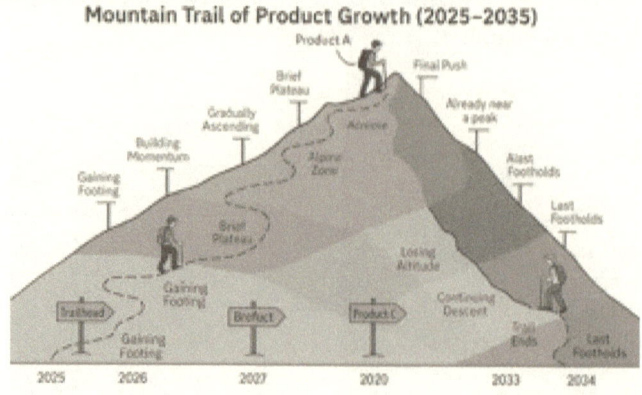

Figure 7.4 Sales Forecast Using Visual Metaphor.

This last graph introduces fun descriptions for yearly milestones such as Gaining Footing, Building Momentum, and the Alpine Zone. As an audience member looks at the three graphs, it is far more compelling to tell a story through the mountain trail and bring the company forecast to life. The first two visuals were Excel outputs, and the final was from ChatGPT with the prompt: "Please draw a stylized mountain image," followed by the raw data in the table.

Some coding prompts help with simple quantitative questions, especially when using smaller LLMs. An example is asking the model, "How many Rs are in the word strawberry?" Interestingly, the results may vary. A solution is to add the sentence "execute code" to the end of the prompt, such as: Write code to count the number of Rs in a given word, starting with the word "strawberry." Execute that code."

Voicemode

Like most search engines and mobile apps, your chatbot likely has a voice interface that lets you speak your prompt. This is ideal for times when you're working from memory and need a few minor fixes, such as a chicken noodle soup recipe. You can ask, "Hey, have carrots, celery, chicken, nd broth, nd need to know what is included in a homemade chicken soup recipe?" The model will return your voice request with their own speaker and provide you with recipes and details of any missing ingredients. You can then keep the dialogue going and ask, "I also have some onions, would these go well with the soup?" A good reply will provide you with both feedback, such as a simple "yes," and likely details on when to cut the onions and when to mix them into the soup. Then you can bring it to a boil (ha) by asking it to provide complete instructions for chicken soup in a crockpot and to list the recipe details.

Interactive

If you are more of the dynamic, interactive type, you may be using your AI to assist you in personal training. Again, you know your body and your goals and need some help with the prompt. Here is an example: "You are my personal fitness coach. I want to gain 10 lbs of muscle. I am a 32-year-old male and am already fairly lean. Ask me questions and act as my coach as you generate a plan for me. The plan can be inclusive of diet and exercise." The model will ask you some baseline questions about your training history, current strength levels, and timeline, and then lay out a plan. When complete, you can export as a .pdf and be ready to go!

Legalese

AI prompting introduces several notable legal risks and compliance challenges that anyone using or deploying these technologies should understand. The core areas of concern relate to copyright ownership, liability for AI-generated content, data privacy, and record retention requirements. Best practices recommend collaboration with legal counsel to review AI use policies, vet substantial outputs, understand the functionality and data retention policies of AI tools, and develop record retention strategies that include prompts and outputs. Where appropriate, deploy technical and legal safeguards to screen for potential copyright violations and to comply with privacy and intellectual property laws before publishing or commercializing AI-generated materials.

Forgot What to Ask

If you are starting your prompt and can't recall a word or phrase, you can always ask your AI to help. For example, a helpful prompt for this is: "I am blanking on a word. It is used to describe someone important, but I think it's also the name of a bird. What am I thinking of? The reply will include "eminence," "cardinal," "majesty," and "titular," narrowing the bird down to "cardinal." The AI may determine this for you and ask if it is correct.

Try an Analogy

You may be working on a creative way to learn science or technology that makes it fun. You ask your model, "Please explain electricity and circuits to me with an analogy to kayaking." The model replies with comparisons of rivers to circuits, slopes to voltages, and rocks to resistance, and then digs deeper, asking: "Why is the steepness making the river more powerful? Please explain like I am 5." Their replies will provide easy examples of steep hills, such as high voltages, and gentle hills, like low voltages. The steeper the mountain, the more powerful the river feels.

Making a List

You've decided to start a new business and need a list of names for the establishment. You enter your prompt: "Please come up with 30 fictitious business names that are about 4 to 10 letters long, easily pronounceable, and have an available .com domain. In an instant, 30 names will appear. After a quick review, you can decide whether to refine the query, expand the requirements, or reformat it as a "list" and create a subset of actions. AI queries are much more than search functions, and the more accurate the request, typically, the more productive the result.

Multi-Contrained

As you become more familiar with the power of your AI model, try a multi-constrained approach. This would typically not be easy in a standard search engine, but with generative AI, it is simple. Imagine the following prompt: "Compare a new Tesla Model 3 and Toyota Rav4 PHEV in a song written in the style of Bob Dylan and add a relevant quote from Barack Obama and Larry Bird." What would you expect from the chorus, perhaps this;

Now the Tesla, she's fast like a hawk on a wire
Zero to sixty in a blink and a fire
Autopilot is watching' like an angel on call
But don't count on it savin' you from wreckin' at all.
So pick up your ride, let the rubber decide
Whether it's data or dirt where your loyalties lie
Me? I'll sit with my boots on the dash
Watchin' the world change in a lithium flash

Master Prompt Method

Hayden Miyamoto introduces the Master Prompt Method—a powerful way to train your AI with comprehensive context about you and your business. He uses the Claude model to leverage personal preferences to give the model a set of information about who Hayden is with respect to his personal and work background, business metrics (products, services, markets, competitors, employees, organization, finance), culture (vision, mission), and goals (KPIs). The form is nearly 30 pages and serves as the "memory" for Claude's thinking. He walks through a simple example of hiring a marketing director using a standard prompt, such as:

"I want to hire a marketing director for company X." Claude replies with a long set of questions due to a lack of information about the query. Hayden then resends the same prompt with the Master Prompt engaged, and it replies with an organized set of questions about the marketing director's responsibilities, based on the 30-page preferences, and then answers its own questions with a fully detailed job description. Ultimately, the prompt asks, "Is this accurate?" After replying "yes," the AI continues with a comprehensive job description, which would save HR over a week in gathering data, conducting internal meetings, and preparing all the nuanced details of a new marketing role. And to take it a step further, the model provides information to pre-screen candidates, asking them for a cover letter and other details that can be collected and analyzed to create a comprehensive summary for leadership before the interview begins. This is similar to the tools used by HR hiring company Topgrading; the AI responses can provide a complete solution in minutes. We all need to consider our own Master Prompt method for our best AI needs.

7.8 ROBOTS & AUTOMATION

As another day begins, you make your way to the kitchen, and the Keurig is already heated with the dark French roast pod inserted. All you have to do is lower the lever and brew your first cup of coffee. You stir in some soy milk and head to the table, where the Wall Street Journal is already neatly unfolded. The TV is on silent with CNBC flashing the latest stock updates. You gesture to your AI assistant, and it responds with a summary of tasks already completed: the bed is made and changed, dirty clothes and towels are in the wash, the house has been lightly dusted, the cat barf cleaned up, the litter trays emptied, and your EV topped off with a full day's charge.

With a single command, you ask for poached eggs with Hollandaise sauce, sautéed spinach, and garlic potatoes. This morning, you want your eggs to be soft and runny, with a dash of freshly ground pepper. Before you even get to the second section of the paper, your breakfast is served next to you—hot, perfect, and just the way you like it.

Later in the day, your agent reminds you that the backyard hedges were trimmed and the flower beds weeded. It also took care of watering the vegetable patch and replanting a few wilting herbs in the raised garden beds. The robotic mower had already cut the lawn at sunrise, and a drone did a quick sweep to scare off any squirrels messing with your tomatoes.

There was also a blinking light on the washing machine this morning —something about the drum being off-balance. Without lifting a finger, your agent diagnosed the issue, ordered a replacement belt, and sent the home repair bot to fix it. The dishwasher also had a leaky gasket, which was replaced before lunch. The agent even managed to recalibrate the thermostat, which had been acting weird after the last power outage.

Reduced Workforce

The significant value of robotics to companies is a healthy return on investment (ROI) for its shareholders. A press release will address the efficiency of an automated production line and offer a path to workforce reduction. That means higher profits to the bottom line. Regarding Amazon, its worldwide workforce is approximately 1.55 million people, and CEO Andy Jassy has recently indicated that continued AI-driven automation may lead to reduced corporate headcount. Over 75% or 1.25 million workers are involved in operations and logistics (warehouses, delivery, and fulfillment centers). This breaks down into about 400,000 drivers and 800,000 warehouse/fulfillment workers.

Additionally, Amazon's robot workforce has expanded from 200,000 to over 750,000 robots operating alongside humans. So they've tripled the number of robots—where is the reduction in the workforce? It's coming in the form of warehouse automation.

In today's Amazon, factory technicians are currently being retrained as robot operators, systems technicians, and automation quality managers. The new tech jobs are for robot maintenance, engineering, and logistics, with smaller fulfillment locations, and a potential for a fully autonomous workforce. With routine or repetitive jobs at risk, Amazon's management team is providing as much advance notice as possible to help retrain or shift workers into software development or AI-related roles. Middle managers are also at risk as fewer and fewer demands are placed on supervision.

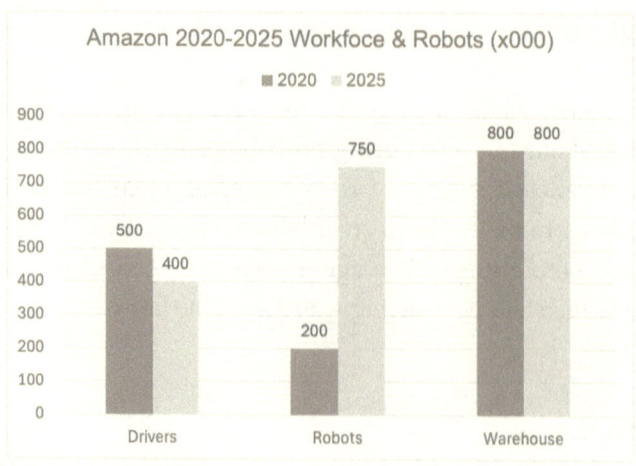

Figure 7.5 Amazon Workforce & Robots

Other companies implementing workforce reductions due to collaborative robots include automotive manufacturing (BMW, GM, Tesla), electronics manufacturing (Foxconn, Jabil), warehousing (Amazon, Walmart), agriculture (Caterpillar, John Deere), healthcare (Intuitive Surgical), transportation (Lyft, Uber), and construction (Built, ICON). In mid-2025, Leslie Stahl from 60 Minutes interviewed the founders of the 3D printing company ICON and their journey to creating 3D-printed homes. The company is currently building residential homes using 3D printing technology to replace the structure from the roofline down to the ground. The fully automated system prints a home in approximately 72 hours, with full completion expected within about 3 weeks. Today, these homes are somewhat of a novelty; however, with improvements in design ease and other cost savings, the ICON house may reduce building costs by 40-50%.

Before the AI craze, early software-as-a-service companies such as UiPath developed robotic process automation (RPA) technologies that enabled organizations to automate repetitive business processes using software robots. The "bots" are designed to emulate human actions — such as clicking, typing, reading, and processing — across various applications, including web, desktop, and legacy systems. Users and developers build automation workflows using a simple drag-and-drop interface that requires little or no programming. The tools use recording functions that capture user actions and convert them into automation tasks. Everyday use cases include data entry (ERP, CRM), billing and payment processing, customer support, HR, and supply chain management. Order tracking, inventory updates, and vendor communications are especially relevant for electronics manufacturing and B2B environments.

Large Robotic Companies

"Will builders lose their jobs when they support robot-assisted construction?"

The list of large company robotics includes ABB, Boston Dynamics, Denso, FANUC, Google, iRobot, KUKA, Mitsubishi, Softbank, Universal, and Yaskawa, with a primary focus on developing collaborative robots, also known as "cobots." These machines operate alongside humans in a shared space. Boston Dynamics has created some of the most exciting robots, including Spot (a dog-like robot), Atlas (a humanoid robot), and Stretch (a warehouse robot). These robots have some of the more advanced AI algorithms to manage visual recognition, environmental awareness, and autonomous movement. Atlas can perform complex acrobatic tasks, while Spot is used for real-time data collection, remote inspections, and security. Uber is on its third generation of autonomous food delivery robots, which incorporate LiDAR, cameras, and ultrasonic sensors to detect obstacles up to 200 feet away, recognize traffic lights, and navigate crowded sidewalks at 5-10 mph. Early versions could hold up to 50 lbs of food and operated in all weather, including rain, snow, and extreme heat. Their batteries last all day with a range of over 30 miles. Next time you order your Uber Eats, look for the robot delivery option at checkout. Google is the primary force behind Waymo, and its self-driving cars are now operating in five metro areas. And finally, Tesla has its humanoid robot, Optimus, and its autopilot software for its EVs, called "FSD" (for free self-driving). Tesla has also begun autonomous ride-sharing in Texas.

7.9 HYPERSCALERS

Hyperscalers are the World's largest cloud and internet infrastructure companies. They operate massive data centers and provide cloud computing, storage, networking, and AI capabilities on a global scale for consumers, businesses, and governments. In 2025, the Hyperscaler cloud market was valued at over $250 billion and is projected to reach over $750 billion by 2035 (an 11.6% CAGR). During the same period, the Hyperscaler data center market will grow from $167 billion to $602 billion (a 13.7% CAGR). The estimated cost of the most advanced AI gigacampus can range from $1 billion to $2 billion, with massive energy requirements and high staffing, cooling, and maintenance costs. Commercial construction can take from 18 to 36 months with ongoing upgrade cycles for new semiconductor devices, liquid cooling, and complex network configurations.

Data Center 1.0 was developed for US federal agencies that required a secure, off-grid, East Coast location to support defense, intelligence, and civilian departments. The data centers in West Virginia, also known as Data Center Alley or Datacenter 1.0, were commissioned in 2024 by Governor Patrick Morrisey, who signed the Power Generation and Consumption Act into law in April 2025. The configuration was part of a sweeping legislative package establishing deregulated, high-capacity, microgrid-powered tech companies. Most of the infrastructure was comprised of "CPUs" to support social media, streaming, and the cloud.

China

The largest Hyperscaler data centers are located in China. They include companies such as China Telecom (10.7 million sq ft), China

Mobile (7.75 million sq ft), Range (6.3 million sq ft), Harbin (7.1 million sq ft), and Switch (two facilities: 7.75 million sq ft + 3.5 million sq ft in Nevada). The Chinese facilities are government-backed and serve the digital infrastructure needs of both the public and private sectors. China Telecom's massive facility in Mongolia Information Park has a footprint larger than 10 million sq ft (approximately 1 million sq meters) and operates with a power capacity of 150 MW. The major US players, including Switch, Amazon, Apple, Google, Meta, and OpenAI, are quickly catching up with huge investments.

Amazon

Amazon's CEO, Andy Jassy, has committed $100B to build new data centers across the US. They are building two mega-campus facilities in Pennsylvania for $20 billion. Another campus, Project Rainer in Indiana, includes seven massive data centers designed for Anthropic and AI workloads, with a power draw of 2.2 GW and extensive water and fiber networks. Additional plans for up to 30 data centers in Indiana alone. Other expansions include sites in Mississippi, North Carolina, and other US states near existing power sources.

Google

Google's CEO, Sundar Pichai, has committed $75 billion in AI spending to expand its infrastructure. The first $25 billion buildout includes investing across the PJM Interconnection grid in Pennsylvania and neighboring states, including Virginia, Ohio, and New Jersey. A 3 GW hydroelectric power plant in PA will power the site. At their annual I/O developers conference, they announced Google Search in "AI Mode" as a response to ChatGPT, Android XR glasses, VEO video tools, and Google Meet with translation.

Meta

Meta has also placed big bets on expanding its data center footprint, committing over $65 billion to new buildouts. Their Prometheus Mega-center is located in Ohio and spans nearly the size of Manhattan, with a 5 GW power consumption. Their second primary site, "Hyperion," is in Louisiana and is anticipated to be similar in size to Prometheus. Meta's new Superintelligence Labs are driving the demand for new server clusters that support generative AI models and handle massive social network loads.

Microsoft

Microsoft has committed to spending $85 billion, with over half of the allocation dedicated to US facilities, focusing on AI model training and cloud (Azure) deployment. They are restarting Three Mile Island nuclear reactors to supply 835MW to data centers in Pennsylvania. Some reports include a shift away or slowdowns in projects in Illinois, North Dakota, and Wisconsin.

OpenAI

OpenAI announced its partnership during a White House presentation with President Trump. The trio included partnerships with Oracle, SoftBank, and OpenAI to build new facilities in Texas (also known as Stargate), Michigan, Wisconsin, and Wyoming. They plan to support up to 10 GW of nationwide power consumption to power millions of AI chips. Their primary focus is on AI workloads to support the ChatGPT roadmap. Oracle will provide the server HW to OpenAI, with Crusoe Energy Systems as the prime contractor for the mega campus in Abilene, Texas.

Switch

Switch is a Las Vegas-based independent Hyperscaler, renowned for ultra-high-density, sustainable, and innovative "exascale" facilities purpose-built for AI, cloud, and enterprise computing. In 2025, Switch launched modular, ultra-dense data halls for GPU clusters, capable of delivering up to 2MW per rack, utilizing a hybrid air and liquid cooling system. These cutting-edge deployments, such as NVIDIA GB300 NVL72 with CoreWeave. They have mega campuses in Las Vegas (>2 million sq ft), Reno (7.2 million sq ft), Grand Rapids (1.8 million sq ft), Atlanta, and Austin. Their five active hyperscale campuses run on 100% renewable power.

xAI

xAI, owned by Elon Musk, has an estimated $50 billion in expenditures for new Hyperscale facilities. They are a private company backed by Morgan Stanley to support new buildouts in Memphis, TN. They currently have sites with NVIDIA Hopper GPUs and are migrating to over 1 million Blackwell GPUs. xAI's strategy is unique in that it's focused on building and directly owning physical data centers and compute infrastructure for large-scale AI model development, rather than solely leasing cloud capacity. This sets a new benchmark for Hyperscaler spend in the AI race.

Company	CEO	AI Spend
Amazon/AWS	Andy Jassy	$100B
Google/Cloud	Sunar Pichai	$75B
Meta	Mark Zuckerberg	$65B
Microsoft Azure	Satya Nadell	$85B
OpenAI	Sam Altman	$100B
Oracle Cloud Infr	Clay Magouyrk Mike Sicilia	$100B*
Softbank	Masayoshi Son	$100B*
Switch	Rob Roy	$10B
xAI	Elon Musk	$50B

Figure 7.6 AI Infrastructure Spend

• Project Stargate is comprised of OpenAI, Oracle, and Softbank and is expected to cost between $100B and $500B over time.

In a July 2025 Wall Street Journal article, Joanna Stern discussed the energy requirements of AI infrastructure. She outlines the task of requesting "a video of a cat diving off an Olympic diving board," and what happens in the data center to manage the response. In her case, the infrastructure was owned by Equinix, which included Superpods equipped with NVIDIA H100 GPUs. The energy required to generate content varies widely depending on the model, GPU setup, and the task. Her report covers demands from text, image, and video searches, along with their associated energy consumption. She then purchases an electric grill, a portable power meter, and a juicy steak. After cooking for 10 minutes and 220 watts-hours, it was time to eat. The energy required to cook was approximately equivalent to generating two AI-generated high-end videos. She summarizes by pointing out that her recent AI short film, which includes thousands of short 8-second 720p clips, required roughly 110,000 watt-hours, or nearly 500 steaks.

7.10 STARGATE

Early planning for the massive Hyperscaler campus started in 2022. In 2024, Project Stargate was formally announced at the White House, featuring President Trump, OpenAI's Sam Altman, Oracle's Larry Ellison, and SoftBank's Masayoshi Son. The initial $500 billion in funding was committed to building new AI infrastructure to meet demand.

The first groundbreaking was in Abilene, TX, for a project called Project Ludicrous. It includes massive buildings spanning up to 4 million sq ft across 875 acres, powered by an initial 1.2 GW of staging capacity to support over 400,000 GPUs for compute clusters. The contractor is Crusoe Energy, with technology partners including ARM, Microsoft, NVIDIA, and Oracle. 50,000 NVIDIA Blackwell GPUs will be integrated into an Oracle chassis, featuring closed-loop liquid cooling to manage the enormous heat generated—a typical rack consumes over 130 kW of power. The estimated total required power is up to 15 GW, making it the most significant data center demand in the World. Note: A typical ChatGPT query requires approximately 10 times the effort of a Google search.

Emily Chang from Bloomberg TV presented a special report on Project Stargate, featuring on-site interviews with Crusoe, OpenAI, and SoftBank. The report, titled "Inside OpenAI's Stargate Megafactory with Sam Altman," aired on May 20, 2025, and provided in-depth, authoritative media coverage. One interesting interview was with Mayor Weldon Hurt, who mentioned new job growth of between 400 and 1,200 jobs, as well as a special tax incentive to attract businesses to Abilene. Hurt mentioned, "Abilene is an old railroad town with lots of Western heritage, but that doesn't mean that we don't want to grow and look forward to the future. We want our city to grow, and we look forward to the opportunities that are coming our way. It could quite possibly be the largest AI data center in the World, and that excites me, to know that we're gonna be a front runner in technology right here in West Texas." Emily inquired about the tax incentive, which equated to an over 85% reduction, to entice them to Abilene and receive billions of dollars in tax revenue.

Stargate's key milestones for Phase 1 will include completing the first two buildings, totaling 980,000 sq ft, by mid-2025 and expanding to eight buildings by mid-2026. Energy demand, carbon footprint, and water usage will stress local and national grids; however, the project is planning to provide all external resources required. The city of Abilene has agreed to expedite permit processing, grant access to the Texas ERCOT energy grid, and offer development partners incentives to reduce operational and construction costs. Stargate has international expansion plans, including Stargate UAE and Stargate Norway.

7.11 AI DEVICES

The AI revolution is so massive that it's calling for an entirely new kind of experience. Some of the most innovative technologists and creative minds are secretly working on groundbreaking new devices. These aren't just updates to your phone or smartwatch—they're aiming for something totally fresh. People are already saying this B2C (business-to-consumer) market could be as big, or even bigger, than the rise of the smartphone. We're talking about products that could break records for how quickly they spread and how many people use them.

Even though we don't know exactly what these devices will look like, one thing is clear—they won't be like anything we've seen before. These aren't just upgraded versions of glasses, watches, or fitness trackers. The people behind them are trying to invent something completely original, something that changes how we interact with the digital World in our everyday lives.

Some insiders believe these devices might blend AI with your environment in a way that feels natural, almost invisible. Imagine a tool that could understand your needs in real-time—without you needing to ask. It might help you plan your day, stay safe, learn new things, or even boost your creativity, all through a totally new kind of interaction.

The excitement is growing, and so are the expectations. As these top-secret projects move forward, one thing is for sure: when these AI-powered devices finally hit the market, they could completely change how we live, learn, and connect with the World around us.

Raymond Loewy and MAYA

Raymond Loewy (1893-1986) was a pioneering French-born American industrial designer famous for shaping the look of modern consumer products, vehicles, logos, and architecture throughout the 20th century. He designed iconic items and corporate identities, including the Coca-Cola bottle, the Greyhound Scenicruiser bus, Lucky Stripe packaging, the Studebaker Avanti car, the exterior of Air Force One, the interior of NASA Skylab, and logos for Exxon and Shell.

Loewy's signature design philosophy was called MAYA, which stood for "Most Advanced, Yet Acceptable." He believed that successful products should be as innovative as possible while still being easily embraced by the public. This principle guided Loewy's approach to creating designs that were futuristic and progressive, yet familiar enough for mainstream acceptance.

LoveForm and OpenAI

In 2019, Jony Ive left Apple to form a creative collective, LoveForm, an independent design company with key brand opportunities, including collaborations with Airbnb and Ferrari and clothing designs for Prince Charles. As a British-American designer, Jony is best known for key designs at Apple, including the iPhone, iMac, iPod, Apple Watch, and AirPods.

In September of 2024, LoveForm began working with OpenAI on the development of artificial intelligence hardware devices that are "less socially disruptive than the iPhone." And finally, in May of 2025, Sam Altman (OpenAI CEO) purchased the AI division of LoveForm, known as "io", for $6.5 billion to build new AI devices.

• • •

Orb

World, a startup in San Francisco, CA, has developed a new open-source AI device called Orb that captures and processes photos to verify uniqueness without retaining your images or collecting other information about you. The device uses a companion application called "World" for authentication and verification. The Orb device scans a person's retina to verify their humanness and is developed by the Tools for Humanity (TFH), a company co-founded by Sam Altman. The Orb "is a privacy-first way to prove you are a human in the world of AI and bots."

So how does it work? As you look into the chrome ball, the Orb uses various sensors (an infrared camera and a thermometer) and a neural network to determine if you are human. During your first scan, the device captures a high-resolution image of your iris, which is then processed by an algorithm into a 12,800-digit binary number known as the Iris code. The Orb filters encrypted data using a secure method that prevents the underlying data from being revealed to check whether it has ever seen your iris code before. Orb anonymizes your iris code by converting it into multiple distinct encrypted codes and sends each to a separate secure server. Finally, once you have "verified" your humanity, a packet of Worldcoin lands in your World App wallet with a value of about $42. You now have a World ID and some Worldcoin.

Alex Blania, CEO of Tools for Humanity, has overseen the deployment of more than 1,600 Orbs globally, with the company on track to install 7,500 by early 2026. He recalls a pivotal conversation with Sam Altman—one that helped shape the company's mission and direction.

Altman told him there were three things he was sure about. First, the development of AI systems smarter than humans wasn't just possible—it was inevitable. When that moment arrived, he said, it would fundamentally change how we trust information: you could no longer assume that anything you read, saw, or heard online had been created by a human.

Second, he believed that cryptocurrency and decentralized technologies would be among the most powerful forces reshaping the World—challenging traditional structures and enabling new forms of economic coordination and identity.

And third, Altman emphasized that scale wasn't just crucial to a crypto network's value—it was everything. Without global reach, the vision would never fully materialize.

Worldcoin, the original project for World, remains a question for the startup. Since 2019, the project has raised $244 million from venture capital firms, with $50 million allocated to fund the Orb device and its software. The total market value of Worldcoins in existence, however, is over $ 1.2 billion. This number is somewhat misleading, as the majority (~75%) of the coins are not in circulation and are reserved for membership or referral purposes. The remaining 25% is split between Tools for Humanity backers and staff, including Blania and Altman.

Humane AI

Humane Inc. is a startup with funding from notable investors, including Marc Benioff, Sam Altman, Tiger Global, Softbank, Qualcomm, Microsoft, LG, Volvo, and Salesforce. Microsoft and OpenAI have announced partnerships with Humane to support their go-to-market strategies. In 2018, founders Imran Chaudhri and Bethany Bongiorno left Apple and raised over $230 million to develop their novel AI device. The design is a wearable pin called the "AI Pin", which consists of two separate parts: a front processing unit and a rear battery. These parts are meant to be attached magnetically, sandwiched between a user's clothing. The voice-activated device features a laser ink projector that creates a holographic image of a touchpad, serving as the user interface.

In May 2023, Choudhri revealed the device during a TED Talk, and in November 2023, formally announced it with a $699 price tag and a $24 monthly subscription. Devices were first shipped in April 2024, but they experienced poor market acceptance. The AI Pin had received generally negative reviews, praising its exterior design but criticizing its limited battery life and poor thermal control, and questioning the usefulness of many of its features. The New York Times reported that, due to overheating, Humane executives would use ice packs to cool the AI Pin before presenting it to its investors. After 6 months, the company had sold fewer than 10,000 units, and more pins were returned than purchased. The company lowered the price to $499, and in late 2024, the US

Consumer Product Safety Commission recalled the device due to a potential fire hazard posed by the lithium-polymer battery.

By February 2025, Humane announced it had stopped shipping the AI Pin and offered refunds to all existing users. HP acquired the company for $116 million and folded it into its HP IQ team.

Amazon and Bee

In July 2025, Amazon acquired the company Bee, which makes a "listening assistant." The device is a bracelet that uses artificial intelligence to continuously listen, transcribe, and analyze everything the wearer says and hears, providing both productivity benefits and personal insights. The wristband resembles a slim smartwatch (like a Fitbit) and is comfortable to wear. With its "always on" listening mode, it actively records conversations and then processes them into searchable text timelines and summaries, enabling the device to recall events, commitments, or personal reflections throughout the day. It analyzes conversations, routines, and environmental data to suggest to-do lists, reminders, and habit tracking. It even summarizes your day, including who you spoke with, what was discussed, and action items generated during the conversation. Imagine no more note-taking during a meeting.

To enhance privacy, raw audio is not sent to the cloud. The bracelet transcribes and processes speech locally, discarding recordings immediately after conversion. Only generated insights and relevant data are stored, not the original audio. Bee claims not to store raw recordings or use them for external AI training. The wearer can delete their data at any time. You can also set boundaries to pause recordings or processing automatically. Users can manually mute the bracelet or predefine contexts (such as locations or specific topics) where the device should not listen or analyze. The subscription is $19/month, with hardware costing $49, and will likely become part of the complete Alexa product line.

Rabbit

Santa Monica-based startup Rabbit Inc. has developed a handheld device that provides an AI assistant on the go. The device is the size of a cell phone, but with one primary purpose: to give an immediate speak & ask" response for unlimited questions and answers. The bright orange device features a single button, a camera, and a small screen display. Other helpful tasks include identifying objects by pointing the camera and querying about anything in the camera view. Using information from the cloud, the device will support bidirectional translation, visual interpretation, memory recall, generative UI, gaming, alarms, and voice recording.

For interaction, the device has a button, voice, eye, and scroll wheel interface. The Rabbit R1 device sells for $199 each and includes a free subscription program. After its initial launch, reviews have been mixed, with concerns about a lack of features, poor integration with third-party services, slow or inaccurate responses to queries, poor battery life, and whether it differentiates itself from a smartphone. Users complained about receiving incorrect results from the AI assistant, about the AI assistant inadvertently playing songs, and about software glitches in which the device continued to play songs despite the user's attempts to pause or lower the volume. Other criticisms highlight a reliance on its Android-based app, suggesting it might be better suited as a software-only app for your phone.

Stream Ring

A new startup, Sandbar, is testing the market with a new form factor and has created a smart ring called "Stream." The founder, Mina Fahmi, calls the ring a "mouse for voice" because it has many features that enable it to handle voice interactions. There is a touchpad on the side, a mic on top, and a little haptic tactile sensor. The user holds the touchpad and then speaks into the ring a stream of consciousness. The device is meant to work alongside the phone, with an app that stores the recorded information for later review and editing.

7.12 SCIENTIFIC DISCOVERY

Artificial intelligence is revolutionizing the entire landscape of scientific research, from data analysis and hypothesis generation to experiment design and the discovery of new phenomena. Below are some key examples, specific research cases, expert quotes, and a roadmap for future AI-driven breakthroughs.

In the field of protein structure prediction, Google's DeepMind AlphaFold cracked a 50-year challenge, accurately predicting structures of over 200 million proteins. This discovery is essential for drug development, vaccine testing, and understanding biological mechanisms. DeepMind can predict protein shapes in minutes, accelerating progress from medical applications to solutions for plastic pollution.

Google and Harvard's connectomics project mapped a human brain segment at unprecedented detail using advanced AI annotation, helping reveal new cellular structures for brain and neuroscience research.

With respect to drug and molecule discovery, CEO of Insilicon Medicine, Alex Zhavoronkov, says, "You can now use AI imagination to create molecules with desired properties that do not exist in the known chemical space. This enables substantial cost and time savings, making drugs more accessible. BioEmu-1 and MatterGen tools facilitate the rapid screening and design of new molecular compounds for therapeutics, materials, and environmental technologies.

For climate modeling and forecasting, Microsoft's Aurora Model utilizes AI trained on Earth science data to simulate atmospheric, land, and ocean interactions, enabling communities to better prepare for cyclones, wildfires, and shifts in air quality. There is now AI for identifying tornadoes and storm precursors, with researchers generating synthetic storms and uncovering new warning signs of violent weather, paving the way for improved disaster response.

AI is also influencing material science. Generative models predict properties to optimize combinations for batteries, catalysts, semiconductors, and green cement, significantly faster than manual trial-and-error methods. Discovery of eco-friendly cement using AI-mixed seaweed, biomass, and faster prototype development for data center coolants using the Microsoft Discovery platform.

A groundbreaking scientific discovery in ecology takes us to Tanzania, where AI processes drone footage to identify and protect endangered giraffes by their unique spot patterns. In urban areas, intelligent garden apps combine sensor data with AI to analyze tree health for sustainability.

Autonomous labs and science factories include companies like Lila Sciences, which builds robotic labs powered by AI that can generate and test thousands of hypotheses and experiments with minimal human input, scaling research exponentially. And a quote from their CEO, Geoffrey von Maltzahn, "With AI-driven experimentation, we can scale that process exponentially. Instead of testing one hypothesis at a time, Lila's autonomous labs can generate and run thousands of experiments, optimizing results in real time.

Professor Yoshua Bengio (University of Montreal) describes scientific AI as a model that aims to understand the World more holistically. This model might encompass, for instance, the laws of physics or our understanding of human psychology. It can generate a set of plausible hypotheses that may explain the observed data and justify predictions or decisions. Its outputs would not be programmed to imitate or please humans, but rather reflect an interpretable causal understanding of the situation at hand. Scientific AI could help us design a safe human-level intelligence and a safe artificial superintelligence (ASI). This may be the best way to guarantee that a rogue ASI is never unleashed in the outside World. Think of Scientist AI as headlights and guardrails on the winding road ahead. [Time Mag vol 205[4], pg 18)

Future discoveries will be strongly impacted by agentic AI platforms from Microsoft Discovery and Google's AI co-scientist. These platforms can now reason, plan, and automate scientific workflows, acting as research teammates that generate hypotheses, run simulations, and refine experiments. AI will help compress what once took years into days for drug discovery, materials screening, and image mapping. National initiatives, such as the NSF's NAIRR project, aim to expand access to AI tools for academia, thereby ensuring broader participation in the next wave of scientific advancements. Artificial intelligence also acts as a scientific generalist, spanning multiple fields, unifying disparate data sources, and supporting cross-domain breakthroughs. Lastly, AI is supporting social and environmental science with real-time climate analysis, rapid disease detection, and modeling of urban and ecosystem change.

7.13 LAWSUITS

One of the key challenges with artificial intelligence is the powerful nature of the results that it can generate, including audio, text, and video outputs. Lawsuits related to AI have increased significantly since 2023, encompassing a broad range of legal domains. The majority of high-profile cases focus on copyright, but there are at least five other significant areas where plaintiffs are active.

Copyright and Intellectual Property: Plaintiffs (authors, artists, publishers, record labels, and news outlets) allege that major AI companies (OpenAI, Microsoft, Meta, Anthropic, Midjourney, Stability AI, and Google) have used copyrighted books, music, art, and journalism without authorization to train their models. There are mixed early court decisions that have found transformative use to be fair in some cases (Anthropic), but copyright liability remains possible for unauthorized/pirated materials. Many cases are ongoing, with billion-dollar settlements and jury trials slated for late 2025.

Privacy and Data Protection: Plaintiffs argue that AI applications (such as Google's search/voice services, Clearview AI, and facial recognition platforms) have violated privacy laws by collecting personal, biometric, geolocation, and voice data without permission. Several large settlements were reached (Texas v. Google, Clearview AI), and new cases were announced regarding biometric surveillance and consumer data.

Defamation and False Information: Individual plaintiffs challenge AI firms for producing and publicizing false or defamatory information (e.g., legal advice bots, ChatGPT-generated news, deepfake apps). Courts have generally dismissed these suits, ruling that current AI outputs do not constitute actionable defamation under existing law.

Bias, Discrimination, and Civil Rights: Plaintiffs assert AI algorithms (used in hiring, lending, facial recognition, and policing) produce biased or discriminatory outcomes that violate laws such as the Civil Rights Act, the Fair Housing Act, or equal protection statutes.

Antitrust and Competition: Governments and competitors have challenged AI leaders (OpenAI, Microsoft, Google, Meta) for exclusionary practices, market concentration, or anti-competitive licensing—major investigations are active in the US, EU, and UK, with preliminary lawsuits filed and outcomes pending.

Contract and Licensing Disputes: Plaintiffs include software developers and open source authors claiming AI companies violated license terms in using code/data for model training. Courts have allowed some claims under state "right of publicity" laws, especially in New York and California.

Consumer Protection and Commercial Torts: False Advertising, Product Liability, and User Harm Cases Against Chatbots, AI Recommendation Engines, and Automated Medical Applications. Early-stage litigation and regulatory compliance actions are gaining traction.

Below are highlights of current lawsuits that are either in litigation or settlement.

Plaintiff	Defendant	Allegations	Judgement
Disney & Universal Studios	Midjourney Inc	Studios allege Midjourney's AI image generator unlawfullly trained on, copied, and sold images of iconic characters	Remedy sought: statutory damages, injunctive relief, jury trial. Litigation ongoing as of Sept 2025
Center for Investigative Reporting (CIR)	OpenAI & Microsoft	CIR claims chatGPT and CoPilot use uncompensated, unauthorized content from its publications, violating copyright and the Digital Millenniu Copyright Act, CIR agrues 60% of chat CPT responses contain plagarized content	
Bird, et al	Microsoft	Authors accuse Microsoft of training on AI on 200,000 pirated digital books using their work for commercial derivative output withou compensation	As of Sept 2025, ongoing litigation
New York Times	OpenAI & Microsoft	Newspaper claims defendant is training AI on millions of copyrighted news articles without permission	Lawsuit is expanding to include Universal Music, Warner, Sony, Atlantic Records, Dow Jones, other class
Texas Attorney General	Google	Texas alleged Google unlawfully tracked and collected users private data, including geolocation, incognito searches, and biometric data	Google agreed to pay $1.375 billion in May 2025
Bartz, et al	Anthropic	Plaintiffs allege Anthropic used millions of copyright books and writings to train large language models without authorization	Seeking statutory damages of up to $150,000 per work with potential damages over $100 billion. Jury trial was scheduled for Dec 2025, however, Anthropic

Figure 7.7 Recent AI Lawsuits

Andrea Bartz, Charles Graeber, Kirk Wallace Johnson, and a class of up to 7 million copyright holders have filed a class action lawsuit against Anthropic, headed for a jury trial. The plaintiffs allege that Anthropic used millions of copyrighted books and writings to train its LLMs without authorization, with potential damages exceeding $100 billion. The co-lead counsel for the plaintiff is Lieff Cabraser Heimann & Bernstein LLP and Susman Godfrey LLP. They have also secured top-level legal support for copyright from Matt Oppenheim and Samuel

Isscharoff. Judge William Alsup's June 2025 split summary judgment provided critical direction on the case as follows:

• Transformative Use of AI Training: The court ruled that Anthropics' use of legitimately purchased books to train its AI model was "spectacularly transformative" and constitutes fair use under Section 107 of the Copyright Act.

• Pirated books infringement: However, Anthropics' downloading and storage of pirated books from sites like LibGen and PiLiMi for its "central library" was not protected by fair use and constitutes copyright infringement. The damages for this aspect could be substantial, likely reaching billions of dollars, mainly if the conduct is found to be willful or in bad faith.

Judge Alsup repeatedly encouraged both sides to settle, suggesting both plaintiffs and Anthropic face grave risks if the cases reach a jury trial (scheduled for Dec 2025).

The coming years are likely to see a sharp increase in lawsuits involving AI technologies. Several factors, including the widespread adoption, rapid evolution of capabilities, and the emergence of new risks across industries and society, will drive this. Deepfakes and misrepresentation will become increasingly realistic. AI safety and product liability will come into question across new vehicles, automated factories, and new medicines. As risk and exposure grow, expect more class actions, multi-billion dollar settlements, and coordinated plaintiff strategies from industry coalitions (authors, journalists, musicians, and programmers). Precedents set in 2024-2025 will shape the market, innovation, and social norms for decades to come.

CHAPTER 8
EMOTIONAL INTELLIGENCE

EMOTIONAL INTELLIGENCE, or EQ, is best understood as the ability to recognize, understand, and manage one's own emotions and those of others. Crucially, managing emotions does not mean suppressing or controlling them; instead, it involves acknowledging and understanding them. Instead, it means being attuned to the emotional undercurrents within ourselves and those around us, and responding with thoughtfulness, flexibility, and intention. High emotional intelligence is reflected in one's self-awareness, empathy, communication skills, and the ability to navigate stress and anxiety with poise and composure.

The concept of emotional intelligence first entered academic discourse in 1990, when psychologists Peter Salovey and John Mayer framed it as a subset of social intelligence—an individual's capacity to perceive, differentiate, and regulate emotional information to guide thinking and behavior. Since then, the idea has evolved into a cultural cornerstone, sparking decades of research, debate, and popular exploration. Landmark books on the topic have helped bring EQ into the mainstream, including Emotional Intelligence: Why It Can Matter More Than IQ[1] by Daniel Goleman (2001), which became a global bestseller. Other influential titles include Sales EQ[2] by Jeb Blount (2017), Emotional Intelligence Habits[3] by Travis Bradberry (2023), Managing Emotions to

Make a Positive Impact on Your Life[4] and Career by Gill Hasson (2018), and Unlocking the Power of Emotional Intelligence[5] by T.J. Bryly (2024). Each of these works contributes to a growing understanding that, in both personal and professional realms, emotional intelligence is often more vital than intellect alone.

Most of these books share common themes about EQ with slightly different approaches to explaining the effects on salespeople. Blount speaks of four pillars of emotional intelligence as 1) empathy, 2) self-awareness, 3) sales drive, and 4) self-control. -

8.1 SCIENCE OF EQ

Anytime the intelligences are evaluated, the underlying science becomes essential. We know more about the brain than we ever have before (ref. Ray Kurzweil's book, The Singularity in Nearer), with artificial intelligence roadmaps forecast to reverse-engineer the human brain by 2030. There is little risk that we will replace the brain with a computer, and yet we need to understand how the mechanisms that function today will be significantly influenced in the future. Emotional intelligence will be transformed into a key support function to artificial intelligence, with each having its place and dominance in our brains.

The science of emotions is shaped by brain activity, specifically in the amygdala. This small structure is the core of emotions, enabling you to respond quickly and instinctively without having to think. It's ideal when you need to move fast. Another part of your brain that influences emotions is the neocortex, which adds the element of conscious thought, language, and spatial reasoning.

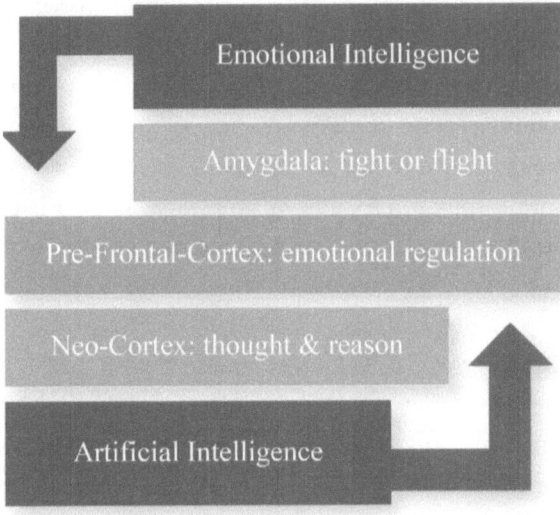

Figure 8.1. The Science of Emotional Intelligence

The science of emotional intelligence goes far beyond simply identifying the brain regions associated with emotion. True scientific principles of EQ are rooted in psychology, neuroscience, and measurement theory, focusing on how emotions are perceived, used, understood, and managed as active processes in human thought and social life.

Emotional intelligence is distinct from general intelligence; it involves the capacity to reason about emotions and to use emotions to enhance reasoning. If we expand on leading models, there are four core abilities, including using emotions to facilitate thought, understanding, perceiving, and managing emotions. Facilitating thought is harnessing emotion to prioritize thinking, problem-solving, and creativity. To perceive emotions is to accurately identify emotional signals in oneself and others, via facial expressions, tone, body language, and context.As we learn to understand our emotions, we recognize nuances, transitions, and how emotions interrelate, including causes and likely progressions. Lastly, managing emotions involves regulating personal and interpersonal emotions to achieve goals, maintain relationships, and adapt to change.

Scientific studies show that effective emotion regulation (a core EQ skill) depends on the interplay between prefrontal cortical systems and subcortical systems (such as the amygdala and the nucleus accumbens/ventral striatum). This balance enables both dampening of adverse emotional reactions and enhancement of positive ones, thereby supporting resilience and social adaptability.

Reappraising a situation to alter its emotional impact is a measurable EQ skill. It encompasses neural mechanisms that connect executive functions, such as planning and inhibition, with real-time emotional regulation.

Emotional intelligence is not a fixed state. It is shaped by experience, learning, and active practice. Neuroscience reveals that brain circuits governing emotion and regulation can be strengthened, thereby enhancing mental health. Training in emotional literacy, mindfulness, and social skills can measurably boost EQ and corresponding brain function.

The most empirically validated ability-based measure of emotional intelligence is the Mayer-Salovey-Caruso Emotional Intelligence Test (MSCEIT[6]) and its updated version, MSCEIT 2. This test is built on the four-branch ability model of EQ (perceiving, using, understanding, and managing emotions) and is widely respected in the scientific community. There are additional emotional tests, including the Situational Tests of Emotion Management (STEM[7]) and Understanding (STEU[8]). MacCann and Roberts developed these with scenario-based tests that present complex emotional situations and require test-takers to select the most effective emotional response. These have been shown to have good predictive and convergent validity, but are less widely used than MSCEIT. There is also the Six Seconds Emotional Intelligence Assessment (SEI), which is not strictly ability-based but combines self-report and 360-degree feedback for higher predictive validity in organizational settings. The Self-Reporting Inventories (SRIET) test is popular, but less objectively reliable for ability assessment due to self-perception bias. It is best considered as a supplement to ability-based tests.

As we covered earlier, performance-based assessments (such as the MSCEIT) gauge how well people interpret, use, and regulate emotions in simulated scenarios, moving beyond self-report bias. EQ operates through complex, dynamic mechanisms, including active perception, feedback integration, regulatory processes, and adaptive behavior, rather than through static brain locations alone. The science of EQ supports the idea that emotional skills can be learned and refined, improving decision-making, relationships, and stress management via measurable biological and psychological processes.

8.2 SALES DNA

It would be wonderful if 23&Me had a test for the percentage of your DNA that drives sales leadership. It would be a skills test like no other, and results might say 60% hunter, 30% gatherer, and 10% uninterested in selling a product or service. There would be a personalized message that read, "Comes from a strong heritage of sales hunters, and your overall well-being is greatly enhanced with prospecting, negotiating, and closing new business. Several key indicators suggest strong communication and relationship-building skills. Ideal life choices include strategic sales, car racing, and mountain climbing. Your energy fuel comes from social interactions, head-to-head competition, and winning."

The DNA of selling characteristics may not spell out the G-C-A-T sequence, but it is true that, at the core, a salesperson must have selling in their bloodstream. Like a strong hormone, the person with the "sales gene" has a genetic predisposition that gives them a natural edge. A groundbreaking study conducted by the MIT Sloan School of Management (Juanjuan Zhang, 2023, https://pubsonline.informs.org/doi/10.1287/mnsc.2023.4879) explored the relationship between genetics and sales performance. They found that top-performing salespeople shared similar genetic traits that enabled them to be superior adaptive learners. They often shared the following attributes: quick customer assessment, flexible product recommendations, efficient time management, a customer-oriented approach, and the ability to seize opportunities. Their findings concluded that "nature" and "nurture" are both critical in the sales profession. Understanding the nature of sales performance can also inform actions to nurture the sales force more effectively. In their concluding remarks, they found;

"Using primary genetic data, we find that genetic variants associated with educational attainment predict salespeople's performance. Genetics is more predictive of sales performance than personality traits. Meanwhile, genetics and effort both contribute to sales performance, suggesting that good salespeople may be born and made. Moreover, we find evidence that adaptive learning, as reflected in salespeople's customer orientation and opportunity recognition skills, partly explains the gene-sales relationship."

The primary genetic contribution stems from variants associated with educational attainment and brain development, such as the polygenic score for learning efficacy. A polygenic score for educational attainment is a genetic summary statistic that can predict a person's likelihood of achieving higher education or academic success. Still, it is not a definitive measure of learning ability. A higher score has been linked to greater self-control and interpersonal skills, which contribute to successful academic outcomes. Salespeople with these markers tend to excel in customer orientation and opportunity recognition, where core adaptive learning skills are crucial.

Research shows that specific genes, such as the OXTR (Oxytocin Receptor) gene, influence a person's ability to empathize, which can enhance relationship-building and customer orientation — crucial for successful selling. The majority of empathy-related traits and skills — approximately 90% — are shaped by life experiences, education, upbringing, and socialization rather than solely by genetics. Most empathy in sales comes from deliberate development, knowledge, and situational learning, making it an accessible skill rather than a fixed trait.

The top 5 traits in salespeople's DNA, according to research on genetic influence, are adaptive learning, opportunity recognition, competitive drive, resilience, and social acuity. The trait with the strongest genetic predictor is adaptive learning, which enables salespeople to excel at adjusting to new information, market dynamics, and customer behaviors. Second on the list applies to "hunters," who often possess a natural ability to spot prospects, interpret signals, and act proactively to generate new business. High-performance salespeople exhibit relentless ambition and a competitive spirit, often driven by genes that influence motivation and reward-seeking. These high achievers set lofty goals and pursue them without settling for mediocrity. The resilience trait enables salespeople to bounce back from setbacks, and their innate ability to read social cues and build rapport with customers is often derived from genes linked to extraversion, emotional intelligence, and trust-building. The table below provides further insights into the key traits that are in salespeople's DNA.

Trait	Genetic Influence	Key Sales Advantage
Adaptive Learning	High	Fast adjustment, solution focused
Opportunity Recognition	Moderate	Proactive prospecting
Competitive Drive	Strong	Relentless pursuit of goals
Resilience	Moderate	Overcoming setbacks
Social Acuity	Moderate	Building deep client rapport

Table 8.2 Salespeople Traits in Their DNA

Ethical challenges persist in the use of genetic data for employment; researchers caution against discrimination based on DNA and recommend focusing on developing adaptive learning skills more broadly. DNA data ignores the proven and significant impact of environmental factors, training, and personal motivation on complex skills like sales. Hiring top salespeople is not the same as breeding racehorses. However, there is a surprising amount of overlap, particularly in the interplay between genetic predisposition and environmental conditioning. In both fields, success depends on a combination of innate qualities (nature) and dedicated development and training (nurture).

8.3 EMPATHY

In 2014, Mary Barra became the first female CEO of a major automaker. She began her career at GM at age 18 as a college co-op student. Throughout her long tenure, she has held various roles, including quality control officer, executive assistant, plant manager, and HR leader. She rose through the ranks by leading with empathy and by considering the perspectives of every GM employee. While delivering the commencement address at Duke University in 2022, she outlined five lessons as follows;

- "Do your best." A call to work hard and go after what you're doing with maximum effort.

- "Find your purpose." Discover the kind of leader you are and understand what drives you, as this will help you lead your organization effectively.

- "Listen to understand." The wisest lesson you'll learn as a leader is to ask questions and listen first.

- "Be honest, always." Always speak the truth and deal with the truth, and be willing to own up to your mistakes.

- "Include one more. Make room at the table." The ethos of Barra's leadership approach is inclusivity and caring for people.

Empathy involves both emotional attunement and cognitive understanding, activating distinct neural networks that help people recognize and respond to others' emotions. Empathic responses in the brain originate in the anterior and prefrontal cortex (see Table x). These areas support emotional processing, with a mix of reactions arising from experiencing and witnessing pain. Empathy also forms a foundational part of emotional intelligence, enabling individuals to connect emotionally and build relationships.

Brain Region	Function in Empathy
Anterior Insular Cortex	Emotional perception & affect sharing
Anterior Cingulate Cortex	Processing & sharing emotional path
Prefrontal Cortex	Perspective-taking, regulation
Mirror Neuron System	Mirroring actions, emotions, auto-empathy
Somatosensory & Motor	Embodied simlutation of feelings

Table 8.3 Brain Regions Supporting Empathy

Empathy enables salespeople to genuinely understand and acknowledge a customer's concerns and emotions, thereby fostering trust and increasing the likelihood that customers will believe in and purchase from the salesperson. Empathy shifts the focus from making a sale to truly helping the customer, making the experience feel personal and authentic rather than scripted or self-serving.

By actively listening and asking thoughtful questions, empathetic salespeople can uncover their customers' true motivations and pain points, leading to more accurate and relevant product recommendations. When customers feel heard and valued, they are more likely to believe that the salesperson has their best interests in mind, which naturally fosters trust. This sense of being understood creates an atmosphere where customers are comfortable communicating openly, willing to share their real concerns and motivations, leading to more honest discussions and fewer misunderstandings.

Empathetic salespeople also establish credibility by demonstrating that they are not just focused on closing a sale, but are committed to helping the customer find the best solution for their specific situation. This approach differentiates them from aggressive or transactional sellers, making customers more likely to return, refer others, and remain loyal over time. Neuroscience research further supports this, showing that empathetic interactions strengthen emotional bonds and trigger trust-building hormones, making customers more receptive and confident in the salesperson's recommendations. Customers are more inclined to trust and believe a salespeople who show genuine concern for their needs, which reinforces the perception that the salesperson is authentic and acting with integrity.

Empathetic salespeople possess a unique advantage: the ability to genuinely understand and adapt to each customer's emotional and situational context. By tuning into the customer's perspective, motivations, and concerns, they can tailor their communication style, tone, and recommendations to align more closely with what truly matters to the buyer. This leads to more meaningful interactions, builds stronger trust, and ultimately makes the sales process more productive.

Moreover, when empathy is combined with a creative problem-solving mindset, sales professionals can go beyond cookie-cutter solutions. They are better equipped to frame challenges in new ways, uncover unmet or hidden needs, and co-create innovative offerings that deliver real value. This flexible, customer-centric approach not only enhances the chances of closing a deal but also fosters long-term relationships and customer loyalty — a critical differentiator in today's competitive market.

When salespeople acknowledge and validate a customer's hesitations, they build trust and defuse tension — key ingredients for successful negotiations. Rather than brushing aside objections or pushing past concerns, empathetic sales professionals take a moment to listen truly. They recognize that hesitation often signals an unmet need, a past negative experience, or a more profound uncertainty. By validating the customer's point of view — for example, saying, "I completely understand why that might be a concern" — the salesperson shows respect rather than resistance.

This approach opens the door to more honest dialogue, allowing the salesperson to explore the root of the concern and respond with clarity, reassurance, or creative alternatives. It shifts the dynamic from adversarial to collaborative, making the customer feel seen and heard rather than pressured. As a result, objections become opportunities: opportunities to demonstrate insight, offer tailored solutions, and reinforce value. Ultimately, this method leads to smoother negotiations, fewer last-minute deal blockers, and significantly higher close rates — not just because the product fits, but also because the relationship does.

In Caroline Fleck's book, "Validation[9]," she covers in detail the subject of equalizing communications and suggests that a person's response is reasonable or justified in terms of the current situation and normal biological functioning and abides by the Golden Rule Approach: "anyone in your shoes would do the same thing." She explains that putting yourself in someone else's shoes, even if it's just through imagination, requires a higher level of cognitive processing that engages the brain's visual, motor, and sensory systems. Research suggests that actively imagining another person's experience enables us better to intuit their thoughts, feelings, and needs. This approach can actually help generate empathy.

Sympathy, on the other hand, is not your friend in sales. Although it comes from compassion, it typically focuses on pity rather than problem-solving. The phrase, "sorry to bother you," should be replaced with "thank you for your time. I wanted to share something with you that could help your business." This approach expresses gratitude and respects the customer's busy schedule. The common misconception is that asking not to bother you comes from a position of weakness or lack of confidence. Instead of honoring the customer, the salesperson is lowering the value bar on their conversation. Save the sympathy talk for condolences or hardship. In the workplace, sympathy can be helpful during challenging discussions, providing support while maintaining distance, helping leaders avoid oversharing or blurring the lines between work and personal roles.

In Brené Brown's book "Dare to Lead," she discusses empathy, self-awareness, courage, and what she terms "Armoured" and "Daring" leadership. Armoured leadership involves driving people with fear, power, and perfectionism. At times of uncertainty, they weaponize fear to their advantage. Having the mentality that knowing everything or always being right is key. Perfectionism is not about healthy achievement and growth; rather, it can be a defensive move and stems from fear of failure, making mistakes, and not meeting people's expectations. Brown describes the armoured leaders as having an acute sense of cynicism and sarcasm as a "get-out-of-contributing-free card." And finally, the misuse of power is dangerous. When someone holds power over us, the human spirit's instinct is to rise, resist, and rebel. As a construct, it feels wrong in the broader geopolitical context; it can mean death and despotism.

Daring leaders cultivate a grounded sense of self that makes room for discomfort instead of armoring against it, and this is where Brown's work on shame and empathy becomes central. Rather than using perfectionism, blame, or sarcasm to deflect shame, they learn to recognize their own shame triggers, name what they are feeling, and stay in connection with others through curious, empathic listening. By practicing empathy —seeing and validating the emotion beneath someone's experience without trying to fix or judge it—they transform shame from a silencing, isolating force into a source of shared humanity, which, in turn, enables accountability, learning, and truly courageous leadership.

Be Nice

In the 1989 film "Road House," Patrick Swayze is hired as a bouncer for a seedy bar filled with raucous cowboys who are willing to drink excessively and fight over pretty women. Swayze is known as a "cooler," with a style that helps diffuse the crowd's emotions. After initially hiring on, he trains his crew to "Be nice" to the crowd of bullies. He shows them how to spot trouble and defend themselves against an impending fight. The first step is a verbal warning by looking the beast in the face and asking them to calm down. This has almost zero effect, and the chaos continues. The second step is to repeat the warning with more cautionary advice. And finally, when only physical restraints will work, the bouncers are to persuade, guide, or drag the victims outside before any fist fights or furniture starts flying. Swayze's emphasis on "be nice" is an empathetic approach that relies on understanding others' feelings, maintaining calm composure, and fostering relational harmony in challenging circumstances. Paradoxically, Swayze suggests the situation at the bar is not personal; it's just a job. He encourages his crew to respond with empathy instead of anger. He turns the bar from a nightly brawl fest to an attractive, live music establishment, with peace and (temporary) harmony.

8.4 HUMAN-TO-HUMAN CONTACT

The definition of human-to-human contact may vary depending on the lens through which it is examined. The most encompassing definition is: the broad spectrum of interactions and communications that occur between people, ranging from casual physical proximity to deep, emotionally connected relationships. This contact is a fundamental human need that influences social, psychological, and even physical well-being.

The top professions that are overwhelmingly involved with human-to-human contact include healthcare, social services, law, education, sales, hospitality, human resources, and direct customer-facing roles. All these roles require direct interaction, communication, and relationship-building as a core part of their daily responsibilities.

At the top of the sales pyramid sits strategic selling, which requires human contact, as there is often a significant dollar value involved in the decision-making process, and the salesperson-to-client interface necessitates considerable trust and emotional connection. We worry that someday artificial intelligence will replace sales jobs; however, when human-to-human contact is needed to close the deal, the robots will have to wait a bit. AI will be instrumental in handling the cognitive and time-intensive data work, allowing salespeople to gain bandwidth for deeper customer interactions that build trust and drive large consultative deals. Strategic selling efforts, such as reading subtle buyer signals, storytelling, and navigating sensitive negotiations, will continue to rely on emotional intelligence and intuition that AI cannot replicate.

During the COVID pandemic, salespeople were forced to rapidly adapt to remote selling, leading to significant disruptions in how relationships were built and deals were closed. Face-to-face meetings, travel, and live events disappeared almost overnight, replaced with Zoom video calls and digital engagements. Salespeople lost the ability to use body language, customer cues, and in-person persuasion —skills critical to building trust and closing deals. Trade shows, plant visits, and in-person sales blitzes were cancelled, and travel became highly restrictive, resulting in a dramatic reduction of live customer engagement opportunities. Digital self-service and remote human engagement have become the norm, with more than 75% of buyers and sellers now preferring this approach over traditional face-to-face interactions. If you were a salesperson in the manufacturing services business, you could no longer host plant visits, which were a key part of due diligence when selecting a supplier. At your Bay Area factory, customers can enter the facility and maintain social distancing (6-10 feet) while performing their tasks. It meant that any simple task became complex, and communicating through a mask was never easy. At night, our General Manager employed a third-party service to spray hydrogen peroxide throughout the facility to kill germs from all surfaces.

Companies that resumed in-person sales meetings after the COVID pandemic gained a competitive advantage over rivals who stuck to remote interactions, signaling a commitment and willingness to go the extra mile for clients. The act of investing in travel or physical meetings became a marker of value, helping salespeople stand out in crowded markets. Active listening and empathizing with clients demonstrated genuine care and understanding, which allows prospects to feel heard, respected, and valued. Expressing empathy reduced negative emotions and helped clients open up about needs and pain points.

B2B players (NVIDIA, Apple, Microsoft, Amazon, Tesla, Netflix, and Meta) leveraged their advanced digital infrastructure and quickly adapted to new buying behaviors, excelling in both B2B and B2C. The post-COVID seller needed to be a subject matter expert, translating complex technical details into clear value propositions and demonstrating thought leadership in client conversations. Leading sales teams have transformed "selling" into "serving," becoming trusted advisors focused on solving customer problems, rather than just pitching their products or services. Hybrid selling became essential, combining both digital platforms (virtual selling) and selective human-to-human engagements, where customers were willing to host in-person visits.

The top traits that emerged during the COVID-19 pandemic and remain instrumental for salespeople today are adaptability, empathy, digital fluency, creativity, and enhanced communication skills. These behaviors initially emerged as crisis responses but have evolved into permanent competitive advantages in sales. We don't use the word' grit' enough when describing a salesperson's attribute, but the willingness to experiment, learn, and persevere in the face of setbacks defines successful post-pandemic sellers. These traits have endured because buyers continue to value responsive, skilled, and trustworthy partners who adapt to their evolving needs and operate confidently in a hybrid environment.

8.5 HUNTER-FARMER SPECTRUM

Time for some visuals and understanding the influence of emotional intelligence across hunters and farmers, as well as the proverbial Venn diagram and the blended, overlapping, mixed area. As you ponder which circle you put yourself in, there is a far more critical challenge: understanding why you may fit into one particular area as your comfort zone, rather than the "other" space you don't relate to or feel uncomfortable associating with. We have discussed the attributes of hunters and farmers in Chapter 2, and most sales professionals can assess themselves based on their strengths, weaknesses, and preferred activities. However, most salespeople fall somewhere on the hunter-farmer spectrum, exhibiting both traits across different situations. For example, a company may have evolving needs to find startups for new business and to nurture existing customers for expansion or retention. In this hybrid role, salespersons may work on both their strengths and weaknesses to become more effective.

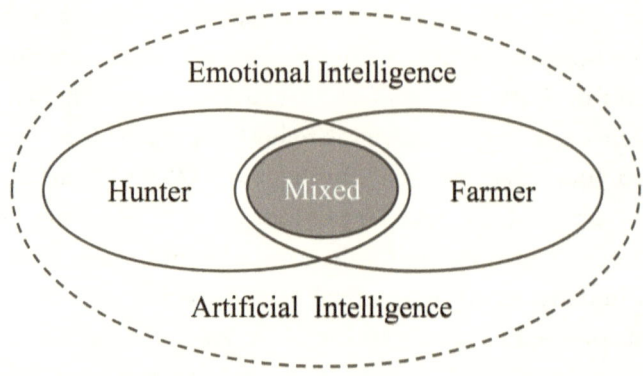

Figure 8.4 Hunter-Farmer Spectrum

When you wake up in the morning and refresh yourself in the mirror, you're not likely to ask yourself whether you are a hunter, a farmer, or slightly to the left of middle on the spectrum. After a cup of coffee, your emotions kick in and guide you in making decisions and planning for your goals, just as you do on any other day. Whether you fit nicely into the hunter or farmer buckets, or have strong attributes as a lone wolf, relationship builder, or challenger salesperson, you will be a better, stronger, and more successful seller when you understand these traits.

It is essential to separate the diagrams from the real world, and leveraging your strengths enables you to be the best person you can be. If you are a farmer who desperately wants to be a hunter (or a wolf in sheep's clothing), you can do so by training your emotions and actions. Be more assertive by changing your relationship-building habits to include pressing your customer on pricing and competition. You may need to manage this change process by simply understanding your current strengths and weaknesses. Writing these down can help with step 1. You might find that you are very comfortable with your current methods, which have served you well for many years; however, change is one of the things all salespeople endure, whether due to job changes, competition, or other dynamics beyond your control. Making up your mind to broaden your skills to include a hunter-farmer blend can be a significant growth factor and deliver immediate impact on your sales. If you are currently an expert in nurturing existing customers, but need to sharpen your new business skills, try some role-playing in a new environment where you are viewed with a clean slate. Move into a new role by telling yourself that you belong and surround yourself with the tools to accomplish this new task.

Attribute	Hunter	Farmer
Primary Focus	New business acquisition	Existing account growth
Motivation	Commission & quota	Customer nurturing
Risk Tolerance	High, embrace change	Low, maintain stability
Skill Emphasis	Negotiation, closing deals	Service, upsell/cross-sell
Communications Style	Direct, persistent	Friendly, collaborative
Key Strengths	Resiliance, independence	Loyalty, long-term

Table 8.5 The Hunter Farmer Attributes

Imagine you want to make a significant physical change, such as losing weight through a combination of diet and exercise. After conducting thorough research, you create new meal plans, commit to visiting the gym (or even upgrading to a club membership), and set milestones to encourage yourself. These include the obvious calorie counting, weight numbers, and perhaps body mass index (BMI), along with other relevant metrics. You may have a particular goal that can be measured by wearing new clothes that fit a smaller waistline, or even by adding new wardrobe items you previously denied yourself because you lost your way from youth to middle age. Imagine trimming your daily intake from 2500 calories to 2000 or fewer —about a 20% reduction. You can keep your coffee drinks, but you have to reduce the alcohol, especially at night, dramatically. You challenge yourself to achieve your goal by a specific calendar date, or even a popular holiday, and meet or exceed internal expectations. This method is old school, before the rising demand for Ozempic medicine took the weight-loss category by storm. In some ways, weight loss achieved through diet and exercise is comparable to sales training achieved through homework and seminars rather than leveraging artificial intelligence. In both cases, there are significant accelerators to achieve similar results.

The purpose of using the weight loss challenge is to reflect on how you can make internal changes to your position on the hunter-farmer spectrum. And as much as you think losing weight is a physical challenge, it is much more about the mental commitment to a goal. So, let's examine a few simple steps to shift your behavior and create a path to performing at any point on the spectrum.

Let's assume you read through the attribute table and you are either slightly or full to the right or left (a hunter or a farmer). That is your starting point. Step 2 varies for everyone and is the most crucial. You need to select the area where you feel most comfortable moving to and make a plan. For example, if you are a naturally friendly and collaborative person, but want to become direct and persistent, this is your next step. Think of a work situation where you would usually control the dialogue with consensus building, socializing a few options, and seeking approval, and then change things up. This time, use a more direct approach to guide the customer along the path you prefer, and be persuasive. You should rehearse your lines a few times and then try the new approach.

In many cases, your fears will be rewarded, as the customer, accustomed to your style and demeanor, will praise your direct, no-nonsense approach and even thank you for being straightforward. You're not completely changing who you are; think of this more as an adjustment where you have now extended your strengths across the spectrum. Try another attribute and work on styles that initially put you out of your comfort zone but eventually give you more tools for your toolbox.

In addition to the hunter-farmer spectrum, there are the key influences of emotional and artificial intelligence. You should picture yourself more as a 3-dimensional (Rubik's) cube, with hunter-farmer in the X-Y plane and EQ in the Z direction. Sorry if this is starting to feel like a calculus equation, but it is good to "visualize" the path you're seeking. We will refer to the Z-direction as your "Zen," and celebrate when we understand the transformation. You started the day by transitioning from your comfortable farming position to a more assertive hunter stance, yet you retained your original emotional intelligence, unchanged. In your former role, you built a strong rapport and deep empathy for your customers' needs; now you need to adapt that approach to your new hunter role. It's much easier than you think, and it will come naturally to you. EQ doesn't force you to be a hunter or farmer, but rather amplifies the strengths of each and enables hybrid success. If you naturally have a high EQ as a farmer, you likely have the same high score as a hunter. Put another way, if you look at two salespeople with widely different EQs, one with poor EQ and one with high EQ. If they make a move on the hunter-farmer spectrum, they will bring their EQ nuances with them. Don't worry — through commitment to change, you can also improve your EQ, should you prefer to.

We then consider the influence of artificial intelligence and how it will operate across the hunter-farmer spectrum. This topic could easily be a book subject in its own right, but for this discussion, we will simplify it. For some people, AI is like adding seasoning to their cooking; for others, it is the main course. Similarly, suppose you are looking to improve your sales skills as a hybrid hunter-farmer. In that case, you can leverage AI tools in almost everything you do, including prospecting, messaging, account planning, and much more.

Aspect	Hunter Benefits	Farmer Benefits	Universal Benefits
Lead Generation & Qualification	Rapidly finds, qualifies leads, automates outreach	Not primary for farmers	Increased pipeline quality
Pitch Personalization	Tailors messaging & demos prospect needs	Crafts personalized follow-ups for clients	Better engagement and relevance
Objection Handling & Negotiation	AI-prepared responses for common objections	Diplomacy in renewal and upsell conversations	Improved conversion rates
Research & Preparedness	Industry/account insights pre-engagement	Account history for deeper relationship	Strategic account management
Customer Onboarding & Success	-	Streamlines onboarding, ensures setup	Faster customer adoption
Retention Monitoring	-	Flags churn risk, prompts proactive outreach	Reduced attrition
Relationship Building	Initial rapport based on data	Manages touchpoints and loyalty	Stronger client relationships
Upsell/Cross-Sell	-	Suggests upgrades and add-ons	Increased account value
Productivity Boost	Automates busywork to focus on selling	Automates account management routines	More time for selling higher efficiency
Collaboration & Knowledge Sharing	Preps handoffs between hunter/farmer	Shares client context for seamless ongoing sales	Harmonized teamwork
Continuous Learning	Surfaces new outreach	Flags account improvement opportunities	Ongoing skills and process enhancement

Table 8.6 AI Influence on the Hunter-Farmer Spectrum

The table above outlines many of the AI influences on a salesperson's routine and segments into hunter-farmer roles. The hybrid role encompasses the "universal" benefits and is akin to a "take-away," to help simplify. Again, the depths to which AI can influence a salesperson are immense, from the tools at your disposal to the endless queries that can be used to help create a path for hunters, farmers, or hybrids. The best approach is to start gradually with work situations and be your own guide about how much AI you want to use. Know that the tools are powerful and allow the salesperson to become a master in record time.

8.6 FAMILIA

We're drawn to the familiar because it makes us feel safe, comfortable, and in control. This tendency is deeply ingrained in both our psychology and biology. Whether we're choosing a song, a restaurant, or a political candidate, familiarity influences our preferences in powerful, often invisible ways. Several key principles help explain this phenomenon: the mere exposure effect, reduced cognitive load, a sense of safety, trust, and the human need for belonging.

Psychologists refer to the mere exposure effect as the tendency to develop a preference for things simply because they have been encountered repeatedly. Whether it's a melody, a face, or a corporate logo, familiarity breeds liking. This effect operates below the level of conscious awareness—our brains process familiar stimuli more fluently, and that ease of processing is interpreted as something positive. Familiar people and settings, such as family environments, provide consistent emotional feedback and help shape abilities like empathy, emotional awareness, and self-regulation. Young adults who grow up in supportive, emotionally expressive families tend to have higher emotional intelligence, showing better regulation and interpersonal skills.

Emotion recognition is more accurate when interacting with familiar individuals. Studies show that people can categorize emotions more effectively in faces they are familiar with, making familiarity a key factor in successful emotional awareness and communication.

Familiarity also conserves mental energy. When we engage with something we already know, it requires less cognitive effort to interpret. Our brains are wired to be energy-efficient, which is why we often choose the path of least resistance. This explains why many people rewatch the same films or return to their favorite restaurants—familiar experiences deliver comfort and pleasure without requiring extra mental effort.

From an evolutionary standpoint, the familiar often signaled safety. A known food source, location, or group was less likely to pose a threat. That instinct still guides us today. Familiar routines and environments reduce anxiety and provide a sense of stability in an unpredictable world.

Familiarity also plays a crucial role in shaping identity and a sense of belonging. The music we grew up with, the traditions passed down through generations, the brands we associate with success—all of these act as cultural touchstones, reinforcing who we are and where we come from.

Too much familiarity, or overexposure, may sometimes decrease emotional engagement and reduce appreciation for emotional novelty. Balancing familiar and unfamiliar experiences helps maintain growth in emotional intelligence.

Artificial intelligence also poses some potential threats to the family, mainly regarding mental health, privacy, social development, and ethical challenges. The increased use of AI-powered devices at home introduces privacy concerns, including risks of data collection, surveillance, and exposure to AI-generated threats such as deepfakes and impersonation. Children and families can be vulnerable to fraud, cyberbullying, and coercion through AI-powered content. AI can disrupt traditional family roles and boundaries, challenging parental rights and decision-making, especially in education and online safety. Children's ability to interpret emotional cues often declines with excessive screen time enabled by AI technologies. Families may experience tension from generational divides in technology adoption or reliance. On a positive note, AI can also enhance communication and support family routines by balancing new digital literacy with somewhat older family values.

In business, politics, and relationships, familiarity builds trust. People naturally gravitate toward what they know because it feels predictable. This is why brand recognition is so powerful: the more familiar a brand becomes, the more likely we are to choose it—often without even realizing it.

Spotify once launched a marketing campaign aimed at increasing music discovery by serving users entirely new playlists filled with unfamiliar artists selected by an algorithm. The campaign flopped. Users didn't respond well to playlists composed exclusively of unknown songs. In a revised approach, Spotify added just one or two familiar tracks into each playlist—and the results changed dramatically. Suddenly, users were more open to exploring the new music. Even a small amount of familiarity gave them a sense of trust and comfort, unlocking the door to novelty.

Ultimately, it's not just that we like the familiar—we need it. It's the foundation on which we make sense of the new. Familia refers to a group of people related by blood, marriage, or living together, often extending to all those within a household. In Ancient Rome, "familia" encompassed not only blood relatives but also enslaved people and servants, essentially all people under one domestic roof.

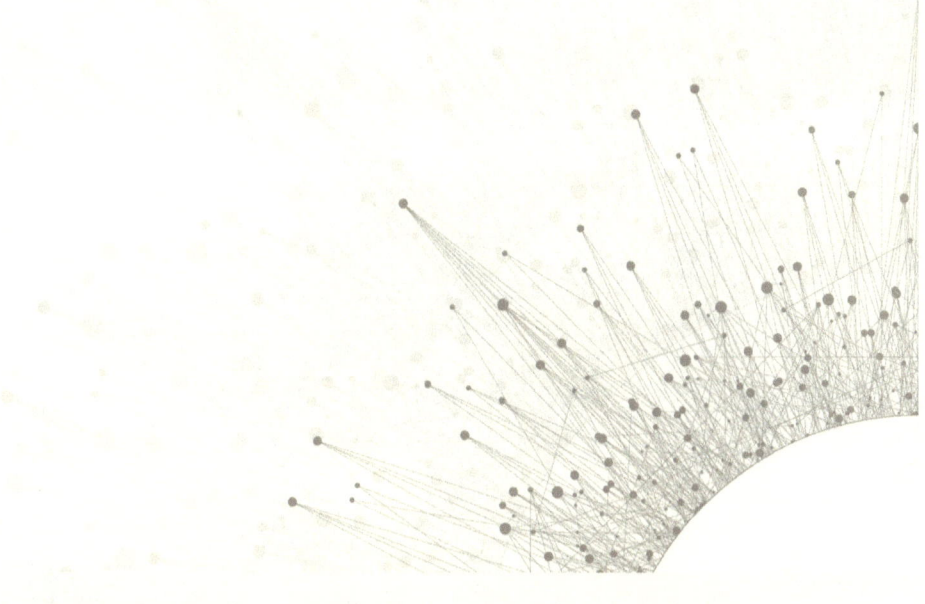

PART IV

CHAPTER 9
SALES EXCELLENCE

THERE ARE leadership positions that require immense knowledge and experience. Seldom do CEOs rise to the top of an organization without demonstrating their skills in management and decision-making. A few exceptions include founders who often possess enough skills, or perhaps a majority of popular skills, to maintain the role until a major hurdle requires a change. Words that usually accompany a leader are brilliant, charismatic, competitive, decisive, emotionally intelligent, financially acumen, great communicator, humble, integrity, knowledgeable, negotiator, relationship builder, risk manager, and understanding. Interestingly, most of these attributes apply to both the CEO and the CRO (Chief Revenue Officer), with some exceptions.

Here is an example of characteristics by role, rated 1-to-3, with 1 for fair, 2 for good, and 3 for excellent. From the table, it may not be immediately apparent where the differences lie between the CEO and CRO; however, there are at least three areas where their goals are nearly opposite. Let's break these down as follows;

- Is the CEO or CRO more competitive?
- A CEO competes in leadership skills to understand the business, define the strategy, build an organization, and execute in all areas of the company. At work, he reports to no one and manages in line with

multiple goals, with fiduciary responsibility to the board. Competition is somewhat self-induced.

- A CRO competes in sales leadership with a focused strategy, a driven organization, and balances tactical and strategic metrics to execute a well-defined goal. Competition is fierce every day, coming from both internal and external forces.

2-Ltr	3-Ltr	4-Ltr	5-Ltr	Number
AI	B2B	ASAP	13485	2.54
BS	BTW	GDPR	CRISP	2.71
DM	FYI	HTML	FAFSA	3.14
IT	IDK	NASA	NAACP	26.2
PR	ISO	SWOT	OSHAI	212
UK	OOO	TTYL	TGTBT	911

Figure 9.1 C-Level Attributes

- Who is a better negotiator, a CEO or a CRO?
- A CEO negotiates with every group in the organization. They are required to weigh in on every significant decision, especially when money, obligations, or liabilities are in question. Negotiating events can be planned or random, and urgent or passive.
- A CRO negotiates every sales deal and puts himself between the customer and the organization. Listen, all big deals require the art of negotiation, and a sales leader manages expectations from two opposing entities.
- So, they both are negotiators, but with slightly different approaches, and yet, common outcomes.
- Why is integrity important?
- A CEO must have integrity to go through challenging situations and come out on the other side with uncompromised results. They must

maintain composure and leadership when significant challenges question the company's ability to deliver its objectives.

- A CRO should also have integrity, especially with sensitive information that may persuade a key decision. Sales contracts often begin with a one-sided approach, where the customer requests the sun, the moon, and the stars, and the CRO must review the language to ensure it accommodates the interests of both parties. Sales integrity includes acting with honesty, fairness, and respect. It involves being truthful in your claims, following through on commitments, and prioritizing the customer's needs and interests. It's about doing the right thing, even when it's not the easiest or most profitable path.

9.1 LEAD BY EXAMPLE

To lead by example, a person needs to have multiple attributes to be truly influential as an effective leader. As you reflect on the managers you have looked up to, the following qualities will likely seem obvious: integrity, self-awareness, strong communication, active listening, vision, and the ability to empower others. C-level executives are hired to lead by example, with the most powerful sword being decision-making. Leaders need to make sound, timely decisions under pressure and amid significant employee challenges. Having high emotional intelligence is crucial to understanding and managing a workforce that may respect authority but needs to see actions that back up words.

Leadership consultant and business author John Baldoni writes in his book "Lead by Example" that one of the best places to see good deeds rewarded is on high school or collegiate sports teams. Look at who the players have elected as their captains. The players are not always the most talented athletes, but they are the most outward-directed. What they do on the practice field is essential for team unity. They are the ones who lead by example, often tutoring fellow players in the art of the game —or, more often, in the art of getting along with a coach, a teacher, or a fellow player.

It all starts with character. What you do when you think no one is watching may be the best definition of character. Character defines who you are and forms the basis for your leadership. People of character command respect because they have earned it through their actions and words. And, as a virtue, if you invest in persons with good character, both customers and team members will benefit. Without it, leadership is impossible; with it, leadership can flourish.

The primary difference between a leader and a manager is that a manager typically focuses on day-to-day operations, planning, organizing, and controlling resources to achieve specific goals within an organization. Leaders, on the other hand, focus on inspiring and motivating people towards a shared vision, driving change, and developing a positive organizational culture. Some key leadership skills, demonstrated by example, include communication, influence, coaching, empathy, and strategic thinking.

Entertainers may be some of the early pioneers in leading by example. They carry their art with them every day and perform at their best, or not at all. Imagine a magician with unimpressive tricks, a comedian with unfunny jokes, or a singer who can't sing. Or, by contrast, watch a performer smash their audition with a rendition of a song that is performed even better than the original artist. An athlete who wins a competitive state championship is inspirational to their team, family, and friends.

But are these entertainers really leaders or just showmen? Let's break it down. The lead-by-example features include integrity, active involvement, accountability, trust, and empowerment. At the same time, the showman leverages charisma, stage presence, storytelling, and emotional connections to captivate the audience. Both of these characteristics are tools for leadership and can be used effectively. A key difference between the two is that leading by example is about substance—demonstrating desired behaviors through actions —while a showperson can sometimes focus more on style and performance.

Dr. Sanjiv Chopra describes 10 key principles of all great leaders in his book, "Leadership by Example[1]." He uses experience and stories to provide practical insights into each principle. In the introduction, he describes a flock of migrating birds flying in a V formation. It is a beautiful sight. Each bird keeps its pace behind the leader, twisting and turning through the air as the leader does. Following is much easier. Scientists have proven that birds in the formation expend much less energy than the leader. But what few people realize is that the formation has no single leader. One bird flies to the point until it tires, then drops back, to be replaced by another. During the long migration, most of the birds have both the opportunity and the responsibility to become the leader of the formation. Chopra states, "True leaders simply move forward doing what they believe is correct and what resonates for them, often without knowing or even being concerned if anyone is following.

L	Leadership
E	Empathy
A	Attitude
D	Dreaming
E	Effective
R	Resilient
S	Sense of Purpose
H	Humility
I	Integrity
P	Packing Others Parachutes

Figure 9.2 Key Principles of all Great Leaders (Dr Sanjiv Chopra)

These principles map efficiently into the key elements of EQ. Recall that emotional intelligence involves managing emotions through empathy, self-awareness, self-control, and sales drive (Daniel Goleman). Empathy and compassion are timeless, and we can find extraordinary examples of them throughout history. Most of these stories involve human tragedy, health and medical wonders, war, and peace. In sales, we recognize that empathy is essential for fostering stronger communication and more meaningful customer relationships. There is also the weakness or toxic side of empathy, where certain boundaries are crossed, and passive and assertive styles are mixed in complex situations. In the well-known Janek Performance Group sales training, empathy is referred to as "the most difficult and valuable sales skill."

Born to alcoholic parents, Glenn Stearns was diagnosed with dyslexia, failed fourth grade, and fathered a child at the age of fourteen. He graduated from high school in the bottom 10 percent of his class. He later became the first person in his family to graduate from college with a degree in economics. Motivated by stories of people who took risks and achieved their grandest ambitions, he boldly moved to California, where he worked as a waiter and slept on the kitchen floor of a one-bedroom apartment that he shared with five other recent graduates. In just 10 years, with no prior lending experience, The Blackstone Group acquired a majority stake in Stearns Lending LLC and became the #1 wholesale lender in the US. Stearn's net worth exceeds $500 million, and despite the lending company eventually surviving bankruptcy, he compromised more than a bit of integrity during his life's journey. (Stearns book: Integrity[2])

Help is on the Way

We hosted a team from an Australian startup called Rocket Labs. The team included subject matter experts in engineering and supply chain management, each with specific tasks to oversee the complex mission of launching unique satellites and other payloads into space. They competed with companies like Blue Origin and SpaceX and had been highly successful thus far. However, one of their new requirements was to "catch" the booster portion of the rocket as it re-entered the Earth's atmosphere. The idea was to reuse some or all of the booster for future missions, as both a cost-saving measure and the task was rather intriguing to watch.

The engineers walked us through the architecture of both the booster and the payload, including various elements such as complex electronics, mechanical assemblies, and pyrotechnics. They were very passionate about how their rocket platform was unique in terms of engineering, safety, and their record of successful launches. About halfway through the discussion, they mentioned a new plan to catch the Stage 1 booster as it reentered Earth's atmosphere. The fuselage was a 3D-printed titanium shell, with diameters of 1.2m (small) and 7m (large), and heights of 17m and 42m. The early plan of record was to have the booster land on a floating barge named Oceanus in the Atlantic Ocean. The barge was later renamed "Return on Investment," as all good engineering projects need a bit of fun. During the discussion, two engineers shared minute details of the analyses they had performed, as if it were an equation from a textbook, with calculations involving weights, velocity, and acceleration. These were very sharp twenty-something engineers with space travel in their veins.

At a break in the action, I asked if I could make a quick phone call, and they awkwardly agreed. I was the VP and had enough clout to either say something or make a fool of myself. I called someone I had worked with in the past, and was lucky when she answered. After putting Angela on speakerphone, I provided her with a brief overview of the meeting and asked for her thoughts on the rocket booster catch. She inquired about the size and weight, and made some mental calculations. She had a military mindset and then ran through the capable helicopters for the job. She discounted the Black Hawk and explained key issues regarding wind speed, timing, and maneuverability. After a mental iteration, she moved to the Sikorsky, which was much better suited due to the challenge of catching the booster and the fine maneuvering requirements. She even went through some pilot details on the Sikorsky S-92. I thanked her (for her service) and her usual excellence.

The Rocket Labs team was taken aback. Although they had all the engineering answers to solve their problem, they had never spoken to a helicopter pilot for their input. In a previous role, I managed Angela, a salesperson with an impeccable record, who had served as a Black Hawk pilot in the Army, bringing valuable mission experience. Asking her for advice about a simple helicopter mission where the enemy wasn't shooting at her was easy. She spoke like a Major in the Army with mad helicopter skills. She even talked about the payload sway after catching it in a net and the challenges of bringing it down safely to the barge. This was an easy lead-by-example moment. We later found out that Rocket

Labs selected the Sikorsky with some minor modifications, such as extended fuel and a capture hook.

Not Too Rich To Lead

I was fortunate to be a part of the second-largest tech IPO in the nineties. Behind Marc Andreessen's Netscape, "D" Multimedia went public as the world's number one graphics add-in card. In this era, consumers would buy a generic PC and then upgrade with a D Multimedia graphics card to improve performance, especially in PC gaming. It was my first IPO, and I was lucky enough to join as their SME for modem technologies. We leveraged the company name to enter the modem business, developed and acquired modems for both Mac and PC installations. The company would also be among the earliest to enter the MP3 player market before Apple.

The company was founded by C.M. Lee in 1982. He was best known for his penny-pinching style, which enabled the company to manage its spending while growing to a historic high. The company grew into the world's leading graphic supplier and leveraged the Windows 95 need for displays. Mr. Lee underwent a leveraged buyout (LBO) and raised over $85 million to pass the reins to a new management team. Mr. Lee's legacy lives on through his name on the Asian Art Museum in San Francisco.

One of his early hires was Dave Smith, who ran sales and was my boss. Dave was a very high-energy leader with a multitasking, charming personality that he used to either praise or scold his team into high performers. Selling into the PC business was chaos, and the demands were intense. There were times when the activities reminded me of hell; it must be like on the NYSE, where traders yell 'buy' and 'sell' tickets. Dave would run an SPIF (sales incentive) and set pricing until the inventory was depleted, and salespeople would make numerous calls to secure sales. POs would flow, and we would meet our monthly revenue quota.

When the company went public, a host of new millionaires emerged, and the parking lot would see a new car appear each day, as Mercedes, Porsches, and BMWs began rolling in from engineers to salespeople.

David bought an SL600 coupe and had it painted a customer's color to match his liking—a very dark purple that looked either black or deep purple, depending on the angle of the sun. He was a class act who wore $300 shirts, $2,000 suits, and $25,000 watches. I remember asking him about why he wore basic dress shoes, and he said, "'Cause I wear them out too fast."

We had brought in a new management team to take the company public, comprising individuals with experience in managing Wall Street professionals. Our new CEO and CFO have disk drive experience, including significant gains in fast-growing markets. Among the top executives, they all earned over $20 million each. I later found out that Dave had the highest wealth based on his vested stock. I knew he was talented, but I wondered how he had managed to have more wealth than the "new" management team. Apparently, during the 13 years leading up to the IPO, overseeing the company's operations was not always easy, and Dave stepped in to help cover Chong Moon's payroll. In return, he received compensation that, at the time, had little or no value. This was my first experience witnessing a lead-by-example situation where one person saved jobs for a few hundred workers and yet took no credit for his actions.

I traveled the world with the sales team at D Multimedia, learning from a fantastic person in a dedicated, aggressive, and workaholic team. On our trips, we would visit many countries at a time and deliver sales presentations to top OEM customers. The days were incredibly long, often starting at 6 am, with extensive traveling to multiple customers, dinners out, and then drinking until late. And then do it again the next day in a new country and new setting. Our group, including the country managers, typically consists of 7-10 persons, and the agenda covers specific details of our products and roadmaps. My role was to explore upcoming modem solutions that were new to D Multimedia, and we were taking a risk by entering the connectivity solutions market. I was typically included in presentations where we knew the audience and could leverage some trust.

Selling graphics accelerators was a challenge, but selling modem hardware proved to be even more complicated, as each country had its own unique telecom requirements. During my presentations, our team remained quiet because the overlap between graphics cards was minimal. However, they owned the customer relationships and put up with my techie slides. I did my best to speak in terms that would be easy to decipher and respect the audience. Feedback from my team was always positive, as I was essentially selling vaporware — since we did not have a product yet —while setting up anticipated products for the future. Our executive management team quickly learned that entering the modem market was very challenging, and the best way to compete with legacy players was to acquire a company already in the modem business and integrate it into our core. We found such a company in Oregon, purchased a small player, and then ignited the D Multimedia graphics sales channel to sell modems—no easy task or investment.

I mentioned the chaotic international sales trips with teams from the US and local country managers. Our global sales director would arrange back-to-back meetings in one country, then continue them across several countries. For our European trips, we would visit France, Germany, Italy, and Spain. In Asia, we would visit Korea, Japan, Singapore, and Taiwan. Most of the travel was by plane, but also included train (including the bullet train in Japan), subway, and extended taxi rides. New countries, new currencies, strange foods, and a new hotel every day. As a presenter, you needed to be on point with no time to get sick or miss a meeting for any reason. It was a work-hard, play-hard crew, and the adventures were hard to replicate. No matter how much alcohol we drank the night before, how few hours of sleep we experienced, the next day was a grind, and we all delivered according to plan. One of the most notable aspects was how the VP and the Director of Sales treated each team member with kindness and respect and kept everyone's whereabouts top of mind. There were times when we had to split the team and send a portion in one direction, then regroup later. Regardless of the situation, we always managed to come together. Traveling with a large team across several countries, time zones, and languages can be exhausting and really lonely if you ever get separated. The simple "no man left behind" attitude was practiced across the team. Cell phones had unique SIM cards for each country, and we would often make game plans for the day in case our schedules changed. As I reflect on the various management and sales teams I have been involved with, I credit this lead-by-example culture style as one that I will remember over the years.

Over the past 20+ years of sales trips and travel to exotic destinations, I have consistently maintained this "no man left behind" approach. I once took two very talented SME's to Thailand to present new technology opportunities to one of our high-volume factories. The general manager was very receptive to us and filled the conference rooms with anxious teammates to hear our case studies on medical and automotive gadgets. Both our speakers were excellent and provided unique insights on technology and manufacturing to support new business. Our evenings were free to explore Bangkok, and I did my best to be a good host. We ate exotic foods, drank a bunch, and went clubbing near Soi Cowboy (or Nanya). On our last day, we were to meet after breakfast for our hotel ride to the airport, and Matt was missing. We called and texted him to find out his whereabouts, but he didn't answer. We were in a foreign country, and he was my responsibility. I started to panic lightly and wondered what might have happened since we left each other the night before. Was he in trouble, lost his phone, or maybe overslept? We checked with the hotel, and they had not seen him. About 20 minutes later, he showed up with a smile on his face, having visited the local market to stock up on fruit and local snacks. It was good to see him, but honestly, we were upset that he didn't pick up his phone or let us know where he was, and we could see the obvious anxiety on our faces as we wondered what to do in a foreign country. Thankfully, no missing person report!

9.2 STAND UP

With a clear marketing presentation, every salesperson can effectively deliver the corporate message to customers. We are programmed to fill an hour meeting with PowerPoint slides that effectively cover every aspect of what we are selling. From the introduction, juicy details, and the "tell them what you told them" summary, each slide will eventually be memorized and played back grandly. We close our notebooks and thank the customer for their time and consideration as we head to our cars, smiling with success. We planned and delivered according to our best sales training, and we documented our weekly status with a check-in-the-box format.

This dated style works well if what you are selling can be easily bound and the buyer needs to hear your pitch. But what if you are facing a highly competitive situation with numerous variables, high stakes, and the buyer holds all the cards? They have done their homework and are currently evaluating a mix of competitors with no clear advantage to any provider. You have become a commodity and need to bring some differentiation.

Oren Klaff, author of "Pitch Anything[3]," provides his solution, called STRONG, which stands for Setting the Frame, Telling the Story, Revealing the Intrigue, Offering the Price, Nailing the Hookpoint, and Getting a Decision. When it comes to customer "Stand up" principles, he suggests that presentations should be concise (no more than 20 minutes), visual, and engaging. As the speaker, it is essential to grab attention quickly; you have only seconds to frame the meeting before the customer wanders off. Get to the point and don't overwhelm the customer with technical details. Communicate value simply and clearly. Present with confidence and don't seek approval. Signal that your solution is valuable and not for everyone. Engage with confidence and a slight air of challenge. You might also evoke curiosity and a bit of tension. Paradoxically, demonstrating a willingness to walk away increases your desirability. Klaff presents the neuroscience of pitching and describes the three parts of the brain: the crocodile brain, the midbrain, and the neocortex. The croc brain is the primal, threat-detecting, novelty-craving portion of the brain. Logic will come later. A pitch must feel safe, novel, high-status, and easy to act on before customers even consider the reasoning behind it. He stresses that the seller should not just present information to the customer. Control the frame, create intrigue, and be the prize; this is how you truly win the room.

A great salesperson's ability to "do stand up," meaning to present, improvise, or command a room in front of an audience, draws on a unique mix of skills developed through both sales experience and classic public-speaking or performance techniques. Great salespeople project confidence, maintain a strong posture, and make purposeful movements, immediately capturing the audience's attention. The best can "read the room," adjust tone, topics, and delivery based on audience dynamics, and smoothly handle interruptions or surprises. These salespeople can pivot easily between humor, seriousness, and storytelling, just as stand-up comedians respond to the crowd's energy. Top performers deliver concise, persuasive messages using vivid stories and real-life examples. They demonstrate high emotional intelligence, sending subtle mood shifts and responding empathetically to questions, skepticism, or enthusiasm. And, like every strong closer, they conclude with a decisive and motivating call to action.

Closing large transactions, especially at the C-suite level, requires not only mastering sales tactics but also embracing the true "art of the deal." Elite salespeople excel when the stakes are high and the audience comprises top executives. They don't just rely on good looks and fancy watches; they prepare, understand value, build trust, and guide the deal to a win.

Preparation for the bigger deals is key. Salespeople should always be overprepared, knowing the customer's organization's strategic priorities, current pain points, the competitive landscape, and key decision-makers. They create an organizational map of key stakeholders, identifying influential decision-makers and each executive's concerns. Review as much data as possible, analyze case studies, and determine the best solution to address any foreseeable future concerns. Remember, C-level buyers want outcomes. They live for return on investment (ROI), growth, risk mitigation, and strategic impact. As a salesperson, you must translate your offering into business results for your customer. Use their metrics, specific language, and industry benchmark. Lead with vision and set the stage by clarifying the "why" and "what's in it for them" before approaching the "how."

In every sales transaction, the customer takes a risk by selecting a vendor, and the larger the transaction, the greater the need to build trust among the parties. Plan with references for third-party validations, major client successes, and industry thought leaders. Sales leaders should be forthright and transparent, admit to limitations (if they exist), as C-suite audiences are trained to spot exaggerations or holes in the story. By demonstrating strong business acumen that aligns with your audience, you build trust and facilitate discussions of strategy, finance, and operational realities.

Command the room with executive storytelling. Open with a compelling narrative that ties your solution to the company's mission or current challenges. Use concise stories that highlight transformational results, not just incremental gains. If you feel the corporate material is overwhelming, be sure to clean it up by using minimal, supporting data that gets right to the point. Please do not waste a C-level executive's time, as they will likely remember and potentially avoid a similar experience in the future.

Conversely, if you're on the right path, the audience should engage with you and ask questions. It's ok to invite questions, especially when you lead them to the correct answer and move the marker in your favor. Be prepared to pivot the conversation in real-time, addressing any sensitive topics that arise. Use active listening skills to validate concerns and reflect what you hear to build rapport.

"Tell them what you told them." Summarize key agreements and reiterate the impact using common words that the customer can relate to.

Clearly articulate next steps and don't leave the meeting with any vague promises. If appropriate, present options that empower the C-suite to make informed choices, positioning them as the deal's protagonists.

It never ceases to amaze sales executives when the dialogue at the C-level comes down to the simplest questions. If you overcome all customer constraints and supply chain hurdles, the final portion of the sale often resembles grade-school dialogue. Be ready when the CEO asks, "Is there anything else they need to know before making a selection?" After presenting tons of detailed information for hours, the closing may be a simple question.

Always project confidence with calm authority, demonstrating you can deliver and support a large deal. Communicate urgency without manipulation and align your timing with your customer's real business needs. Send a tailored, high-level recap of the meeting within hours of your conversation. Provide only the actionable items, next steps, or strategic documents to respect the executive's time and attention. Use language that speaks to executives in clear, concise terms, emphasizing outcomes and benefits. Assume the note you are sending will be repurposed for internal use at the operational or board level. The higher the transaction level, the more straightforward, direct, and concise the messaging should be delivered.

When the Planets Align

In early 2025, as demand for generative AI and cloud infrastructure reached historic highs, hyperscalers rushed to secure next-generation GPU (Graphics Processing Unit) clusters. NVIDIA's top enterprise sales director recognized the opportunity to establish a strategic partnership and secure a deal valued at over $800 million. We will refer to her as "Suzy Smith" in this book. Suzy wasn't just a product expert; she was a market visionary with deep relationships across the Hyperscaler landscape. She tracked capital flows, listened closely to CTO whisper networks, and anticipated the rare window when customers would bid on n'Vidia's flagship processors, known as the Blackwell GB300 NLV72 cluster.

Her journey began at the Citadel campus in Nevada, where the company Switch was preparing to double its AI compute density. Suzy arrived with a custom analytics dashboard showing every Hyperscaler's competitive gaps, projected revenues, and power efficiency metrics against global benchmarks.

She met with Switch's CTO and key data center architects. Rather than sell specifications or speeds & feeds, she led with outcomes. "Deploying Blackwell across your next build isn't just an upgrade; it captures $250 million annual incremental revenue in new AI services and reduces per-rack operational costs by 19%. She then presented case studies and a timeline to stay ahead of Meta and Alibaba.

When conversations turned technical, Suzy anticipated every question on compatibility, cooling, and a competitive chip roadmap. She had pre-negotiated NVIDIA engineering support on liquid-cooled rack deployments and mapped out supply assurance for delivery amid global chip shortages.

Suzy also orchestrated executive-level alliances, connecting Switch's CEO with NVIDIA leadership for strategic planning and alignment of the future roadmap. Every meeting concluded with clear decisions and next steps; contracts, due diligence, and deployment phases were all summarized in concise, one-page executive memos.

Her competitor tried last-minute discounts, but Suzy's trusted, date-driven approach and commitment to joint innovation won the deal. By the following quarter, Switch signed an $800 million GPU contract, launching one of the world's largest AI factories powered by NVIDIA's latest technology. Her success wasn't just technical; it was built on anticipation, consultative presence, and the artful ability to frame NVIDIA's value in terms that make Hyperscaler leadership move quickly. NVIDIA's top salesperson built enormous trust, sold value, and helped define the future for C-suite executives leading the AI data center race.

9.3 CLEAR THE ROOM

Over the past 25 years, I have participated in dozens of sales meetings, where keynote speakers provided direction and mission statements to guide sales teams. Interestingly, speakers with lower management titles would often fill their slides with too much information and complex strategies that required several slides to convey. They would come from engineering or marketing folks who knew every word and inch of the material and could clearly communicate the messages.

Interestingly, as the speakers rotated from managers, directors, and vice presidents to the C-level, the amount of material per page had one thing in common: less is better. If a CEO/CFO/COO had more than three or four slides, they were speaking too much. The messages were elegant, direct, concise, and unambiguous. If the company vision needed a refresh or reminder, that would become clear. Perhaps the competition was intensifying in a key area of the business, and a simple graph could illustrate market share or a significant competitor's win.

Room A or B

One of the most memorable sales meetings was held at a corporate venue with a conference room that accommodated several hundred people. After a few cups of coffee and some small talk among competing salespeople, we assembled in the main room. The CCO welcomed everyone to the event and proceeded with the agenda. Just one slide that read the following message: "Please see your email and room assignments." After which, everyone glanced at their phones to read their emails and assignments. My email was a bit cryptic and said Please attend the 10 a.m. session in Room A. I wondered if this was an alphabetical assignment or some other crazy order. I topped off my coffee and heard several folks talking about their assignments, which seemed to include either Room A or Room B. I took my seat and glanced around at what looked like about half the team. When everyone was seated, the CEO appeared and, with his usual commanding voice, praised us all for our hard work and dedication. He expressed concern that the business would become more competitive, our solutions would become increasingly complex, and that we needed to improve our team. Everyone was fully attentive and listening to every word spoken. No slides, no BS. As the great storyteller that he was, he described a famous sales challenge which resulted in one winner and many losers. He touched on the methods employed by the winning team and how they navigated through adversity.

The Cut

Then came the news. He said the folks in room A have been selected as the "go forward" sales team and will be reassembling later with the following assignment. On three slides, list your top three accounts and how you will win them over. We were to be specific in our approaches and identify anything in the organization that may be required to complete the win. There should be enough details to execute a strategy and schedule, and this would become our marching orders. He closed by wishing us good luck and said he would see us all in the afternoon. The others, in room B, would be sent home. Suddenly, half the team was gone, and those of us who remained would be the new strategic sales team. It was quick, concise, and very effective. No waiting to see what might happen or who "might" be affected. I headed back to my hotel room and began to assemble my trio of strategic accounts with more clarity than ever.

Amazing, how well this method works. It may not be suitable for everyone or every situation, but it was effective for a team that had become complacent. At the same time, the competition sought to dislodge us from our #1 position. It was also my first time working for a company that had established a leading position in the market, characterized by a dominant market share, high customer satisfaction, and effective factory utilization. Our company was the envy of our competition, and they used every easy trick to gain share, including price dumping, stealing employees, and telling our customers unbelievable stories to try to displace our leadership. After all, when you are on top, everyone wants a piece of you and will try every tactical scheme to beat you down. It was one thing to study market leadership in business school; it was another to be on the winning team and watch your management team reduce the salesforce by 50% to motivate top performers to become great performers.

9.4 INTERVIEWING SALES LEADERS

Finding top salespeople is notoriously challenging for several reasons, and standard interview processes often fail to identify the best talent. When seeking a complex skill set, it isn't easy to find that rare combination of drive, emotional intelligence, resilience, strategic thinking, and adaptability. For many companies, past success isn't always predictive due to differences in industry, customer type, and sales cycle complexity. Traditional interviews alone are insufficient; however, some methods may help weed out the chaff. The most effective interviewing methods combine structured behavioral assessments, live skill demonstrations, and rigorous simulations to evaluate candidates.

Before starting the interview process and collecting a massive amount of resumes from a job posting, spend a few minutes looking for new candidates. Ask the hiring manager to write down a short list of "wants," and condense these into a filter to begin your search. If you want someone with dual degrees, 15 years of experience, and a history of multi-million-dollar achievements, ensure the pile of resumes has these qualifications as a minimum. Be specific in your search and don't settle for anything less than what you want. Please treat this as an opportunity, not an exercise; it should feel like an invitation to a club with very high standards, from which only a select group is qualified. You are building a SWAT team and have a direct mission. If you hire four strong candidates and one weak one, the team will struggle to respect you.

The strongest hiring managers have assessment tools that require candidates to complete before they begin the interview process. Examine the responses to cognitive and personality tests to identify aspects such as drive, competitiveness, emotional control, and problem-solving abilities. Can the candidate respond to difficult questions or think on their feet? Ask about wins and losses, and listen carefully to how the candidate describes each experience, noting the authenticity and quality of the responses. Did they provide sufficient responses to warrant a full interview?

Some role-playing will open new doors, especially the unexpected ones. I endured a challenging interview with a CEO who brought two bottles of water to the meeting. The role was for a VP of Sales at a very complex semiconductor manufacturing company with extensive technical requirements. I had done all my homework and was prepared to answer a host of questions with well-thought-out responses. After handing me one of the waters, he asked me to sell him the bottle. It was a quick curveball and icebreaker to see if I could handle a simple request and adapt to what was probably more challenging than discussing the technology in his factory. I proceeded to describe the sparkling water's features and benefits, as well as the brand's key attributes. I referenced the origin of the water and the health properties to improve one's everyday lifestyle. The CEO inquired about competition, pricing, and the delivery schedule, which were the exact questions he would later ask regarding the technology job. Thankfully, I passed the "water" test and successfully navigated the rest of the technical questions, followed by a series of interviews with the entire executive team. This form of role-playing is excellent for checking the box on adaptability, but it is only a small gate to pass through in the overall process.

The Name Game

When in doubt, time to play the "Name Game." My father, a brilliant physicist, was also well-known for his exceptional hiring skills. He was responsible for research and development in thin-film optical coatings during a period when the industry's most advanced work was being done. Still, candidates also needed a strong academic foundation. Typically, this meant a PhD from the University of Rochester, UC Berkeley, or Arizona State University. During the interview process, candidates would visit the plant, observe the advanced methods, meet with several key team members, and then have the opportunity to address their biggest challenge. Remember, this was a person who grew up teaching his teachers about science and determining how many metal layers were ideal for achieving the proper translucency in the windows of the Space Shuttle.

The interview would start cordially, allowing the would-be candidate to explain their background and perhaps their academic thesis. If there were any questions, the dialogue would often be brief, since there weren't many experts in the field. After a while, Dr. A. would go up to the whiteboard and start jotting down several terms in a matrix. The following conversation began with a mix of acronyms, random or significant numbers, and letters. He would ask the candidate to explain any or all of the terms and what they meant to them.

2-Ltr	3-Ltr	4-Ltr	5-Ltr	Number
AI	B2B	ASAP	13485	2.54
BS	BTW	GDPR	CRISP	2.71
DM	FYI	HTML	FAFSA	3.14
IT	IDK	NASA	NAACP	26.2
PR	ISO	SWOT	OSHAI	212
UK	OOO	TTYL	TGTBT	911

Figure 9.3. The Name Game

Affectionately known as "The Name Game," candidates might pick a number like "2.71" and explain that it is Euler's number and how it is used in natural logarithms. And then, perhaps "NASA" and what the space agency meant to them - maybe the Apollo missions to the moon. But, more importantly, the fun would be around the softer terms like "TGTBT" or "TTYL" when the person might know what the letters stood for; however, they would struggle to explain what is meant by "too good to be true." Assuming the conversations continued and sufficient dialogue covered all the necessary points, a dinner out with the candidate and their significant other (as applicable) was the final step.

Recruiters

There are mixed reviews on whether recruiters are necessary in the hiring process. The benefits are evident: top recruiters use their skills daily and have developed a reputation for finding excellent candidates. The top recruiters will list their past successes in placing C-level executives and managers across diverse industries. The top retained recruiters include Heidrick & Struggles, Korn Ferry, Russell Reynolds, and Spencer Stuart, which charge upwards of 35% of the hire's first-year salary. They typically assign a small team to the task and use organizational charts, databases, and a well-established network to accomplish the job.

However, there is one drawback to using recruiters. Statistics suggest that top recruiters have a success rate of approximately 60% (with some estimates as high as 80%), corresponding to a 40% failure rate, with many searches remaining uncompleted. These poor numbers may not reflect the firm or the search; instead, the task has a very low success rate. It is believed that artificial intelligence is improving the hiring process by over 50% and more internal human resource teams are taking on the challenge of pre-screening candidates. Unfortunately, every company has unique hiring criteria, and they are likely the best people to know the company culture and, hopefully, the hiring manager's hot buttons.

For many reasons, interviewing can be one of the more challenging tasks for sales leaders. Like most managers, recruiting is a more strenuous exercise than motivating your existing sales team to achieve better results. They organized a plan to staff with the right team elements, including SMEs, hunters, farmers, and sales operations, which can be a nightmare. However, one of the most important things to remember is that dream teams are only built once. If you invest in the process, you can assemble a highly competitive group of sales leaders.

9.5 ABSOLUTE FOCUS

Several professions require the highest level of focus, including Formula 1 racers, surgeons, concert musicians, airline pilots, and legal professionals. These roles demand extraordinary concentration, decision-making under pressure, and sustained cognitive and physical effort, with even brief lapses having significant consequences. Brad Pitt's new movie, "F1," depicts the life of a Formula 1 driver, offering an intense, full-throttle, and immersive cinematic experience. The racing scenes are considered hyper-realistic, providing a visceral feeling of speed and motion, particularly through the use of cockpit-mounted cameras and actors driving real

F1-modified cars. Similarly, the TV series "Pitt" draws you into the intense daily activities of an ER medical team in Pittsburgh, with footage so realistic that it is almost hard to watch. It's just gory enough to make you look forward to the next episode. Pilots and air traffic controllers are responsible for hundreds of lives on each flight, making split-second operational decisions while monitoring many variables for hours. Their focus must not lag for even a moment.

Salespeople often have a high-pressure job that requires significant focus and resilience, although the intensity and type of focus differ from those of an F1 driver or surgeon. Salespeople must maintain concentration to navigate complex negotiations, meet quotas, manage rejection, and stay organized across multiple opportunities, often in a fast-paced and stressful environment.

Sales roles require multitasking and focus to hit targets, find and nurture leads, and close deals while filtering out distractions. The best performers enter a "flow" state, prioritizing key activities and balancing simultaneous client interactions, administrative tasks, and strategy sessions.

The often relentless performance targets create daily pressure, demanding constant attention to numbers, prospects, and deal flow. Salespeople are always on and in competitive environments, and frequent rejection can lead to anxiety, requiring mental discipline to refocus and persist. Always being available at all hours and maintaining strong client relationships make it difficult to fully disconnect from work, further heightening stress and demanding ongoing focus.

While intense focus on sales is usually directed toward people skills, deal management, and mental resilience, rather than split-second life-or-death decisions, it is still essential for success and well-being in the field. Many experts and studies identify sales as one of the most mentally demanding and stressful careers, requiring stamina, resilience, and sustained attention to succeed.

As an avid tennis player when I was younger, I always admired the top professionals who could manage their game during intense competition. In recent years, Jannik Sinner, from Italy, has been widely recognized for his hyper-focused approach, characterized by supreme mental resilience and the ability to stay fully present and calm under pressure on the court. Sinner has emphasized the importance of remaining mentally focused, especially during intense matches, such as his five-and-a-half-hour battle on clay (against Carlos Alcaraz in the 2025 French Open), where he maintained concentration despite missing critical match points. His ability to stay "mentally focused without any complaints," as he describes, is seen as a key factor in his rise to Grand Slam contention.

Where to Focus

A good friend tells a story of an event where he was nearly killed and saved by mental focus. It was at a time in his life when long-distance running was his vice, helping him escape his mind from work and other troubles. He was not a runner, but the activity would draw all his resources and had a self-satisfying effect that made it worthwhile. Most of the runs were over 5 miles long, and he picked new routes to keep him curious, always wanting to explore more places.

On this particular day, he found himself on a run with an overpass bridge up ahead. Halfway across the bridge, he noticed it wasn't complete and was still under construction. In fact, the path he was on changed from a smooth road to a more and more narrow path until he realized it was just a 16" beam and a 100-foot drop to a dry riverbed. His mind quickly shifted from worrying about his stride and breathing to maintaining balance and managing the fear of falling. One of the key messages he shared was that if he looked straight down and worried about the very next step, he would likely drive himself crazy and likely fall. However, if he looked ahead to the end of the bridge, there were over 50 strides to safety, and that was challenging to the point of panic. In an instant, he raised his arms to support his balance, slowed his pace, and focused on the steps just about three or four strides away. His eyes watched the center of the beam, and he took a step with confidence that he could reach the mini goal. By keeping the task as a small win, he broke down the longer challenge into small steps that led to more small steps until he reached the other side of the bridge.

9.6 ELITE SELLING

When I was in my late 20s, I visited the US Olympic Training Facilities in Colorado Springs, Colorado. My passion was to enter the world of sports medicine and solve complex problems for athletes who suffered injuries or chronic diseases. During the visit, a group of elite runners on the track caught my attention. They were in fantastic shape and gliding around the track like gazelles. I asked one of the trainers about the study (every exercise regimen was part of it), and he said they were studying blood flow and lactic acid production.

They had several groups of some of the nation's top distance runners, and they participated in short 1-mile runs at altitude (6,000 ft above sea level). They started with 5:00-minute mile times and performed blood draws after each set. During the cool-down periods (under 5 minutes), the test results were reported, and then another set was conducted at a slightly faster pace. The next race was run at a 4:45-minute pace, followed by a 4:30-minute pace, and finally a 4:15-minute mile pace.

There were over 30 men and women in the group, each a local record holder in their community. Their ages ranged from 16 to 28, and most were heading to the early Olympic trials with hopes of making the team. What was even more impressive than their speed and efficiency on the track was the results of their blood test. For the majority of the group, they did not produce any lactic acid—a condition where the blood is starved of oxygen—until they ran below 4 minutes and 15 seconds. Remember, this was at a mile-high altitude and at speeds fast enough to win many collegiate races. To qualify for the Olympic trials, the men needed a time under 3:50, and the women under 4:20. These were elite runners!

CHAPTER 10
SELL SMARTER

THE ART of selling may be aging gracefully as we move into the next phase of technology influence. Over the past 25 years, there has been significant growth in sales tools, informational databases, social media platforms, and the ability to survive through a pandemic. After 2025, we will forever be known as the generation that embraced artificial intelligence and became "smarter" salespeople. Every aspect of our daily lives will use technologies that incorporate some form of AI, and we will assess our current skill set —empathy, active listening, and self-awareness —to become the best we can be.

For some salespeople, being considered intelligent may be a compliment, while being intimidated by software tools that automate the "selling" process by leveraging repetitive tasks may be a threat. However, the elite salesperson will take on the challenge of learning how to use a combination of artificial and emotional sales and thrive in the new paradigm.

To "Sell Smarter" is to leverage our unique abilities in emotional intelligence, which have been our strengths in managing human relationships, and to incorporate the key strengths of artificial intelligence, thereby undoubtedly enhancing our sales persona. The new sales leaders will be those who know their strengths and manage their AI and EQ to achieve superior results.

10.1 KNOW YOUR INTELLIGENCE

Salespeople need to understand their unique blend of intelligence, including a mixture of the "intelligences." We spoke earlier in Chapter 1 that we can categorize dozens of intelligences that reside in our basal ganglia (the center of the brain) or surge to the forefront in our frontal cortex, where we support reasoning, problem-solving, planning, and working memory. Knowing your own intelligence is not a science experiment; rather, it is about gaining a better understanding that several factors influence how we process information. As salespeople, we want to understand how we respond to conditions that impact our daily activities.

We have all endured standardized testing, in which we are subjected to scientifically validated personality and intelligence tests that assess logical reasoning, analytical thinking, problem-solving, and core cognitive strengths. We also offer personality-focused emotional intelligence exams that measure empathy, resilience, adaptability, self-awareness, and impulse control. For those who want more granularity, sales personality and ability tests are available, such as SalesDrive, TestGorilla, and Hire Talent Sales Ability. I can count on one hand the last time anyone shared their scores on these tests or even had the experience of being part of a sales team focus group to better understand their aptitude in selling. The pessimist would say these tests don't work, but the honest criticism is that the data don't predict whether you are skilled at selling. The data can be collected and stored in an HR file with other assessments, but very few managers will single out the "winners" of the standardized test challenge. Keep your GPA and IQ scores to yourself.

To know more about yourself is to pause and reflect on your style in key situations. In sales, this is a daily occurrence: customer issues can swing the pendulum from rejection to celebration, and from uncertainty to closing deals. As you become your own coach, you may analyze how you handle business "swings" and how you respond to them. Evaluate your recent transactions, both good and bad deals, and assess which intelligence profiles were most active and effective for you. Gather multi-dimensional feedback from your peers or managers, and if appropriate, even leverage client feedback about your greatest strengths and weaknesses. You may uncover information during the post-mortem that will help you in similar deals in the Future. Receiving transparent feedback is also a healthy path to closure, helping you with the painful reminder that you spent months or even years putting a deal together, only to find that the customer has selected another vendor. The longer the sales cycle, the more self-help should be applied.

Be careful, some of your intelligence may change over time. Let's break down a few of the more apparent changes. Your IQ score, if you have one, was likely taken in your youth and should remain relatively stable into adulthood. However, your "fluid" intelligence—the ability to reason quickly and solve new problems—declines gradually after early adulthood, but "crystalized" intelligence—the knowledge gained through learning and experience—increases with age. Similarly, emotional intelligence (EQ) can increase with age, particularly in understanding and regulating emotions, empathy, and stress management. EQ can be significantly improved through training, self-reflection, and targeted interventions. Studies show workplace and academic EQ training drives lasting improvements in emotional skills. Older adults often exhibit higher emotional intelligence due to lifelong learning and accumulated experience, which enhances their ability to navigate challenging situations and relationships.

Both IQ and EQ are dynamic and influenced by life circumstances, learning experiences, and deliberate personal development. EQ, in particular, is not a fixed value. It can be intentionally developed and tends to show measurable gains with maturity, education, and training. In Travis Bradberry's book, "Emotional Intelligence Habits," he dedicates a chapter to increasing your intelligence. He says IQ explains about 20% of you, with the other 80% coming from EQ. He asks a few simple questions, such as whether you were an early reader, if you are left-handed, if you took music lessons as a kid, and whether you are funny. If you answered "yes" to many of these questions, you may have enjoyed a higher-than-normal IQ growing up. He shares other interesting facts about using a graph in a report and about using a middle initial in your name, which can increase your perceived IQ. He cautions against being or acting too bright in simple situations and reminds us of the simple problem. "A bat and a ball cost a dollar and ten cents. The bat costs a dollar more than the ball. How much does the ball cost? Hint: if you blurted out ten cents, you should reconsider your answer, take a deep breath, and lean in on five cents.

There is no doubt that a higher EQ score will enhance sales skills and support sales in more complex environments. The Journal of Applied Psychology showed that individuals with a higher EQ earned \$29,000/yr more than their peers with lower scores. Add to our intelligence mix the integration of artificial intelligence into our sales operations, web searches, and customers' toolsets, and we may need to perform IQ/EQ quick checks, much like changing the oil in our cars. If there are new updates every quarter on how both sellers and buyers operate across their purchasing and networking platforms, we will need our own "intelligence dashboard" to manage ourselves. Like a software update, we will upload our daily experiences to our EQ headquarters. Those engaged in professional development, such as sales, leadership, or coaching, prefer to refresh their EQ skills every 6 to 12 months. Have you had your EQ checked recently?

10.2 ACTION FALLACY

In Martin Gutmann's TED Talk, "Why Do We Celebrate Incompetent Leaders[1]," he cautions that we often mistake charisma, action, and dramatic storytelling for actual leadership competence. He uses examples of two famous explorers (Ernest Shackleton and Roald Amundsen) who each undertook remarkable expeditions. He carefully runs through each of their experiences, where Candidate A was the first explorer to successfully reach the North & South Poles, as well as the Northeast and

Northwest passages. Candidate B set off for the Antarctic four times and failed on three of these attempts. Gutmann poses the question, "Who should we hire for our expedition?" Of course, the obvious answer is Candidate A, the successful one.

However, the truly gifted one is Candidate B (Ernest), who has been the most celebrated polar explorer of all time. His leadership role models have been captured in best-selling books, blogs, documentaries, podcasts, and an endless stream of social media posts. Meanwhile, (Roland) by any metric, the most successful explorer has largely been forgotten. No fewer than 26 books have been written celebrating Shackleton's leadership qualities.

The action fallacy in leadership is the mistaken belief that great leaders are those who constantly act, generate drama, and respond to crises visibly, regardless of whether those actions lead to meaningful or positive results. This bias causes organizations and societies to favor leaders who are highly vocal, bold, and dramatic. These are the ones who "save the day" during emergencies, while overlooking those who achieve success through careful planning, prevention, and quieter, less conspicuous efforts.

Shakleton

Gutmann describes Shackleton as a classic example of the action fallacy, celebrated for his epic struggle for survival and dramatic crisis management during his Endurance expedition. Shackleton's leadership is marked by energetic attempts to overcome harrowing odds, surprising stories, and constant heroic action, which business schools and books often highlight as the quintessential model.

Amundson

In contrast, Amundsen is portrayed as the unseen leader. Gutmann notes, "Amundsen dedicated his life to understanding the polar environment and made every decision, in planning and in execution, with a nuanced awareness of the environment around him. The result was a series of immensely successful expeditions, but so drama-free that they fit poorly with our conception of a master leader." Amundsen's achievements stemmed not from crisis management but from methodical preparation, keen adaptation to reality, and the prevention of problems to such an extent that his results were often attributed to "luck" by traditionalists.

True leaders are authentic and bring out the best in people. This authenticity comes from self-awareness and integrity. These leaders build trust through transparent relationships and consistent moral values. Authentic leaders welcome and thoughtfully consider dissenting opinions, encouraging honest feedback within their teams. They follow through on commitments and model dependable, disciplined behavior for their teams.

Planning and action behind the scenes are crucial for effective leadership because they lay the foundation for organizational stability and trust, often in ways that are not immediately visible but that directly impact outcomes when challenges arise. Quiet planning and preparation enable leaders to see storms before they become hurricanes, allowing them to anticipate potential problems and address them proactively. The prepared leader fosters a positive environment within their team by mentoring, facilitating collaboration, and recognizing individual contributions. Strategic planning allows leaders to allocate budgets, time, and talent where they will be most effective. Leaders who operate in the background encourage others to step forward, take initiative, and innovate, empowering teams rather than dominating the spotlight.

I was in charge of our recent sales team meeting and put together an agenda for a 2-day event with each hour planned and topics well-defined. To energize the team, the day began with a gift presented to each of them. On the first day, these were puzzles, fidgets, and a few flying saucers. It was like a kid's birthday party, complete with some fun over their coffee. Lunch on the first day was provided by a guest speaker from the factory, who described some unique challenges that customers often overlook.

When we returned after lunch, I presented them with a quiz, each question about the factory. The questions were multiple-choice, made learning fun, and helped the sales team remember key metrics about our sales offering.

The training ended in the early afternoon, in time for a freshen up before dinner out. We visited a local brewpub and invited several managers from engineering, quality, and IT to join us and contribute to discussions with the sales team. We limited the alcohol and went back to the hotel before midnight. Day two also started with a wrapped gift. This time, each salesperson received a gift that reflected their strengths or passions. Although these were inexpensive gifts, they were each very well received, and it was clear that thought had gone into each purchase. We went through more sales strategies, and then it was time for lunch. We went to a cafe nearby and rented a large room. This time, we added a few executives to the mix and increased our anxiousness a few notches. For some of the salespeople, it was their first time meeting with these folks, and the exchanges were priceless. After returning to the sales meeting, we ended with awards, trophies, and a custom t-shirt. Those who had to catch flights headed out, and the rest returned to their hotels before a late dinner, followed by some pool time, darts, and bourbon shots. While sitting at the bar, several of the salespeople praised the meeting as one of the best they had attended in a long time. They had fun, learned more than they ever expected, and the planning paid off. A year later, at the next sales meeting, groups from other sales departments decided to join our team, causing a stir among the other leaders. Speak softly, and carry a big stick.

Senior "Loudership"

Over half the companies I have been lucky to work with have held the notion that leaders are those who speak often and loudly. Group meetings are about who controls the narrative, regardless of the content. I am always amazed by senior leadership who feel it is necessary to speak up regarding a matter they are neither an expert in nor knowledgeable about, and yet they rant about potential outcomes. They build a house of cards and invite you to watch as it collapses during any rebuttal.

Conversely, it is always a pleasure to listen and watch a leader who is unconcerned with what other people are thinking and willing to give credit where credit is due, even if it's not blowing their own horn. Say "no" to self-aggrandizing words. When a senior leader references a key contribution from a peer or lower manager, it is a sign that they are about improving the overall good. This behavior is even more respected when they use this example to illustrate a new direction they want to pursue and provide evidence that shows they have done their homework.

During a conversation with Sir Jony Ive (Ref "A conversation with Jony Ive, YouTube[2]), the moderator asks about the design team rituals. Jony replies: There is nothing more important to me than the creative team, and declaring them, being clear about this is my contribution, and therefore I need to be part of an extraordinary team. He goes on to express his concern about working with a small team that really trusts and loves each other, and you'll be in danger of actually listening. He says," To be quiet and to listen - and one of the things that terrifies me, I know that I have missed really amazing ideas that came from a peaceful place, from a calm person."

It often feels like senior leaders are paid to talk rather than to listen. They plan their day around meetings in which they are the key speaker, and even in casual settings, they need to dominate the conversation. How many remember that the talk-to-listen ratio should be under 50%? In fact, most recommend listening up to 80% of the time. The simplest measure is a talk-to-listen ratio near 1:2 (33% talking, 67% listening). This style emphasizes the team and what's on their minds. The more leaders ask of their team, the more they should look for feedback, openness, and decision-making from the team. Impactful leadership works when the entire team is aligned, and everyone in the room has a voice.

Informal Gatherings

A common technique for building support from your team is to use informal gatherings to expand your circle of influence. Instead of having just coffee and donuts during break, consider an immersion event to spice things up. A good friend of mine is an event planner in the Bay Area who works with multi-billion-dollar "search engine" companies to host events at their larger venues. Over the past couple of months, he hosted a Southeast Asia-themed gathering to celebrate ASEAN Day, featuring Thai food and Vietnamese desserts. At another conference, they wanted to celebrate Led Zeppelin, complete with their music, posters, and other merchandise, creating a concert-like experience. Employees became increasingly interested in the sessions, as each break was filled with fun entertainment and buzz.

Understanding the action fallacy is critical because it encourages reflection before action and helps prevent inefficient, impulsive, or wasteful decisions. Leaders who rely on a high listen-to-talk ratio will inspire and empower their teams. And finally, those who feel that they must take credit for someone else's work are like stealing or even plagiarism. For many companies, there are no immediate consequences, but the organization is much more innovative than they may let on. Most CEOs can identify bad seeds over time and will take corrective actions before this behavior becomes a habit. Reward the strategic thinkers, promote those who lead by example, and publicly recognize high performers who prioritize results over style or volume.

10.3 2-AXIS GOSPELS

Leadership and self-help books are renowned for creating phrases or acronyms that encapsulate a new approach to solving a problem. Whether the author is famous for inventing Atomic Habits, SPIN Selling, STRONG, Radical Candor, or The Challenger Sale, they each have their place on our shelves. The 2-axis approach is perfect in that it exudes simplicity. There are just two axes and typically four or fewer categories (one in each quadrant). High-paid consulting firms have passed down the infamous "4-blocker" grid to support a path to new decision-making. The method forces the author to summarize any situation into four key topics.

In Kim Scott's book, "Radical Candor[3]," she describes a unique management philosophy that combines caring personally and challenging directly, soliciting criticism to improve leadership, and providing guidance that helps others grow and develop.

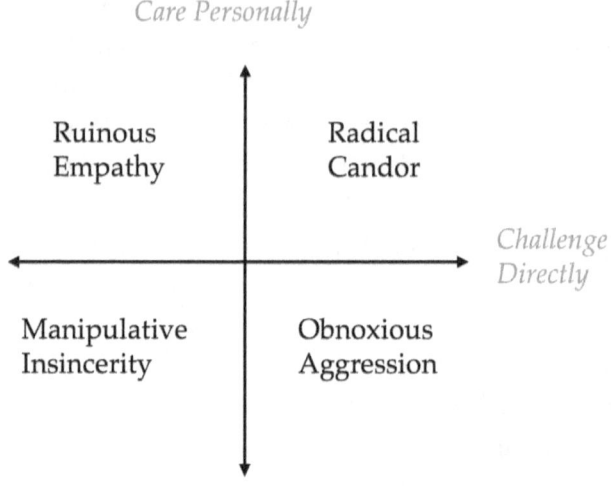

Figure 10.1 Radical Candor

Urgent / Not Urgent

Another popular visual is the Eisenhower Matrix (ref: The Champion Leader pg 93, Christopher Conners, and The AI Edge, pg 54 by Jeb Blount), which helps teams define what is urgent and essential ("Do"), and then compare these activities to the lesser quadrants of not urgent and not necessary (or "Eliminate"). In each of the four quadrants, the "intake" or inputs for a program are defined and placed in their respective boxes according to urgency, risk, ownership, and schedule. After conducting this simple exercise with your organization, the strategic implications will guide you on the tactical tasks you need to accomplish and the distractions you need to avoid.

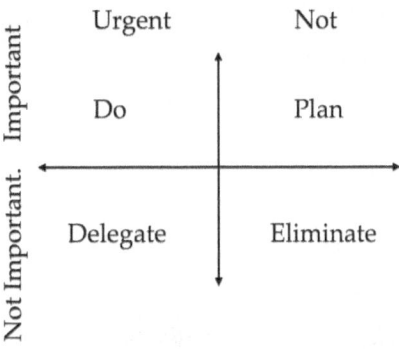

Figure 10.2 Eisenhower Matrix

Early in my career, I was the CEO of a startup with a limited budget to hire enough engineers for our project. It involved both analog and digital semiconductor designs, and we had a plan of record, laid out by our head of engineering, complete with detailed incremental tasks, to complete a very complex chipset. The engineering managers were excellent and understood the process steps, enabling them to assign risks and approximate completion schedules easily. During one of the more challenging and early design phases, we met as a group with the founders and faced the reality that we had more work than time or money to spare. After some heated discussions and nearing burnout, I slowly drew the Eisenhower Matrix on the board and asked the team to help categorize the key tasks into the four quadrants. I then realized how powerful this simple matrix was, and it started to make sense. Although not everyone agreed with the assignments or definitions of importance or urgency, we settled on the groupings. At the end of the meeting, we understood the "Do" quadrant as key to what would later become the funding milestones, which enabled near consensus.

For those who have experienced a RACI exercise, you'll greatly appreciate how the simplified 2-axis approach can reduce a complex set of tasks to a set of priorities and a new plan of record. The RACI method is ideal for assigning clear roles within an organization and allocating accountability, with the following designations: R = Responsible, A = Accountable, C = Consulted, and I = Informed. These two methods can be complementary, with RACI clarifying "who," and Eisenhower clarifying "when and what," to achieve success.

Givers, Takers, & Matchers

In Adam Grant's book, "Give and Take[4]," he proposes that people operate in one of three reciprocity styles in the workplace and other interactions. He categorizes individuals as Givers, Takers, and Matchers. The givers are people who consistently help others without expecting anything in return. Givers can be found at both the bottom and top of the success ladder. Successful givers are often strategic in their giving, focusing their efforts where they can have the most impact and creating a culture of giving around them. They usually build stronger relationships and networks over the long run, as others come to trust and appreciate their generosity. Takers are individuals who seek to gain more than they contribute and prioritize their own interests over others' needs. They are cautious and self-protective in their interactions and may strategically help others only if it benefits them. In the long term, takers may struggle to build trust and lasting relationships, which can hinder their success. And finally, matchmakers are individuals who strive to maintain a balanced approach between giving and taking. Their approach is characterized by a "you scratch my back, I'll scratch your" mentality, expecting reciprocation when they help someone. Matchers tend to reward givers and punish takers, contributing to a sense of fairness and reciprocity within a group.

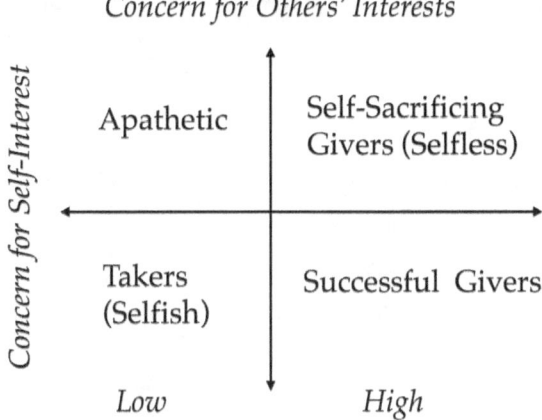

Figure 10.3 Adam Grant's Give and Take Matrix

Leveraging the 2-axis visuals helps clarify a key direction while presenting either the opposite behavior, nearby or similar traits, and eventually spells out the obvious direction as the author's main point. Across leadership books, these simple x-y graphs allow readers to identify common behaviors and draw on examples that are very common in the workplace. Additionally, many of these methods serve as the framework for teaching, consulting, and mentoring. Below are some additional author/matrix examples used in sales or management leadership.

Book & Author	2-Axis Framework	Notes
To Sell is Human, Daniel Pink	Attunement vs Assertiveness	Compares skill sets, finds balanace crucial in modern selling
The Challenger Sale, Dixon & Adamson	Teach vs Tailor	Profiles reps using behavior axes
Coaching Salespeople into Sales Champtions, Keith Rosen	Skill vs Will	Coaching approach based on rep's motivation & capability
The Qualified Sales Leader, John McMahon	Influence vs Authority	Identifies true power in sales opportunities
SPIN Selling, Neil Rackham	Need-Payoff vs Situaion Implication	Map questioning and positioning strategies
Eat Their Lunch, Anthony Iannarino	Value Creation vs Competitive Displacement	Positioning for winning customer over competitors
Cracking the Sales Management Code, Joran & Vzaana	Activity vs Results	Optimizing what managers measure and prioritize

Figure 10.4 2-Axis Book & Author Examples

10.4 4D SELLING

The next generation of high-performing salespeople will require a more complex set of traits to match the world they are selling into. The buyers are raising the bar in terms of height to satisfy their needs, and all essential deals will include more transaction pathways. If this were a game, the length of the field has just gotten longer and broader, and the smooth grass is now an all-terrain mess with hidden obstacles. The days of surfing the web, networking on LinkedIn, plugging data into Salesforce, and sending out a routine HubSpot sequence are the most table stakes in your arsenal. The best will become multidimensional and chameleon-like to set themselves apart from the competition. Why would anyone settle for just a farmer when they can have a hunter-farmer hybrid in two dimensions, add emotional intelligence for a third dimension, and complete the mix with artificial intelligence for a fourth dimension? An actual "4D salesperson" fluidly transitions between winning new business and maximizing existing relationships, all while blending technical and human skills to outperform in hybrid environments.

Accordingly, the buyer-seller relationship is undergoing a fundamental shift with the advent of artificial intelligence. The new seller can
deliver highly personalized messaging by analyzing vast amounts of
real-time data about buyer behaviors, preferences, and intent signals.
Repetitive sales tasks — such as lead qualification, data entry, and
proposal comparisons — are now automated, freeing up salespeople to
focus on relationship building and strategic engagement. Sales and sales
operations team members should make proactive proposals as a standard matter of new approaches. A well-written prompt (perhaps several
pages in length) will generate a pre-meeting strategy and supporting
data to outline a proposal. A first meeting with the customer transitions
from introductory small talk to a more engaging discussion, using
customer information to address the buyer's needs. Data does not replace
face-to-face interactions; however, it should accelerate the conversations
with early buyer-seller collaboration.

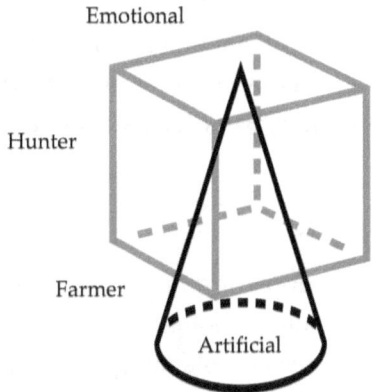

Figure 10.5 4D Selling

In turn, buyers can leverage AI tools for more innovative research,
product comparisons, and informed decision-making, thereby
compressing sales cycles and enabling more effective negotiations. AI
empowers buyers to be informed well beyond their local domain. At the

time of this writing, the US was implementing tariffs that had a dramatic impact on the global supply chain from its trading partners. Parts and services that utilize low-cost regions, such as Asia, are often subject to significantly higher fees. One popular analysis is the iPhone, which Foxconn produces in China and India. With Chinese tariffs ranging from 34% to 55%, the price of an iPhone 16 would increase from $799 to over $ 1,100. A meeting with a buyer that was once bound by simple supply chain constraints has now become a discussion about the global economy, where the price of doing business is highly determined by the location of your factories or the relationship your CEO has with the White House.

In Bruce Willis' movie "The Fifth Element," the four classical elements—earth, air, fire, and water — are described, and then love is added as the fifth element. This "love" refers to the aether, a mysterious substance believed to permeate the celestial sphere and to be purer than any of the four material elements. Historically, the notion of a fifth element was broached by Plato and later by Aristotle, but neither philosopher used the term. Is there a possibility of a fifth dimension in sales? Hang on, Star Trek fans, perhaps when we teach our AI models to incorporate strategic reasoning, we will experience another dimension.

Not everyone who is a top-performing salesperson will require 4D selling skills, and simply adding another AI browser bookmark will not make prospecting easy or account planning a one-button solution. One of the main reasons salespeople enjoy their jobs is that they appreciate interacting with customers and guiding them through the process — from initial introductions to details, negotiations, and ultimately the close. No software tool will add a physical dimension to the conference table, nor will the best-crafted account plan be a compelling read. Like any expert, you must hone your craft by listening to your audience, reviewing your material to assess how well you are meeting customer needs, and finally, executing your strategy. Never doubt your strengths and be willing to expand your skills with emotional and artificial intelligence. Rehearse, role-play, and deliver your pitch with one, two, three, or four dimensions. I recall a story from years ago about an early AI experience with an overhead projector. During a presentation, while the speaker was flipping to the next viewfoil and making a gesture on a line grid, a second person, simultaneously at the smartboard, was drawing an upward line onto the projected graph. It was as if the first speaker's finger was magically drawing in free space. The audience could barely "connect the dots" and watched in wonder. We've come a long way from plastic viewfoils and overhead projectors, and the next phase of supreme selling skills will encompass all dimensions.

10.5 LOVE OF SALES

There are many paths to becoming a salesperson, and almost none have common roots. If your parents are in real estate sales, you will likely follow in their footsteps with a similar career, such as selling real estate, insurance, or home loans. If both your parents are well-educated, it is likely that you will also be educated and may prefer the more complex or technical aspects of sales. And although sales is one of the world's oldest professions, there is no college degree with a major in sales; well, indeed, it is in the school of business. Northwestern's Kellogg School of Management is one of the nation's highly ranked business schools and offers a 10-week Mastering Sales course. The course provides a toolkit for success, suggesting it will transform you into a high-impact salesperson and ultimately drive business profitability. For $2,600, it is probably the best way to add this label to your LinkedIn profile and claim you attended the University of Chicago's Kellogg School.

If you have spent your career in sales, it is likely because you love selling and are good at it. Selling is a demanding profession, and living with the stress of "what have you done for me lately?" can be annoying. Unless, of course, you answer that you just closed a megadeal worth millions of widgets or dollars. Winning charisma is like a pheromone — an invisible, often inexplicable quality that attracts others and subtly motivates them to trust, follow, or buy from you. Studies show that charismatic leaders and salespeople make deeper connections, spark enthusiasm, and create emotional engagement, helping them win deals, followers, or opportunities almost effortlessly. Charismatic presenters capture the room with voice, body language, confidence, and passionate belief.

The overlapping effects of high emotional intelligence and charisma compound to enhance influence and persuasion. High EQ sellers handle objections gracefully and motivate action—not pressure—through understanding and connection. Loving sales often means loving to solve problems and serve others. EQ helps salespeople identify actual pain points, communicate value in a personal way, and deliver solutions that resonate emotionally rather than just logically.

We know that a salesperson's daily routine is filled with ups and downs. Based on specific events of the day, the mood can be swayed by rejection, challenging negotiations, or significant shifts in the business's path. Deals often begin with the hype of a new program, accompanied by excitement for volume manufacturing and a go-to-market ramp. Remember, the best-laid plans of mice and men usually go awry. Tesla launched one of the most game-changing pickups with the new Cybertruck. It offered a new EV platform with autonomous driving capabilities, unbreakable glass windows, and 845 hp, achieving a 0-60 mph time of 2.6 seconds. The forecasted build plan for 2025 ranged from 300,000 to 500,000 units, while the current sell-through is only 5,000 units per quarter, or 20,000 units per year. That's off by a factor of 25x in the wrong direction.

Loving what you do as a salesperson stems from an intrinsic motivation rooted in your core. Some or all parts of the sales cycle must resonate with your ego and motivate you to drive deals and achieve the rewards you desire. This positive cycle of increased job satisfaction, hard work, and rewards drives higher confidence and better performance. A recent major compensation survey (ref: ACI Central, June 2019) found that sales reps and managers cite "enjoyable workplace environment and culture" as their number-one job priority, with high compensation (including commissions) coming in a close second.

Thankfully, a love for sales can last for decades, given the field's dynamic, ever-changing nature. Salespeople are constantly learning from their company about the variable nature of their customers. Unlike other staff employees who may get stuck in a routine of coming to work each day and suffering the same grind, a salesperson has a new play to visit every day. There are always more prospects and new territories to explore. Every day is different, and this can be just what a salesperson looks forward to. One day can be spent on data mining and customer research, while the next is filled with multiple meetings, presentations, and negotiations on the road. How many jobs provide you with the freedom to travel and a car allowance? Take advantage of the opportunity by delivering new business and new customers, which constantly change the work routine. Align your personal goals and values with your work purpose, avoid burnout, and remain open to change. A 20+ year career in sales means you will experience a long list of stories filled with stories. If it's been a while since you last celebrated a significant win, reset your targets and continue pursuing your lifelong passion for sales success. Bring a stakeholder a customer-appropriate gift and shift your focus from your goals to how you can better serve your audience. People do business with people they like and trust. If you can't remember the last time you were outwardly kind to a customer, then it's time for a refresh. Do more than just sending emails; make it a point to provide human contact by getting in front of your accounts. Every visit with a customer is an opportunity to gather more information and a step in the right direction. Love what you do, and you will be rewarded.

Play More Golf

. . .

It is well understood that business is done and won on the golf course. If you laid out our sales strategies, where in the list does playing golf appear? Elite salespeople consider golf a requirement for winning and leverage the game to build high-value relationships and influence key decision-makers. Amongst the other requirements are dining, VIP events, and, depending on how high the stakes are, an exotic travel trip, jewelry (e.g., a watch), and elegant gifts delivered to the front door, such as a rare bottle of whiskey.

C-suite executives play golf in their limited free time, at worldwide team building sessions at resorts with PGA-approved golf courses, and with other three-letter "C" execs. For a few hours on the grass, CXOs swing the hell out of their clubs, navigate the fairways, and methodically manage the short game for a win. The "C-level" crowd can easily keep a conversation about themselves or their business for 18 holes. It is not whether they play golf or have a handicap under 75; rather, it is where to draw the lines between sport, strategy, and sand traps.

For Lalida. Being a good golfer is associated with having high emotional intelligence. Golf requires players to manage their emotions under pressure, recover quickly from errors, and maintain focus for extended periods. Overlapping similarities between golf and EQ include self-awareness, self-regulation, resilience, and empathy.

10.6 STRATEGIC SELLING

In preparing to write this book, I reviewed over 50 books on selling, artificial intelligence, and emotional intelligence. About a third were best-sellers, and not a single one had "Strategic Selling" as its title. There was Sales Enablement, Sales EQ, Sales Management Simplified, Sell Different, Sell or Be Sold, Sell with a Story, Selling with Nobel Purpose, Spin Selling, Challenger Sale, The Sale, Sales Survival, Science of Selling, To Sell is Human, Atomic Habits, Fanatical Prospecting, Never Split the Difference, Radical Candor, and Lead by Example. One of my favorite authors, Adam Grant, writes in his book, "Hidden Potential[5]," about character, motivation, and systems of opportunity. He has a chapter called "Diamond in the Rough," in which he describes how to identify hidden potential in uncut gems—and the challenge of interviewing astronauts for NASA spaceflight missions. Grant also provides insights into grade point average (GPA) and grade point trajectory (GPT), and explains why the trajectory may be a better predictor of talent.

Jeb Blount, the mastermind behind Sales Gravy and numerous books on sales leadership, has yet to use "strategic sales" in a title. He does offer online training courses that include selling strategies. Over 20 years ago, in 1985, Robert Miller and Stephen Meiman wrote a bestseller called "Strategic Selling[6]." The book presents a systematic approach to B2B sell-ing, mapping decision-makers and managing through each person's influence in the decision-making process. Several consulting firms (esp. Korn Ferry) offer sales training using the Miller-Heiman method with the "Blue Sheet" used for strategic planning.

Emotional intelligence and sales strategies are distinct yet comple-mentary forces in driving sales success. Emotional intelligence is about connecting with people, while sales strategies focus on structured, repeatable approaches to win deals. EQ in sales means reading clients' emotions, showing empathy, and building genuine trust, which enables deeper connections, smoother negotiations, and authentic loyalty. High EQ sellers stand out through adaptable communication, resilience in the face of stress, and the ability to navigate objections with empathy rather than force. Emotional intelligence drives long-term success, particularly in consultative and enterprise sales where rapport and influence are crucial.

Emotional Intelligence	Sales Strategy
Builds trust and rapport	Structures sales process
Reads and adapts to emotions	Targets, tracks, closes deals
Drives relationship value	Provides consistency and scale
Key for complex deals	Key for process optimization

Table 10.6 Emotional Intelligence vs Sales Strategy

Strategic sales strategies are data-driven plans that encompass targeting, solution design, pipeline management, closing techniques, and post-sale follow-up, ensuring consistent sales outcomes and scalability. Strategic sellers utilize tools such as CRM analytics, segmentation, and refined outreach processes to move prospects through the sales funnel efficiently. These methodologies help teams achieve quota, align resources, and improve forecasting accuracy.

The most effective salespeople blend emotional intelligence with sharp strategies, using EQ to personalize interactions and strategy to anchor process, measurement, and scale. Studies demonstrate that EQ amplifies the effectiveness of any strategy, as emotionally attuned reps execute plans with more resilience, creativity, and customer connection.

Is the sales strategy becoming woke? No. The term "sales strategy" itself is not "becoming woke"; however, confusion may arise because marketing strategies are increasingly incorporating social consciousness ("woke") messaging or themes. In contrast, sales strategy remains focused on systematic approaches for closing deals and driving revenue.

Instead, we see an evolving Blue Sheet resulting from AI. The Miller Heiman Blue Sheets are evolving from a static planning artifact into a live, collaborative digital tool that automatically keeps them up to date with actionable milestones. AI will make strategic selling "smarter, faster, and more adaptive," ensuring Miller Heiman's core principles are easier to implement and extremely potent in today's data-driven sales landscape.

10.7 COLLABORATION

Over the next five years, collaboration platforms are expected to undergo significant improvements. Today, there are millions, if not billions, of active users on these platforms who send and receive electronic messages daily. The word "collaboration" originates from the Latin "collaborare," which means "to work with," formed from "com-" (meaning "together" or "with") and "laborare" (meaning "to work"). Its whole meaning is the act of working together with one or more people toward a common goal, emphasizing joint effort, partnership, and teamwork to accomplish shared objectives.

The top collaboration platforms include: Asana, Figma, Google Workspace, Miro, Notion, Slack, Trello, Monday.com, MS Teams, and Zoom. These platforms are widely recognized for their ability to support remote, hybrid, and in-person teams with features such as messaging, file sharing, project management, visual collaboration, and seamless integration with other tools.

Slack was founded in 2009 as a tool that excels at real-time communications with searchable channels, DM's, huddles (voice/video), and a vast integration library with advanced AI features. The name Slack is an acronym for "Searchable Log of All Converstation and Knowledge." In 2020, IBM installed Slack on over 350,000 user computers, making it Slack's largest customer to date. In 2021, Salesforce acquired Slack for $27.7 billion and integrated it into its platform to create what it calls the "digital HQ" for business, aiming to redefine the Future of enterprise software. The Slack integration roadmap at Salesforce included several AI-led products, such as Agentforce with AI agents and Tableau Next with AI dashboards, as well as further unified collaboration across platforms, including Confluence and Microsoft.

Slack has over 65 million monthly users sending 700 million messages per day. Zoom became one of the most popular collaboration platforms during the COVID-19 pandemic, and its user base grew to over 300 million daily active users. Microsoft Teams has over 320 million users, primarily due to its integration with Microsoft 365. Google claims over 3 billion active Workspace users, making it the most widely used productivity and collaboration suite globally.

So why do salespeople need to collaborate? Salespeople need to collaborate because effective sales today requires working with teammates, subject-matter experts, marketing, and even customers themselves to deliver the best solutions, learn from past deals, and navigate complex buying groups. Collaboration boosts efficiency by sharing best practices, avoids costly information silos, facilitates warmer client introductions, and enables faster, more successful deal closures in increasingly complex environments where multiple stakeholders are involved. Collaborating means learning from others' successes and failures, which accelerates onboarding, boosts win rates, and prevents the repetition of mistakes. Shared knowledge can include real-world experiences, such as case studies, where lessons from a previous example may help guide the upcoming project to a better outcome. Consider what it's like when you embark on a home remodel. The first people you approach are contractors with similar experiences, such as those with skills in cabinetry, windows, and flooring. Having the right subject-matter expert on your team can be invaluable as you collaborate with external folks, including customers or influencers. Engineers and other members of technical teams, on both sides of the table, often enjoy introducing complex information that can potentially disrupt business momentum. The best way to counter this is to have an SME who can carry the conversation or even persuade it your way.

Interestingly, the key traits of top collaborative leaders include empathy and openness, vision and community building, leading by example, flattening of hierarchies, and celebrating diversity of thought. The collaborative leader welcomes feedback and maintains transparent communication, regardless of position or authority. They unite teams around clear, shared purposes and values, building environments of trust, safety, and shared achievement.

There is no single universally accepted "best" leader for collaboration, but several leaders and organizations stand out for their exceptional practices and impact. Notably, Google is frequently cited as a global model of collaborative leadership, characterized by a culture that empowers employees to share ideas, minimizes hierarchy, and fosters psychological safety, ultimately driving legendary innovation. Collaboration is now non-negotiable for high-performing sales teams, and the leading digital platforms fundamentally improve how teams work together, share information, and close deals more efficiently.

10.8 BITCOIN

Bitcoin was created in 2008 by Satoshi Nakamoto, who launched the first Bitcoin network and mined the "genesis block," thereby implementing the first decentralized digital currency. Today, the Bitcoin market capitalization is over $2.24 trillion (as of August 2025), making it the largest and most dominant cryptocurrency globally. Only 1.3% of the global population (or 106 million persons) owns Bitcoin. Before NVIDIA's stock skyrocketed, no US stock had ever reached a trillion-dollar market capitalization. Today, NVIDIA has a market cap of $4.4 trillion, with Microsoft closely behind at $3.7 trillion, and Apple at $3.2 trillion.

AI has an estimated market capitalization of $244 billion, roughly one-tenth that of Bitcoin. However, Bitcoin's growth rate is slowing to 5-7% per year, while AI's CAGR is astronomical at 35-38%. Both markets are dynamic and transformational, but they serve vastly different needs and have contrasting risk profiles and investment rationales. There are AI-powered trading models that utilize vast datasets to forecast Bitcoin price trends, optimize buy-sell timing, and manage portfolio risk, far surpassing traditional strategies. The AI algorithms analyze blockchain activity and transaction patterns to detect anomalies, prevent fraud, and enhance security, thereby reducing vulnerabilities and fostering trust in the Bitcoin ecosystem.

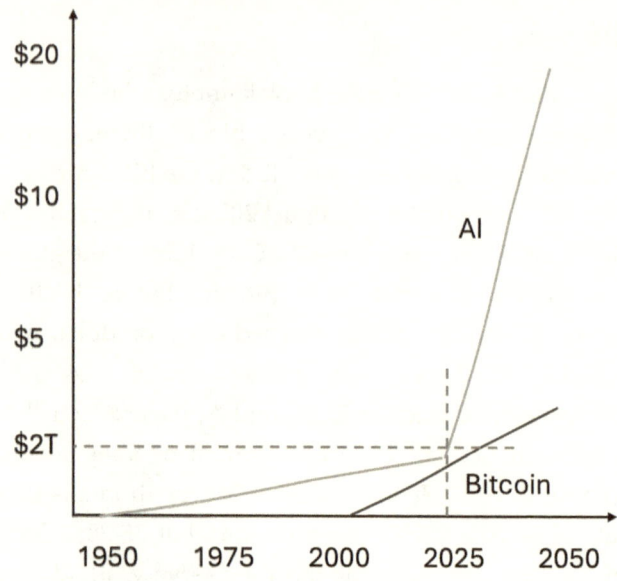

Figure 10.7 AI vs Bitcoin Growth Projections (2025-2030)

There is a belief that traders who develop and apply emotional intelligence are more likely to achieve success and consistency when navigating the dynamic fluctuations of the cryptocurrency market, such as the Bitcoin market. EQ leads to more rational and profitable trading decisions. Studies have found that emotional signals, such as fear, greed, and sentiment, are potent predictors of cryptocurrency prices, often outperforming technical signals in market forecasting. EQ provides a competitive edge for navigating the psychological stress and uncertainty inherent to the crypto market, helping traders stay calm and focused amid drastic price swings. While a high EQ significantly boosts profitability in crypto trading, it must be paired with technical expertise and, perhaps, AI for better overall results.

If projections hold, by 2030, both Bitcoin and AI will have approximately 1 billion users each, or about 10% of the population. Bitcoin's largest markets are financial institutions, ETF products, and large-scale corporate and treasury adoption. At the same time, AI will become more pervasive across healthcare, finance & banking, retail, self-driving cars, customer service, education, cybersecurity, and entertainment. In my opinion, the AI market capitalization is under-estimated at $1.8 trillion by 2030, with some high estimates exceeding $15 trillion. This kind of volatility forecasting is a testament to the impact AI will have on nearly all markets in our economy. The overlapping Venn diagram of Bitcoin and AI has a small area; however, it is essential to recognize the immense impact of these technological phenomena.

10.9 FUTURE SELLING

A powerful blend of advanced AI skills and high emotional intelligence will define the future salesperson. They will adapt to new technologies and methods that enhance their top performance. Some of these skills are covered throughout this book, and others will be played out as artificial intelligence matures from early-stage (now) to middle and post-maturity. We can only speculate about what these new requirements entail and prepare for the upcoming updates.

The 21st-century salesperson is tech-driven and human-centric. They are skilled at leveraging AI for lead research, predicting buying behavior, automating workflows, and hyper-personalizing at every touchpoint. They use AI for analytics, forecasting, and efficiency, but center the sales process around genuine relationship-building and customer trust.

In the 2-axis view of AI and EQ, we have two intelligence scales that intersect in elite selling. On the AI spectrum, we have the continuum from low to high: ANI (artificial narrow intelligence), GPAI (general-purpose AI), AGI (artificial general intelligence), and ASI (artificial superintelligence). We are quickly moving through the phases as more and more advancements in AI become available in our workplace, tools, and lifestyles. AGI is emerging as we shift to reasoning, learning, and problem-solving. ASI is still a bit like science fiction as we develop more intelligent systems that compete with human intelligence and autonomous self-improvement.

Emotional intelligence (EQ) has its own parallels to AI, with direct parallelism in our emotional states. We have all experienced emotional recognition when interfacing with early AI technologies to request query results or perform minor tasks. However, as we ascend the AI hierarchy, the emotional intelligence ladder grows to support heightened awareness, root-cause analysis, and advanced emotional awareness at the highest levels of AI, known as superintelligence.

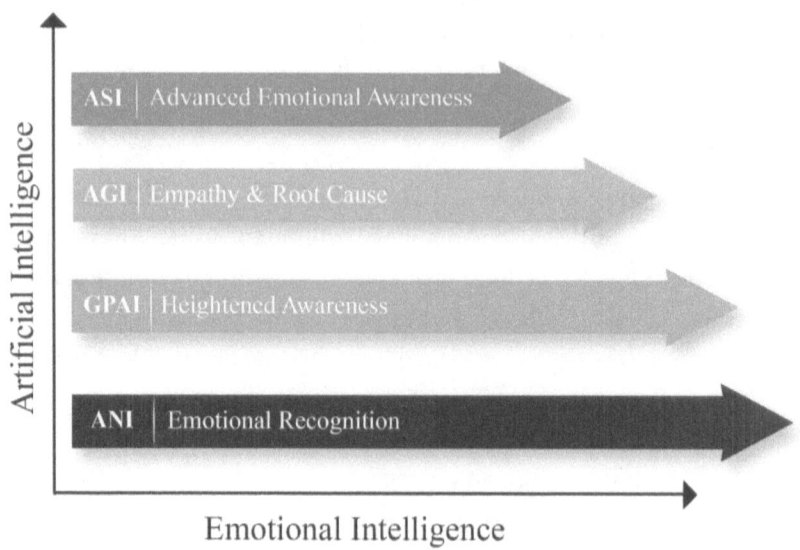

Figure 10.8 AI & EQ Spectrums

They are also masters of self-awareness and self-regulation, managing their own emotions and reactions while remaining attuned to buyer cues. They practice empathy and active listening as part of their everyday routines. They anticipate customer emotions and needs during every stage of the sales cycle.

The elite salesperson leverages new tools to provide an in-depth understanding of their customers' industries, pain points, and motivations. They combine consultative selling with value-driven presentations to address customers' strategic challenges. This commitment ensures that no two presentations are alike and that each presentation is tailored to each customer meeting. When the audience is part of these presentations, they are engaged and voice their support throughout. The salesperson knows when to bring in subject matter experts, when to use executive power, and whether the presentation should be 10 pages or just 1 page.

The new style is very subtle with emotional intelligence on the outside and artificial intelligence on the inside. Customers witness value from the start of the relationship and develop trust across the buyer-seller boundary. Complex sales cycles are broken down into organized phases with both data-driven and human-centric elements.

Next-Gen Call to Action

New call to action (CTA) for sales blend AI-driven personalization with emotional intelligence, inviting prospects to collaborate, co-design, and experience value in interactive, low-pressure ways. These CTAs are less about hard closes and more about creating genuine, insight-driven part-nerships, reflecting the new reality that sales success now depends on both advanced technology and deep human understanding.

CTA Approach	Leverages AI	Leverage EQ
Personalized Analysis/Benchmark	Yes	Yes
Co-Design Session	-	Yes
Candid Pain Point Conversation	-	Yes
ROI Prediction	Yes	-
Guided Workflow Experience	Yes	Yes
Micro-commitment Follow-up	Yes	Yes
Mutual Value Proposal	Yes	Yes

Table 10.9 AI and EQ Leverages to CTA's

In the era of advanced AI and heightened focus on emotional intelli-gence, the most effective sales CTAs have evolved beyond "Request a demo" or "Sign the Contract." Modern CTAs are designed to be more personalized, consultative, data-driven, and emotionally engaging, lever-aging both AI insights and genuine human connection. AI is trans-forming CTA messaging, making it more intelligent, more relevant, and emotionally aware. Businesses will need to rethink how they invite prospects to act, favoring personalized, interactive, and context-driven CTAs that fit each customer's journey. The new CTAs are dynamic, learning, and deeply attuned to the person receiving them.

10.10 HUMANS & HUMANOIDS

We are familiar with the art of selling to humans, and thankfully, this practice will continue, at least for most of us. There is a general concern that new technologies, including automation, robotics, and other "human substitutes," will replace humans in the workplace. Some of these may be threats or just distractions; regardless, they are changing the sales landscape.

Let's review and dispel the apparent points of automation. Let's skip the early water wheel (1st Century BC) and move directly to industrial robots that assemble, paint, weld, polish, label, and package products on factory lines. Giants like Amazon utilize robotic picking, sorting, and packaging for both manufacturing and logistics. The state-of-the-art, lights-out factory has machine vision, automated inspection, quality control, and sensors to manage a production line without human intervention. Some common examples of fully automated factories include those that build cell phones, printed circuit boards, and food or beverages. Philips operates a light-out factory in the Netherlands that assembles up to 15 million electric razors per year, using 128 robots for part delivery, assembly, testing, packaging, and shipment. Humans are present only for quality assurance, which is increasingly automated as machine vision advances. GE has lights-out factories for its appliances, IBM has a major plant that builds keyboards with full automation, and Tesla's gigafactories employ advanced robotics and automation to develop batteries and electric vehicles.

Believe it or not, not all robots are used for automation. Some robots, such as collaborative robots (cobots), logistics mobile robots, or experimental/humanoid robots, may serve roles in collaborative work, research, or service rather than purely automated tasks. Mobile robots, such as those used in warehouse robotics, automate tasks like transporting goods but can also be used for exploration or inspection across sectors beyond manufacturing. Service robots perform tasks like cleaning, surgical assistance, or delivery that may not be classified as pure manufacturing automation. Educational, research, and entertainment robots, including humanoids or social robots, may be autonomous, but are usually not deployed for industrial automation.

Salespeople do not yet need to routinely transition from selling solely to humans to selling to humanoids. Still, the groundwork is being laid for future scenarios when humanoid robots could act as buyers, intermediaries, or support staff in sales environments. Humanoid robots are being piloted as sales assistants to provide product information, personalized recommendations, and conduct interactive presentations; however, humans still drive the actual purchase decisions. Projections by Goldman Sachs and others suggest that the market penetration of humanoid robots could begin to impact sales roles, with robots gradually assuming more autonomous buying tasks in industries such as retail and healthcare. As AI advances, salespeople will increasingly interact with and sell to humanoid robots acting as corporate agents, procurement bots, or automated decision-makers. Studies show that a hybrid model is likely, with salespeople selling to humans augmented by AI agents and occasionally negotiating with robotic procurement systems, particularly for mundane or repetitive transactions. For now, human-to-human sales remain dominant, with humanoid robots augmenting, rather than replacing, human buy-ins and sales in most markets.

There is a growing but nuanced corollary between artificial and emotional intelligence in both humans and humanoids. AI systems, particularly recent generative models, can now outperform the average human participant on standard emotional intelligence tests, demonstrating high proficiency in recognizing, interpreting, and simulating emotional responses. However, crucial distinctions remain regarding authenticity, depth, and the origins of emotional experiences.

Artificial intelligence, even when highly effective at recognizing and "expressing" emotions, does not truly experience feelings. Its empathy is simulated, not lived, and it cannot understand emotions at the subjective or conscious level. This distinction means that while AIs may demonstrate EQ behaviorally, their empathy is not intrinsic, but programmed or learned. Humans possess an intuitive, context-driven emotional understanding shaped by culture, life experiences, and self-awareness, enabling profound and authentic connections that current AI agents often lack. Genuine emotional engagement and the ability to form deep, meaningful relationships remain essential human strengths.

Humanoid robots designed to mimic human features, such as expression, tone, and gestures, can elicit feelings of connection and trust from users, especially during short or task-focused interactions. However, in more complex or prolonged exchanges, humans often sense the absence of genuine understanding. Leading research suggests that artificial and emotional intelligence should be seen as complementary. AI delivers speed, data-handling, and scale, while EQ in humans anchors judgment, trust, and authentic connection. As workplaces automate, the uniquely human facets of EQ become even more critical for leadership, culture, and innovation.

10.11 SELLING SMARTER

We recognize that the future will require each of us to adopt new technologies and manage their impact on our daily lives. The influence of artificial intelligence will be literally everywhere, from our time in the workplace and at home to leisure, travel, space, and likely beyond. What used to be future predictions are now today's realities, and it's not when you will be faced with decisions on AI, it's more a matter of how much AI will be used, useful, or distracting.

To "Sell Smarter" is to embrace both artificial and emotional intelligence and combine their strengths to be the most successful salesperson you can be. Sales situations are inevitably complex and filled with variables that require the leader and the support team to rely on their strengths in managing the process. Each phase has elements where it is beneficial to rely more on artificial intelligence or perhaps emotional intelligence. Therein lies the importance of managing both influences and adjusting your behavior accordingly.

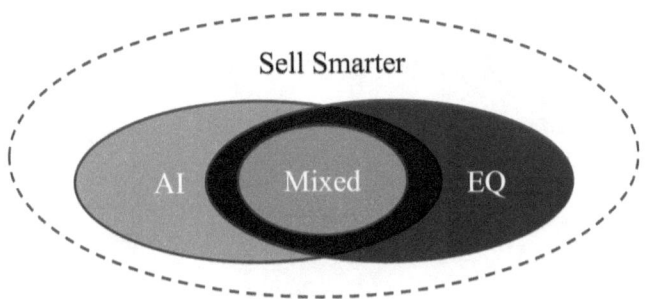

Figure 10.10 Sell Smarter with AI and EQ

Sales leaders will shift their approach from a static emphasis on strategic selling to a dynamic focus on the influence of emotional general intelligence, combining traits from artificial intelligence and emotional intelligence, known as AI+EQ. When we "harness the power of AI and EQ to drive sales success," we don't just hit the "AI Mode" button; we adopt a new approach that enables us to win in complex sales situations by blending our best attributes. We truly sell smarter when we upgrade our "human" tools and deliver with superior sales intelligence.

The "Sell Smarter" process is a life journey that requires nurturing, attention to detail, informed integration of tools, and the constant excitement that makes us want to be better.

NOTES

1. EMOTIONAL GENERAL INTELLIGENCE

1. Daniel J. Levitin, "Successful Aging," A Neuroscientist Explores the Power and Potential of Our Lives, Penguin, 2020
2. Lisa Early McLeod, "Selling with Noble Purpose," Drive Revenue and Do Work That Makes You Proud, Wiley, 2020
3. Daniel Goleman, "Social Intelligence," The Revolutionary New Science of Human Relationships, Bantam, 2007
4. Matthew Dixon, Brent Adamson, "The Challenger Sale," Taking Control of the Customer Conversation, Penguin, 2011

2. SALES CHI

1. KSBW, "The Salad Bowl of the World, " Salinas, CA 1953
2. Ferdinand Porsche, the Lohner-Porsche Mixte (aka Semper Vivus), the world's first hybrid car in 1901
3. Michael Solomon, PhD, Psychologist, NYU university study, 2018
4. "Chi" can refer to the Greek letter X (chi) the 22nd letter of the Greek alphabet

3. PSYCHOLOGY OF SELLING

1. Sir Alexander Crichton (1763-1856), physician and author, known for his early work on mental disorders
2. Dr. Charles Bradley (1902-1979), a psychiatrist credited with medicine for headaches
3. Vanderbilt ADHD Diagnostic Rating Scale (VADRS), 2003
4. Forbes Health, Best Online Therapy for ADHD in 2025, https://www.forbes.com/health/l/best-online-therapy-adhd
5. Thomas Erikson, "Surrounded by Idiots," Essentials, Oct 2020
6. James Taylor, "Carolina in My Mind," 1968
7. Sarah McLauchlan, "Angel," 1997
8. W.H. Auden, "Funeral Blues," 1938
9. Gary Guller, "Make Others Greater," May 2013
10. Sales Are Dope (S.A.D.), Amazon Prime Video, Comedy, 2025

4. SALES CHALLENGES

1. Richard Bernstein, "Dr. Bernstein's Diabetes Solution," Little, Brown Spark, Nov 2011
2. UT Southwestern Medical Center, Alcohol and Alcoholism, Oct 2024
3. Chris Voss, "Never Split the Difference," Harper, May 2016
4. Roger Fisher, "Getting to Yes," Penguin, May 2011
5. Matthew Walker, "Why We Sleep," Scribner, Oct 2017
6. "A Clockwork Orange," Stanley Kubrick, 1971
7. Nokia 9000 Communicator, Nokia smartphone, 1996
8. iPhone, Apple, announced Jan 2007
9. "The Gods Must Be Crazy," 20th Century Fox, Sept 1980

5. SALES DRIVE

1. An AI Pioneer Thinks Everyone Is Wrong - Again, Meghan Borrowsky, Wall Street Journal, November 15, pg. B3

6. SALES CYCLES

1. First-mover advantage, Wikipedia Feb, 2014
2. Augusto Solomon, "Moonshot Sales," May 2020

7. ARTIFICIAL INTELLIGENCE

1. Frank Rosenblatt, "Electronic Neural Network, Mark I Perceptron," National Museum of American History, 1958
2. Joseph Weizenbaum, "ELIZA" a natural language processor, MIT, 1966
3. Wall Street Journal, researcher Alexandra Samuel, Monday, November 3, 2025, pg R10
4. Time Magazine, "Introducing the 2025 TIME100 Next," Vol 205, May 12, 2005

8. EMOTIONAL INTELLIGENCE

1. Daniel Goleman, "Emotional Intelligence, Why It Can Matter More Than IQ," Bantam, Sep 2005
2. Jeb Blount, "Sales EQ," Wiley, Mar 2017
3. Travis Bradberry, "Emotional Intelligence Habits," TalentSmart, Aug 2023
4. Gill Hasson, "Emotional Intelligence, Managing Emotions to Make a Positive Impact on Your Life," Capstone, Nov 2024
5. T.J. Bryly, "Unlocking the Power of Emotional Intelligence," Dec 2024
6. Mayer-Salovey-Caruso Emotional Intelligence Test, Wikipedia 2016
7. V. Allen, N. Rahman, A. Weissman, C. MacCann, C. Lewis, R. Roberts, "Situational Tests of Emotion Management", Article, APA PsycNet, 2015

8. C. McCann, R.D. Roberts, "Situational Tests of Emotion Understanding," Database record, APA PsycNet 2008
9. Caroline Fleck, "Validation," Penguin, Feb 2025

9. SALES EXCELLENCE

1. Sanjiv Chopra, "Leadership by Example," Thomas Dunne Books, May 2012
2. Glenn Stearns, "Integrity, My Slow and Painful Journey to Success," Forefront Books, May 2023
3. Oren Klaff, "Pitch Anything," McGraw-Hill, Jan 2011

10. SELL SMARTER

1. Martin Gutmann, "Why Do We Celebrate Incompetent Leaders," TEDx Berlin, May 2024
2. Jony Ive, "A Conversation with Jony Ive," YouTube, May 2025
3. Kim Scott, "Radical Candor," St Martin's Press, Oct 2019
4. Adam Grant, "Give and Take," Viking, Apr 2013
5. Adam Grant, "Hidden Potential," Viking, Oct 2023
6. Robert Miller, "Strategic Selling," Grand Central Publishing, Apr 2005

ABOUT THE AUTHOR

James L. Murray grew up and lives in California. He is an accomplished sales leader with experience selling technology products and services for companies ranging from early-stage (startups) to multi-billion dollar enterprises. His career started in space and satellite communications, semiconductors, and professional services. He has developed business plans, raised venture capital for early-stage, Series A, and Series B rounds, served as a key representative at roadshows and NASDAQ IPOs, and participated in several mergers and acquisitions.

Over the past fifteen years, James has been instrumental in leading strategic sales teams in professional services. His management style is characterized by leading by example and active listening, and he is recognized for his high emotional intelligence. He is well-educated, holding advanced degrees in engineering and business administration. His passions include abstract art, exotic fish, tennis, and vintage muscle cars. He holds a US patent, has written multiple books, and enjoys days spent with his family and the beaches in the Central Coast.

Roasted Garlic & Brie, Vintage Camaro, Caymus Cab, Discus Pairs,
Forty-Love, Picasso, Ro-cham-beau, Route 432, 26.2 < 3hr

AFTERWORD

Before embarking on Sell Smarter, I read over 400 books, newspapers, journals, blogs, video's, and TED Talks on subjects ranging from leadership to strategic selling, from psychology to self-awareness, from genius makers to sales survival, atomic habits to let them theories, from tipping points to challengers, from radical ideas to active listening, and from time management to self-control.

On the subject of artificial intelligence, the key sources went well beyond books in print and included contributions from the source and from large language models themselves.

To complete the survey of artificial and emotional intelligence, it became clear that the book would become a living document, requiring updates to keep pace with the massive changes in AI.

If another update is requested, I'd be happy to write another book, as many more topics tease our intelligence and raise the question of what's next. I'll promise to write it if you agree to read it, even if you use your chatbot next time to save time and get a quick summary.

Embrace the unknown chaos of artificial intelligence, enjoy the good parts, and learn to manage expectations.

www.ingramcontent.com/pod-product-compliance
Lightning Source LLC
Chambersburg PA
CBHW030909120626
46554CB00001B/75